Trave
Fortune

An African Adventure

by
Christina Dodwell, F.R.G.S.

ISBN: 1-59048-213-1

The Long Riders' Guild Press 2005

First published in 1979

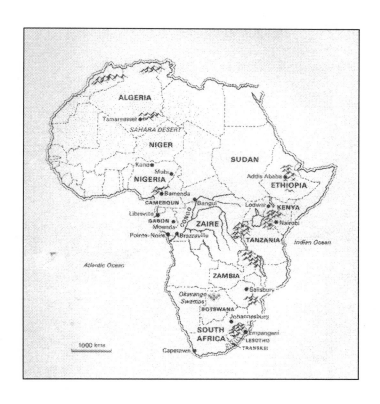

Map labels (as visible):

ALGERIA

Tamanrasset

SAHARA DESERT

NIGER

Kano • Mubi •
NIGERIA • Bamenda
CAMEROUN • Bangui
Libreville •
GABON •
Moanda •
Pointe-Noire • • Brazzaville
Congo
ZAIRE

SUDAN

Addis Ababa •
ETHIOPIA

Lodwar • KENYA
• Nairobi

TANZANIA
Indian Ocean

Atlantic Ocean

ZAMBIA

Okavango
Swamps
BOTSWANA

• Salisbury

Johannesburg •
SOUTH
AFRICA • Empangeni
LESOTHO
Capetown • TRANSKEI

1000 kms

To my family, friends, and all the people who helped me on my way.

Contents

Author's Note

When I told my parents that I was planning to travel round Africa, they immediately replied: 'How lovely.' Had they been negative, I would not have wanted to write and share my experiences with them. Had they worried constantly, I would not have done what I did. Throughout my travels I always treasured the knowledge that my family had faith in me. It gave me the confidence to go ahead.

I wish there was room in the book to name all the people whose kindness and hospitality I shall never forget. It is not possible to list all the people to whom I am grateful, but I want them to know that without them my journey would not have been so wonderful.

Among those I particularly wish to thank are:
in Nigeria, Victor Okonedo, and the Waters family;
in the Congo, Albert Loureko, the Gilroy-Scott family, and all the missionaries and foresters;
in Rhodesia, Flops and Jeremy Lewis, the Robertson family, Ura and Jo Deworonin, Pauline and Sandy Ward, the Adams family, the Simleit family, the Revill family, Kevin Evernett, Yozz, Jan White, and Nicky Kleine;
in South Africa, the Klugman family, Cuan McCarthy, Aunty Planty, Erica Goss, the Boyd family, the Elliot family, David and June Summerhayes, Winkie Girdwood, Klaus Hoge, Joelle, Pascale, Gillian and Martin Seaton-Smiths, the Ogden family

and Scott;

in Botswana, Les and Barbara Hearn, the Riggs family, xd, and Jill and Kingsley Butler;

in Kenya, Rogue Barkas and family, Bill and Bimbetta Ryan, Sandy Birkbeck, Peter and Mary Johnson, Denis and Denise Fisher, Hugh Jones, Gordon Martin, the Pollacks, Jean, the Barkas family, the police force and the army.

Part One

Equatorial and West Africa

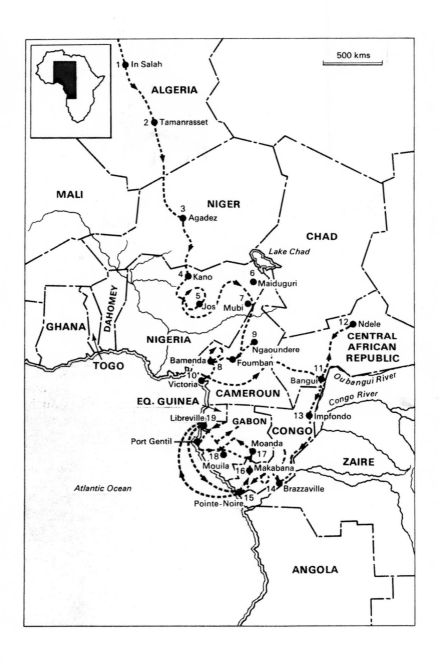

I
Abandoned

I left England on 11 March 1975 intending to spend a year as an overlander driving through Africa. I had three companions: two boys and a girl. I made contact with the boys through an advertisement in a travel magazine, after looking in vain for suitable travelling companions among my friends. The two boys were an inseparable pair who had been together since childhood and had spent the last few years travelling by Landrover in India and Australia. The way they described their journeys – stopping at interesting places, meeting the local people, visiting the wonders of the world – it all sounded exactly the way I was hoping to travel in Africa. They also knew a great deal about the mechanics of Landrovers, an important consideration. The fourth person to join us was Lesley Jamieson, a twenty-eight-year-old nurse from New Zealand. A nurse seemed a wonderful asset to an overland trip, and in addition she had spent a year travelling through South America.

And me? I was twenty-four. I had held an assortment of jobs from secretary of a society column in a fashion magazine, advertising manager of an engineering firm, interior designer, to manager of the Mayfair branch of a car-hire company. I was home-loving, materialistic, possessive, insecure, and very afraid of the dark. For years I had longed to travel but had done nothing about it. Events pushed me into making the decision, and once having decided, I saw no reason to back out.

I expected that some last-minute catastrophe would prevent us leaving and was amazed when everything went as planned. We bought a very modern Landrover and equipped it with everything one could possibly need or want. We drove across Europe, through Spain and landed in Morocco. From there we set off for the Sahara. Our journey had begun.

The stoniness of the desert surprised me; I had expected day after day of endless, rolling sand dunes. Some evenings we wandered across pebbled wastelands with cores of red rock jutting out of the gravelly grey; other evenings were spent sitting on high perches above vast seas of rock, watching their colours change as the sun set over the desert. I tried to absorb the immensity of it all. Occasionally we would spot the dark brown tents of nomads camped in the middle of nowhere, people with no possessions except a kettle which was always on the boil. As soon as they saw us they would call us to join them for tiny cups of hot strong mint tea. It didn't matter that we couldn't speak their language. We managed very well with smiles and gestures. Conversation consisted of them exclaiming and touching our clothes, while Lesley attended to anyone who was sick or injured; I either helped her or sat and sketched my surroundings.

The nomads were Tuaregs, also known as the blue men because their robes are dyed with indigo which stains their skin. They are a graceful people who carry themselves proudly, heads held high; their features are finely defined and aquiline. The younger ones sometimes spoke a bit of French. The children had their heads half shaven leaving a line of woolly hair running from their foreheads to the nape of their necks or with just a tuft on the crown. Many had been corrupted by the overlanders and everywhere we stopped they clustered round the Landrover, poking their hands through the doors or windows demanding: '*Cadeau, donnez-moi un cadeau.*' Their faces distorted with rage when we gave nothing. But in their homes they were shy, quiet and helpful.

4

After each day's driving was over and the Landrover parked, we would cook a supper of dehydrated meat and vegetables. Then the boys either went straight to bed or, if we were camped beside other overlanders, they would hurry over to say hello and sit for hours telling stories about their previous trip to India. After supper Lesley and I usually walked together, exploring the land around us and enjoying the twilight of the fading day. We were not yet friends; we rarely talked on our excursions, but our silences were comfortable, an easy sort of companionship.

As we journeyed there was always something to interest us. Crumbling mud walls showing above the palm trees would lead us to ruined towns with abandoned forts and watchtowers, all slowly dissolving back into the dusty pink landscape. Wherever we found sand dunes we spent hours running up and down them, ploughing through the sand laughing, or tobogganing down the slopes on our skirts. If we were camped near an oasis, young boys would show us how to knock ripe dates down from the palm trees; others elected to be our guides and took us to see hot springs, or crusty salt flats, or puzzling beds of seashells, or rocks with delicate pink stone clusters. The children often invited us into their homes to eat *couscous*, the local dish of semolina with meat, and they showed us around the towns which were an enchanting collection of shapes moulded out of the earth and carved into the hillsides, dominated by mosques or battlemented fortresses.

One of our jaunts was to Timimoun, an ancient town built by the Sudanese as a stopover point for camel caravans. It was a beautiful town: the entrance was through beehive-shaped gateways; all the buildings were made of red mud and their walls were decorated with intricate patterns of holes and spiked columns. A rabbit warren of narrow alleyways led us between houses and arches, under the floors of the mosque, and into a walled garden full of exotic flowers and singing birds.

The way across the Sahara was marked by cairns or stone posts

at intervals of about half a mile and, on the long stretches where
the sand was too soft to support a vehicle, distinctive tracks of
hard-packed sand had been formed. They were rutted, dusty,
and badly corrugated. The constant vibration caused havoc in
our Landrover. Door bolts broke, hinges fell off, nuts sheered
through, fuses blew, the gaz-holders snapped, an oil can split,
and one of the jerrycans exploded. The heat of the desert was
fierce. Inside the engine the petrol was evaporating before it
reached the carburettor. Inside the Landrover everything metal
was burning hot, and the water in the filter unit was hot enough
to make coffee.

The nights and mornings were cold. I felt a bit stupid wearing
an overcoat and jerseys in the Sahara; I reflected that perhaps
I was still in England and just dreaming that I was in the
desert. I could see the landscape flashing past, but I wondered
where it was all going and if we were really moving. According to
my diary we had left England ten days ago, and according to the
map we were approaching In Salah, which means 'buried in
sand'.

Our route led over the Hoggar Massif, where at Tamanrasset
the dusty mountains rise to heights of 10 000 feet in strange
pillar formations, orange and grey volcanic rock pinnacles spiralling upwards, and mountains made entirely of hexagonal
basalt columns which looked like the fingers of many hands
standing in a long row. We were now halfway across the Sahara.
The Landrover needed some repair, so we decided to stop and
overhaul it at Amsel, a little oasis ten miles from Tamanrasset.

It was a calm and peaceful place. Groups of huts made of mud
and sand with palm-leaf roofs were dotted among the sand dunes
and clumps of palm trees. We camped outside the village, beside
a spring which fed into a small lake which in turn trickled out
and down to irrigate a glossy green valley where the villagers
grew their *couscous*. Our first priority was to put the Landrover
back in order. Every single nut and bolt had rattled loose, the
wheels needed refitting and tightening, the doors were falling

off, and the whole body was about to fall apart. The food storage cupboard was in chaos: the pop-top containers had all popped their tops and flung their contents out, screw-tops had become unscrewed, tins of food had spilt and exploded, and the bottom of the cupboard was inches deep in a sticky, soggy mess of cooking oil, tea leaves, soap powder, rice and dried vegetables. We cleaned it all out. Even the bright yellow curtains had turned brown with dust, so we washed them and all our clothes, pounding them on the rocks as the local women did and spreading them over the ground to dry.

One day as Lesley and I walked to the village to buy a loaf of flat unleavened bread, we were befriended by a Tuareg called Moktar. He was the village silversmith, and he took us to his forge where we drank cups of mint tea, watched him making crosses and jewellery of silver filgree, shared the very last of my cigarettes, and Lesley treated his younger brother who had cut his leg. Moktar's mother took us to her home and taught us how to bake bread in the sand.

That afternoon Moktar visited our camp. He came galloping across the sand on his white racing camel, his blue and white robes flying out behind him; he was a superb sight. I was thrilled when he let me ride his camel, though in truth I think I was more terrified than anything else. He had come to invite us to the *fête de Mohammed*, the Moslem celebration of the birthday of the prophet. We accepted with great pleasure and he arranged to collect us in the evening. Before he left he gave me a present of a tin of local tobacco and a small metal pipe. He had made the pipe himself, from a strip off a Landrover. I treasured it and used it constantly for the next two years.

As promised, Moktar escorted the four of us to the village and into his mother's house where we were to have supper. We were introduced to everyone. The young women were wearing their finery. One had a flamboyant red party dress; another was in fluorescent yellow; the third had spruced hers up with strips of glittering tinsel because it was so faded. The old women wore

7

black, while the men were dressed in the traditional blue *djel-labas* (like caftans) and *shesh* (turbans). We all sat down around a huge bowl of *couscous* and camel meat, helping ourselves with our hands. Of course we couldn't understand a word of the lively conversation, so we listened to the flow of voices, praised the food and smiled at everyone.

After supper Lesley and I went to the Moslem dance. A wide empty space was lit by flaming torches, illuminating men in white robes who shuffled heavily round in a circle firing gun-powder-packed rifles into the sand, moving to the noise of six drums in different rhythms. The air was thick with dust. The other villagers were chanting and singing. Moktar's mother took us among the women, who tried to teach us to ululate, which is a high trilling sound of the tongue and throat. They thought our efforts were hilarious. Their lovely, soft, sighing chant was backed by a stirring hand-clapped rhythm, and as they clapped the women danced with their hands and arms in synchronised flow, while a girl from Mali sang a solo harmony above it all. The sky overflowed with stars, the night grew cold, and the ground shook with the stamping circle of flickering men. Then there was a thud as one of the men fell flat on the ground.

'Ah,' said Moktar, who was standing unnoticed beside us, 'he has drunk too much music.'

One by one they all slowly crashed down in an exhausted stupor. The dance had come to an end.

In the morning we set off on the last half of the Sahara crossing, heading out of Algeria, through Niger and to Nigeria, still nine hundred miles away. The desert was empty, devoid even of fea-tures, just an endless expanse of flat sand. Sand, sand, sand and sand for mile after hot mile. We were grimy with dust, our clothes and faces were dripping with sweat. I remembered Moktar's words: 'This is the land of thirst and mirages which is called Emptiness.'

After three days the sand gave way to a dried-up salt marsh. I imagined that until recent years there had been grass and water here, but now the expansion of the desert had claimed it and instead I saw only mounds of bleached white skeletons and the skulls of camels and donkeys. They made convenient cairns to mark the track. The dust cloud churned up behind the Landrover was visible for several miles. When the nomads saw us coming, they would grab a bowl or a cup and start to run towards our path, begging for water. Ignoring my requests to stop, the boy who was driving accelerated and swerved to avoid their pleading faces.

The Sahara was over. It had been a strange experience, close-confined in a Landrover crawling across the vast dry expanses fanned by the scorching sun. Now the land slowly changed from utter barrenness to savannah with dry, dusty scrub. It became more populated, and with each step that we made south the people's skins became blacker, and their faces flatter with broader noses. Everyone smiled and waved greetings to the Landrover as we passed. The girls had their hair plaited in many rows over their heads; the women wore huge earrings and carried their babies on their backs; and the men wore long robes and swords in decorated leather sheaths. The land became more colourful: red dust, yellow flowering trees, vibrant green grass, white cattle-egrets, and humped cattle with very long horns. Anthills rose like spires ten feet high; tobacco and cotton grew in the fields. Finally, on 10 April, only one month after leaving England, we reached Kano in Nigeria – and our expedition came to a sudden end.

In Kano we parked the Landrover at a camping-cum-car park and unpacked our gear. Then the boys disappeared – with the Landrover.

'They'll turn up again,' Lesley said confidently, so we waited. Another day passed but there was no sign of them. We tried to keep calm. I was glad we were in an English-speaking country and that Lesley and I were together. We decided that we had better look for the boys, but we had no idea where to start. Eventually we found them sitting at a table in a town bar. As we walked in the atmosphere froze.

It was an angry bitter meeting. It seemed that they had sold the Landrover to the first bidder for a ridiculously low price. Lesley pointed out that as partners in the expedition and equal joint owners of the Landrover, we were justified in questioning their actions. To cut the argument short they agreed to pay us half the money, but first deducted a large figure as commission for some Lebanese man and an even larger figure which they said was import duty. Without any attempt at explanation they solemnly divided what was left into two and gave us a thin sheet of Naira notes. I refused at first to accept the money and started again to protest. Tempers flared, but Lesley intervened, realising that there was absolutely nothing we could do.

'Let's go,' she muttered in my ear. Defeated, we took the money and left.

Naira, Nigerian money, is only valid in Nigeria. The banks refused to exchange it and directed us to the black market. My parents had told me never to go near the black-market dealers, but we were desperate. They offered to exchange our Naira for the pathetic sum of £400. I reckoned that the Landrover and equipment had cost us at least £3000.

We felt confused and hurt. We couldn't understand what had happened or why. I was sure that the boys had not intended to do this to us when we first set out. I kept wondering what had gone wrong. As a group we hadn't squabbled and bickered half as much as most of the other overlanders we met. Since I dislike arguments, I had tended to ignore the undercurrents of friction and unpleasantness that had developed on the trip. I had expected that once in Kano we would all sit down together and discuss our differences which at the time had seemed no more than the normal strains that might be expected on such a journey. But now the more we thought about what had happened (and about the loss of so much money), the more we boiled with anger and rage. The heat didn't help either — it must have been 40°C in the shade.

So ended the Landrover trip. All our hopes and dreams came crashing down and we were left with a heap of clothes and paraphernalia piled up in a car park. We couldn't leave it for fear it would be stolen; we couldn't move it because we had nowhere to go; and we couldn't keep it because we had no use for most of it. We sat down to think of a plan.

Neither of us mentioned giving up and going back to England. It didn't cross our minds, and if it had we would have dismissed the idea as pointless. Why come all this way just to turn round and go home? Obviously we were going to continue, but the question of how, when and where made our minds boggle. We decided to tackle the problems in order, starting with our possessions. We briefly considered sending most of them home by post, but many people had warned us that most parcels went no farther than a back room in the post office where they were unwrapped and distributed.

An African sauntered up, ignored our stony glares, admired our heap of gear, and offered me three Naira for my boots.

'They're worth at least six!' I objected.

'It's a deal,' he said, putting six Naira in my hand and dashing away before I had time to change my mind.

This seemed to be a signal to all the other Hausa men who were loitering about. They descended like a flock of vultures on our pile of goodies, squawking excitedly, pulling and grabbing at shirts, jeans, jerseys, blankets, books, cassette tapes and gadgets, fighting over who saw what first and demanding to know the prices.

'Stop, bring back my towel,' Lesley cried. 'No, you can't take that. They're my washing things.'

I had a tug-of-war with a man who wanted my sketchpad, but our protests were drowned by their shrieks of delight as they opened our cosmetic box, spilling out the contents, and clamouring to know the use of each lotion. There were men squatting down to examine things, more men leaning over them to grab other things, and it seemed that hundreds of bodyless hands were reaching between people to grope wildly around in the hope of finding something.

It was an instant public auction, and so ludicrous that we forgot our anger and started to laugh. Fifty Hausa men all bidding simultaneously; prices being shouted from the back. We were haggling and bargaining in every direction. My umbrella was sold as a sunshade; my shoes went to a man who said they would be sure to fit one of his four wives; bottles of scent were seized by the young men for themselves, not their girlfriends; and my entire cassette collection was bought for one tenth of its value. Lesley kept discovering that she'd bartered goods for other equally useless things like strings of beads, leather purses and pottery.

The Hausa tribe are famed throughout West Africa for their trading abilities. They were such skilful bargainers that somehow we happily sold things at insanely low prices against our will and better judgement. As a carcass is picked clean down to the bones, so all that remained of our pile of goods half an hour later were the barest essentials. We found we had sold all our jeans and trousers, but were left with two long skirts each, an assortment of shirts and T-shirts, evening dresses, a pair of sandals each, and my Chinese silk jacket which I couldn't bear to part with. Our paraphernalia was down to two needles and thread, one cup, two spoons, a torch, Lesley's travelling clock, some nivaquine pills to prevent malaria, some aspirin, washing things, towels, sleeping bags, and my hammock which ingeniously folded up to the size of a clenched fist. In the excitement of it all I had inadvertently sold my watch.

2
A New Life

'Stop. Lesley, stop. Wait for me,' I yelled. But she was marching down the road half a mile ahead and didn't hear me. I couldn't go on. I was finished. Dead. I had never carried a backpack before, and I couldn't carry that one any further, it weighed a ton, my shoulders and arms had pins and needles.

'I'm not cut out to be a hitch-hiker,' I muttered to myself as I stumbled along miserably, 'and if this is what it's about then it's not for me. Stop, Lesley please stop. It's sheer torture.' My useless skinny ankles gave way and I grabbed hold of a tree for support.

'Right, that does it,' I announced loudly. 'I give up. I'm going home. I'll hail the first taxi I see, go to the airport, and take the next flight back to England.' My spirits lifted, and I looked for Lesley so I could tell her my decision. She was way ahead and, since I could not leave her without saying goodbye, I set off in pursuit.

The problem had started that morning in Kano. After breakfast we had made ready to leave, heaved our home-made rucksacks onto our shoulders, but the weight toppled me over backwards and I collapsed on the floor in a giggling undignified heap. I felt like a tortoise turned upsidedown and no matter how hard I flailed my arms and legs I couldn't get up. I finally managed to roll over, raise myself to hands and knees, then to my feet, but I still couldn't stand upright.

Lesley assured me it would be easier once we were walking, so we set off. She marched along while I plodded from tree to tree longing to stop and take off my pack, but knowing that if I did I'd never have the courage to put it on again.

Two days earlier our future had looked like a vast empty void. When I wrote to my parents telling them what had happened they replied by telegram strongly advising us to fly to Nairobi, which would be safe, civilised, and where it would be easy to travel about on buses and trains. Lesley said we must get backpacks and hitch-hike. I was not sure about that, I had never tried it and was still a bit inclined to recoil from the unknown. But there wasn't much choice. If I wanted to see Nigeria I would have to hitch-hike. The most important thought in my mind was that I wanted to see Africa, and the fear of hitch-hiking was certainly not a good enough reason to stop me. We had already delayed a week in Kano; there were no backpacks to be bought and we had to make our own – and the days had slipped by. It was time to make a move. 'Where to?' Lesley had asked. We thought for a while, and we had decided to go first to Jos because it was on a high plateau where the heat would be less overwhelming.

Just as I caught up with Lesley a lorry came rumbling along and we waved at him to stop. It was an empty gravel truck. We scrambled into the back, freed ourselves of our packs, and stood with our elbows leaning on the cab roof, which was dented and scarred with countless accidents. The engine roared into motion, the tailgate rattled noisily, loose chains clanked and jangled, the wind whistled in my ears and whipped my skirt against my ankles. I held tightly onto an iron pole; it felt solid and reassuring. The road was single track and led across vast open plains of red earth, dry grass, and dead-looking bushes. The only other vehicle we saw during our journey was a yellow, blue and red painted mammy wagon emblazoned with the slogan 'God is Here'. It came hurtling up behind us, overtook on the wrong side, and careered on. The interior was jam-packed with people, while those who could not fit inside were standing outside on wooden bars and hanging onto the roof.

Our lorry trundled along slowly, passing through clouds of wood smoke where some Africans were making charcoal. I could smell the kebabs roasting as we drove through another village and see the women pounding grain and the men re-thatching their mud huts. Everybody waved to the lorry, though when they saw two white girls in the back their jaws dropped open and their eyes bulged. The track reached its destination, a small red mud village where it stopped to load up with bricks that the villagers made down by the well. We watched them for a while, then wandered back to the road. Our journey had begun in earnest.

Our second lift was on a lorry going all the way to Jos, and sporting the slogan 'Thy Will Be Done'. The driver stopped at every village to collect or off-load passengers and goods. When we climbed in there was a party of women dressed up to go to town, wearing *kohl* round their eyes and thickly painted eyebrows. I noticed that a couple of the women had bleached their skin to make it paler. I asked them why, and they replied that the paler one's skin, the more beautiful one was considered. The effect was an ashen grey-brown, and Lesley told me that the cream they used stimulated skin cancer.

The lorry stopped in a village where we all got out to drink palm wine, which had been tapped directly from the palm trees by plugging bottles in to their trunks and leaving them to accumulate the liquid. The newly tapped wine was refreshing and tasted like lemonade, unlike the older wine which was thick and fermented. The driver drank several pints of the fermented wine before he couuld be persuaded back in the lorry; we set off in a series of kangaroo hops, and charged down the road at such a speed that every pothole and bump threw us all into the air.

Standing beside me were two women whose hair was plaited and bound full length in patterned brass rings. Their tribal markings were intricately designed diamond shapes on their foreheads, their skin was scarred with lines resembling cats' whiskers cut outwards from the corners of their mouths. Other women had plaited their hair flat in lines on their heads, and their fringes were strung with rows of beads; they had heavy metal earrings, necklaces, twinkling, toothless smiles, wizened, wrinkled black skin, flapping, withered breasts, henna-stained hands, and weathered, split feet.

More people to pick up, these were equally fine looking women in glittering headscarves over brightly patterned headscarves and more headscarves tied to hold them on, with babies slung on their backs tied into their voluminous clothes. And yet more people climbed aboard: some children in blue school uniforms, plus a bedstead, a six foot table, and eight sacks of spiky grass. We drove on. At each stop people climbed out and people climbed in, with oildrums, loads of firewood, and some scraggy sheep. The lorry was piled high. A man with a deckchair made of palm stalks clambered onto the top, set up his deckchair, and relaxed into it. I stared incredulously. I joined the man with the deckchair on top of the lorry. With the wind in my hair, and the view stretching out panoramically, I felt a sense of elation that I had never thought possible.

'Look at those balanced rocks!' Lesley shouted, and before long everyone on the lorry was helping us to spot them. They were extraordinary configurations of several rounded boulders sitting vertically one on top of the other as though a giant had balanced them there, and some were so off-balance and over-hanging that it seemed to me they should have toppled down years ago. We emerged on top of the plateau of Jos at an altitude of over 4000 feet; it was still hot but the air felt less sticky. Climatically it has always been regarded as the most pleasant area of Nigeria, and was the centre of one of the early civilisations of the world. Approximately 1500 BC the Nok people who inhabited Jos plateau learned the art of smelting bronze, presumably from the ancient Egyptians or Greeks who had developed it in the same era.

Jos was a fascinating mixture of eras and styles, combining ugly modern air-conditioned bungalows in half-acre plots and residential areas of impressive old colonial mansions with arched verandahs, windows with shutters, graceful gardens, and the servants' quarters set apart behind the kitchens. In contrast the African sectors had mud houses built in the Arab style with points to the roof corners and decorative battlements; some with shiny new corrugated tin roofs, others with rusty old ones; tall gateways of cracked mud, and red mud walls sculpted into raised mouldings or painted with large primitive snakes, fish and flowers.

We roamed the town on foot, exploring every corner. On the outskirts we found some tin mines; the man in charge showed us around, then took us to the tin miners' club where a load of drunken Irishmen were singing rugby songs, but we couldn't think of any rhyming words to fill in the obscene blanks. We visited brothels by mistake, but chatted with the girls, and found ourselves in dives from the most disreputable to the highly select. We slept the first night in the Anglican mission, then met a man who offered us his room in the Hillstation Hotel as he was going to be away for the weekend. It was a very grand place; there were champagne parties both evenings, but all I remember was that a man from England told me that our hitch-hiking was a disgrace to society, it was the duty of every European in Nigeria to set a good example, we must maintain our distance from the Africans, observe the rules of conduct pertaining to young ladies, and immediately cease to travel in lorries. I walked off in disgust. We hadn't 'gone African', we were just people who wanted to see how things were, by looking at the difference in our cultures, not in terms of good and bad, superior or inferior, but as totally separate worlds.

The fact that we were hitch-hiking did not automatically imply that we were dirty scruffy people. We dressed as we felt happiest, wearing long skirts and our hair twisted up on top of our heads. We couldn't travel on lorries and leave our hair loose;

it would have become tangled and we were so much cooler when we put it up. I usually twisted mine into a bun – I was cultivating the schoolmistress image – because as single white girls we were constantly approached by hopeful men, and I had the notion that a schoolteacher naturally commanded respect. We always wore long skirts, partly because I'd sold our jeans in Kano, but mainly because we found skirts more practical, they were cooler to wear than jeans, they washed and dried in ten minutes, they felt much freer and more comfortable. A girl in a flowing long skirt is something which no driver will pass without stopping to offer help. You fit in nowhere, and are acceptable everywhere.

I ought perhaps to mention that I was born and brought up in Nigeria. It bore little relevance to our present situation as I had never been to the northern regions, and besides the outlook and character of Nigeria had changed so dramatically from what I had known, that at first glance it seemed like a different country. I had known Nigeria as an obscure poverty-stricken land, but now fabulously rich oil fields had been discovered off her coast and she was suddenly rolling in immense wealth.

I was born in 1951 in the colonial days when Nigeria was a federation of the British Empire, and I spent the first six years of my life living deep in the bush. There were few other white people in Nigeria, just some missionaries and government officers. Unlike South or East Africa, there were no British settlers. Nigeria was considered to be part of darkest Africa, the climate was so unhealthy that it had become known as the white man's grave, and the phrasebook contained useful expressions such as: 'Why has this man not been buried?' As Nigeria moved towards independence the government officers were replaced, and my family returned to England. When I was thirteen the company for which my father worked offered him a post in Nigeria which he accepted. I continued my education in England but joined my parents for the holidays. Then came the Biafran war. I was in

Lagos for two military coups and also during the Biafran war, but it wasn't particularly dangerous for us, it was a tribal war and both the Ibo and Hausa stressed that they had no quarrel with the British. The Africanisation of commerce and industry had already begun, the whites were replaced and we returned again to England, but there were never any hard feelings or bitterness on either side.

In all I had lived for about eleven years in Nigeria, but now it was strange to be back. I didn't want to visit the south and the places where I had spent my childhood, but I did want to show Lesley as much as I could of the changes and stages that Nigeria had been through, starting from pre-colonial times. I knew that isolated pockets of the ancient ways still existed, like the Oba's palaces with their dark tunnels and shrines with sacred offerings of goat's head, or the queen's rooms with rows of *juju* dolls which represented every member of the palace and enabled the queen to manipulate and control their activities. We had the advantage that I knew something of the history of chiefs like the Awujale of Ijebu Ode, the Orangun of Illa, the Alarke of Egba, or the Alarphin of Oyo who in 1700 had ruled a great land stretching from the Niger River to Dahomey. People who nowadays talk of 'savage Africa' overlook the ancient kingdoms, culturally, politically and militarily well developed, whose armies rode into battle on horseback carrying spears, wearing chain mail and helmets with ostrich plumes, hundreds of years ago when tribe fought tribe in endless warfare; or the Holy War; or the Moslem invaders who swept in from the Sahara to establish their sultans as rulers of Sokoto and Bornu, where there are still sultans today.

Wherever we knew there was a palace we would go to visit it. One of the most traditional we saw belonged to the Emir of Zaria. An Emir is an important man, ranking between a chief and a king, and his large rambling palace was enclosed behind high red mud walls with magnificent double gates set in a thick archway. As we walked in through the gates we met one of the Emir's body-guards, who told us the Emir was due home shortly; in the mean-time he offered to show us around.

We crossed the courtyard and went from brilliant sunlight into an enormous dark chamber. We could see nothing but black-ness, so we stood and waited for our eyes to adjust. I nearly died of fright when the bodyguard loomed up beside me, all I could see were his teeth and the whites of his eyes. He led us through a chain of dark chambers, pointing out the dome-shaped palm leaf ceilings, the bats hanging from the rafters and heavy ornate mud supports; we emerged in the council rooms which were furnished with rich carpets, tasselled wall-hangings and deep-cushioned armchairs; all the other rooms were bare, but pinned on the crumbling walls of one was a faded photograph of Queen Eliza-beth as a young girl, flanked by pictures of emirs past and pres-ent. Then the bodyguard showed us his own living quarters, and introduced us to his three wives and two horses.

The Emir arrived just as we were leaving the palace. He was greeted by ecstatic blasts on an old trumpet and someone came running with a chair which was set under the middle of the arch. The Emir sat down. He was a fat man and had no doubt been fat-tened deliberately since the Africans thought that a man who was not fat could not be wealthy or important. He was dressed in thick white robes up to his nose, and a white turban on his head.

Suddenly three horses came thundering down the avenue towards the gateway, their blue-cloaked riders brandishing swords, and urging their steeds faster with spiked wheel spurs. They were heading directly for the Emir, and they reached within two paces of him still at a fast gallop. At the last moment the riders leaned back, hauled on the reins, and in one stride the horses all came to a halt in a cloud of dust, just one step away from trampling the Emir flat. The riders saluted him, turned, galloped back down the avenue, turned again and repeated the performance. By the third charge the horses were splattered with blood and foam, and I realised that their beautiful silver-inlaid bridles had bits with a long metal spike which jabbed into the horse's mouth and forced him to stop so dramatically. This colourful display is the customary greeting of subject to chief.

Our hitch-hiking was a carefree, boisterous affair. It took us around northern and central Nigeria in an amazing assortment of vehicles – Chinese water-tankers driven by rather taciturn yellow men working with agricultural projects; an old jalopy with some Scottish Quakers who said that Moslems couldn't go to heaven because they didn't read the right Bible; a van full of students from the Archaeology department of Ibadan University on their way to dig for prehistoric men in the Central African Republic; air-conditioned Cadillacs driven by Englishmen at 120 mph; clapped-out Landrovers with hot-blooded Italians who drove like maniacs.

The maddest drivers of all were the lorry drivers. I couldn't resist noting some of their slogans in my diary: Why Worry, Jesus Saves, Alleluia, Beauty Is No Virtue, Thine is the Glory, Easy Boy Easy, Where Will you Spend Eternity? God's Will, God is True, and Trust in God – good advice because you certainly couldn't trust in the lorry which howled along like a bat out of hell, lurching and swaying, screeching to a halt four times a day for Moslem prayers or at every roadside bar where the thirsty driver drank his fill of alcohol. But there was no point in being afraid, it was just part of this thing called hitch-hiking, and though I still disliked the idea, I always enjoyed the journeys.

Lesley and I had no schedule, we made plans according to our mood of the day: it was lovely never to have to be anywhere, never rushing to get somewhere, and we laughed when we remembered our neatly mapped-out itinerary with the Landrover. As each day passed, our rage against the boys who had abandoned us diminished; we were beginning to adapt to a new life and a new style of travelling. I loved being part of the ever-changing load of passengers and goods; our destination seemed irrelevant, it was the journey now which was an experience in itself.

3
First Impressions

It was ten days before we were faced with the harsh reality of
having nowhere to stay. We were in a town and we had a note of
introduction to an English couple, but they were not at all
friendly. We contemplated going to a hotel, but decided that,
since we were now hitch-hikers, we had better learn to sleep in
the bush. We walked out of the town, beyond a place labelled
'Military Academy' and found a grassy valley with a lovely grove
of mango trees dripping with ripe fruit. I pulled out my
hammock and we tied it to the trees. The hammock guarantee
stated that it would hold two people, so we both climbed in and
ate some mangoes that hung within arm's reach.

Our first visitors were three young schoolboys who stopped to
say good evening. They were very formal, and spoke in charming
English. They asked where we were coming from and going to,
and they watched curiously while I tried to repair our broken
torch. When I turned it on nothing happened. The boys shook
their heads sympathetically and said:

'Torchey no agree.'

'The power disappoint greatly.'

'The light be quenched.'

When they left they said:

'Farewell, and may you have the wealth of God.'

'Farewell, and may you travel with fortune in Nigeria and
unto your journey's end.'

'Farewell, and may you suffer no discomfort, and arrive in Kaduna free from diseases.'

Our next visitors were a group of young men from the military academy, who couldn't believe that they had seen two white girls swinging in a hammock. They were most concerned that we were intending to sleep there, and suggested that we ought to be afraid of wild animals, snakes, lurking vagabonds, and the approaching storm. We started assuring them that we were quite happy, then suddenly there was a sharp crack as one of the hammock ropes broke and both Lesley and I fell in a heap on the ground. All we could do was lie there laughing helplessly, so the men took control of the situation. One man ran off to fetch more rope, another to find a hammer, and a third to bring nails. They returned with everything except the rope, but had brought a length of electric cable instead. To re-sling the hammock we only needed to tie one end back onto the tree, but somehow it turned into an army exercise with twenty men all trying to tie one knot. Each man had a different idea of how it should be tied and everybody argued about the merits of each idea. Layer upon layer of knots were added. The storm was not far away and it was almost dark by the time they judged the hammock safe again. We thanked them and gazed in admiration at the splendid sight of the tree, so securely trussed up that it looked more like a macramé exhibition.

We could already see distant flickers of lightning, and we wanted to be comfortably installed before the storm broke. Ten men held the hammock steady while the others helped us to climb back into it, tucking our large sheet of plastic around us to keep us dry. The lightning flashes illuminated the night clouds in magnificent, multi-cumulus silhouettes. A breeze stirred and rustled through the leaves of our trees. Then it turned into a wind, gusting strong and cool, and stronger; soon it was howling, racing along, tearing anything in its path; the branches were straining sideways, yielding to its force, and the hammock rocked gently. The lightning flashed on and on, cracking the sky in jagged forks; several of them hit the earth and a bush on the horizon burst into flames. I heard the first roll of thunder rumbling towards us as the storm gathered momentum. The wind became a gale and the thunder exploded overhead in deafening chaos. A new sound emerged, the hissing of rain as it swept across the land; large, wet, heavy raindrops splashed on our faces, blown in advance by the wind. We pulled the sheet of plastic up to our chins and snuggled further down into our sleeping bags. Torrential rain poured down, hammering on the thick, leafy mango trees which sheltered us. The storm howled and raged; it was marvellously wild, and the swaying hammock rocked us to sleep.

Any doubts I may have had about sleeping in the bush had vanished during the night. I woke to a lazy, sunny morning and leaned out to pluck mangoes for breakfast.

Ironically, we were safer sleeping out in the open air, or in village huts, or schoolrooms, than we were in towns. Although people sometimes offered us a spare room, we soon learnt that the African men didn't mean it as a free invitation. When it came to bedtime, they would say, 'Sorry, you can't have that room after all, because I've invited a friend over and he's sleeping in it, but one of you can share my room and the other can share with him.' We always said a firm no. Their suggestions were never ill-intentioned, they were always very polite, and our refusals were accepted with good grace, except that sometimes they didn't believe that we meant it, and the night would develop into a farce with Lesley and me sharing a single bed and everyone else trying to climb in too. We would pretend to be fast asleep and, just as they slid under the covers, one of us would roll over and make sure the intruder was pushed onto the floor. When they tried to wake us, we snored and snorted, and tried hard not to giggle. One of my best tricks was to fake a coughing fit which sounded so wretched that, when it finally subsided, they patted my head and said, 'Poor girl, we'd better leave them in peace.' But we knew we were never in any danger of being raped or harmed, they just wanted to check, in case we had changed our minds.

Village life was surprisingly strictly organised and each person had their role to fulfil. It was the work of the men to build the huts and keep them repaired, to erect and renew the pens for the animals, to clear the bush and undergrowth from places that the women had decided to cultivate, to make tools and weapons, to go fishing, hunting or gathering, or to be craftsmen. The women's duties were to fetch water, to till the land, and to provide food for their families. The boys were responsible for herding the sheep and goats, which gave them the opportunity to learn about plants, nature and the outdoor world. The older girls were expected to help prepare the food for the daily meals and also to carry water, while the younger girls were in charge of minding the babies, and sweeping the huts and yard. Every person demanded of their juniors the same respect and obedience as they gave to their seniors, and children were taught to imitate their elders, thereby learning to behave in an adult way. It was almost unheard of for a child to disobey its parents, and though the family system had disintegrated in towns and civilised areas, it was still the rule in the more remote villages. We developed a great respect for the village people, and knew that we could rely on their strict code of conduct and their natural warmth and friendliness for our safety.

The town Africans were not quite the same; many of them seemed to have lost their integrity and adopted a set of values taken randomly from the white community. We found that, when an African had attended school, he considered he was now educated. To farm the land was work fit only for peasants, and no educated man would do such a menial task. He wanted an office job, which he couldn't find in the bush, so he went to live in a town. But there were not enough jobs and unemployment was high. He became twisted with disillusionment and had no option but to turn to stealing. The pick-pockets in Nigeria rank among the finest in the world and burglary is so common that virtually every expatriot house has a nightwatchman who sleeps outside on the doorstep. The young Africans who succeed in finding work move towards their next goals, which are to throw off all vestiges of their village backgrounds and become sophisticated and fashionable men of the world.

But for us the real Africa lay in market-places which we never tired of visiting. Most markets are devoted to fruit and vegetables, meat which is covered in flies, and piles of cattle and goat hooves, mouths and skinned heads. When an animal is slaughtered, nothing is wasted; even the hide is cut into two-inch squares and sold as flavouring for soup. Every rooftop is lined with vultures, waiting.

We stopped in one market-place to watch calabash carving, the traditional art of the people of Oyo. They used big, watermelon-sized gourds which they cut and carve into primitive designs; we visited a local potter who turned clay pots by hand; we went to the dye pits, deep hollows scooped in a centuries-old sunbaked clay area. Each hollow was a vat of bubbling colour, red-brown produced from bark, saffron, and indigo which had two sources, a plant and a grass – the pungent smell of which lay heavily in the air. People with dye-stained hands were busy dipping and wringing out their cloth. The women's faces were tattooed with finely drawn blue feathers below their cheekbones and lines down their foreheads. Beside the women was a group of men, folding, looping, tying and knotting the cloths so that they would dye into the correct pattern. One of them showed us how he made a spiralling swirl of stars to symbolise the Emir surrounded by his councillors and courtiers, each circle representing official followers and subjects. The last process was performed by a row of men sitting lotus-position on the ground, rocking backwards and forwards, wielding heavy wooden clubs and beating the cloth continuously.

The market in Kano was divided into sections; we wandered down alleys lined with booths selling brightly coloured materials; inside every booth and under the shade of every tree were treadle sewing machines with men sewing elaborate embroidery on robes or caftans; and every branch, door and wall was hung with glittering displays of their craftmanship. Sewing and needlework was men's work. The women's domain was the food market where wooden bench stalls were heaped with mangoes, melons, avocadoes, grapefruit, bananas, pineapples, pawpaw, coconuts, dates, tomatoes, yams, onions, aubergines, okuru and all types of spinach. Other women sat on the ground, surrounded by old bottles full of red palm-oil, and baskets piled high with dried beans, groundnuts, pimentos, chilies, various types of grains and a multi-coloured patchwork of spices of different smells and textures. Guinea foul and chickens were stacked in palm leaf cages, or hung by their legs from poles and wires.

At one stall we stopped to buy some eggs – or so we thought. But the woman took them all back again, put them in a bucket of water, and gabbled crossly at us. It transpired that she was scolding us for not testing the eggs to see if they were rotten. When they are put in water the good ones sink and the rotten ones float. Ours all floated. The woman laughed heartily, selected some others, and gave us the ones which sank.

At another stall we watched a woman who had just acquired a scarlet bra. She did it up round her, turned it round a bit, shrugged and wriggled until it was comfortable. One of the cups was fitted nicely on her shoulder and arm joint, the other cup hung empty between her breasts. She tucked her handkerchief inside it and walked off happily humming to herself.

What I loved most about the markets were the *juju* sellers. Nearly every market had a *juju* seller, who would sit slightly apart from the main trading area with his wares spread out on a sack beside him – shrunken, dried monkey heads, hands, bird and snake heads, bones, claws, strange scaley skins, and a small range of old bottles filled with murky fluids.

A *juju* man is simply a native doctor. His approach is similar to that of faith healers, and his medicines are often little different from those used by European herbalists or old wives' remedies. In fact, several hospital drugs, such as anaesthetics, are developed from plants that the Africans have been using for centuries.

Juju is West African medicine and magic, and, depending on the ailment, the charms can either be hung round one's neck on a string, or they can be pounded into a powder and eaten, drunk or pasted on the affliction. Without certain rituals, the charms are worthless, and the *juju* man is responsible for giving power to his medicine. The rituals usually involve incantations, sounds or shapes, but it is all highly complicated and very secret. For example, certain plants are only potent if they are picked at the time of the full moon, and their preparation can be spoilt by anything from the crowing of a cockerel to the pattern of the maize which is accidentally dropped on the floor.

The *juju* man also sells a variety of spells and he can often make them to order. Most common, I found, were spells for the love of someone you fancied, success in your ambitions, fertility, and once I was even offered one for twins.

Juju also refers to the more violent and occult use of magic, but this is the territory of witches, not the doctor. The one thing which nobody doubts is that *juju* works, and it is indisputably true that, when a curse is put on someone, he will die. Most Europeans agree that it is all in the mind; Africans have such a strong belief in the power of *juju* that, if one is cursed, he gives up all hope, falls ill and dies. But the old timers whom we met shook their heads and said they were not sure, they thought there was more to it than met the eye. People would not admit the existence of things which could not be explained or submitted to their tests of logic and reason. I know that a few people in the western world think that there are things we cannot understand because we have not yet reached the stage of advancement where we can comprehend them. Maybe these things are not mysteries, just mathematical formulas so sophisticated that we cannot yet conceive how they work. In 10 000 years' time it might be as obvious as the rotation of the earth and the force of gravity, and as simple to engineer as electricity from a stream of water. Some people recognise that there are unusual forces and influences connected with certain sounds and shapes, like the mantras of transcendental meditation which induce a different state of consciousness, and the power of shapes such as the pyramid experiments which seem to prove a pyramid's ability to rejuvenate and suspend decay. People will admit that there is something uncanny about Ouija, but they don't like thinking about those things; it frightens them.

The African's mentality seemed to me to be pre-logical. They accept the power of *juju* as part of their cultural heritage and, in contrast to the Europeans who laugh at *juju* and don't understand what it is about, the Africans laugh because they believe it works and they don't understand why it has to be understood.

Lesley and I had now been on our own for three weeks. What had begun as a relationship of convenience was now developing into a genuine friendship. Lesley's was a large, reassuring presence and she seemed fully prepared to adapt her own natural ebullience to my more reserved nature.

Some days, we learnt so much we could hardly absorb any more; some days, we were so exhausted that we couldn't decide when to walk, when to stand and look, or when to sit down; some days, I would follow Lesley, letting her make every single decision as though she were alone and I was her shadow; some days, she would follow me; and some days, we would both follow each other without realising that the other one wasn't leading. We both wanted to live a slice out of every type of life in Africa; and I particularly wanted to absorb it all and think more deeply as I travelled.

4
Deep in the Bush

Our career as hitch-hikers ended abruptly. Nigeria had run out of petrol, the refinery had closed for overhaul, and although ships carrying emergency supplies of fuel had arrived at Lagos, apparently they could not dock because the harbour and offshore area were blocked by over 400 ships laden with cement. Shipping was at a standstill, and without fuel all road traffic came to a grinding halt.

We had just travelled through Bauchi, which is a Hausa word meaning 'slavery'; the town was founded initially as a slave-collecting centre. There was still a duck-billed tribe who insert rounded plates inside their lips, I think it was originally done because it made them too ugly to be sold as slaves, but nowadays it is done for beauty.

The last vehicle we saw was on a lonely road heading to Maiduguri in the north-east near Lake Chad. We had been walking for hours when a Range Rover appeared going in the opposite direction. The driver stopped anyway. He was an Italian called Georgio, and didn't speak any English but knew a little French. He said he was going to a remote place deep in the bush, and he urged us to come and see for ourselves, and stay as long as we liked.

We agreed and I wondered why we even bothered to make plans as they rarely bore any relation to where we went. Things just seemed to happen and change with each day. Georgio took us to the camp of a small group of Italian road-construction engineers. It was certainly remote, but it wasn't what I called roughing it. There was a generator for electricity, refrigerators and air-conditioning, hot and cold running water. Each man had a funny little bungalow built of paper and plywood which was meant to last two years but threatened to fall down at any moment. The only thing these Italians lacked was female company.

Dinner was great fun with every course a different type of pasta. None of the Italians spoke English, so we said they must sing to us. They kept popping up with melodious arias, booming operas, and tender love songs. Everyone sang different songs at once, while Lesley joined in with 'Old MacDonald had a Farm', and I started up with 'Rule Britannia'. I refused to sit beside Georgio because he continually lunged at me with open arms, so I made Lesley sit between us. Georgio would pat Lesley's knee and ask her to pass it on to me; I sent back an imitation of a shotgun aimed at his head; he sent kisses; I threatened to pour a bucket of cold water over his head. It was 3 a.m. when we got to bed, but we slept untroubled.

The following day we went for a walk and in the dry bushland behind the camp we found, to our surprise, two horses. They were remarkably thin, but nevertheless they were horses. The Italians told us that they belonged to the camp, but they were wild, or at least no one had tried to ride them. One of the horses was a black stallion called Diablo, and the other, Cara Mia, was a brown mare who looked slightly pregnant but she was so skinny that it was impossible to tell. The land was barren and dry with only a few odd stalks of dead grass, and I was amazed the horses had lasted so long.

'Nonsense,' said Georgio in broken French, 'they could easily carry you for miles.'

I retorted that I'd love to take them away to some place where the grass was green and they could grow fat and happy. And before we knew it we had acquired the horses. Lesley and I

32

looked at each other in astonishment.

'Well,' said Lesley in her matter-of-fact voice, 'it's a good way of getting round the petrol crisis.'

We then pondered as to where we should go. None of the Italians could agree on where we might find grass; we knew the Sahara lay to the north so we wanted a southerly direction, but we didn't have a map. Lesley had heard of a town called Bamenda which was in the mountains of south-west Cameroun, and since highlands are generally green we decided to go there.

The next step was to see if the horses were rideable. They didn't object to being led round in the two halters we had made out of string, so we borrowed the cushions off Georgio's sofa and tied them like saddles on the horses' backs. We found a large rock to use as a mounting block, and I climbed onto the mare's back. She was obviously surprised but she made no fuss and walked forward when I told her to. Lesley chose that moment to admit that she didn't know how to ride, and said that she would lead the stallion while I tested the mare. We walked for a while, and when I decided to put the horse through her paces, she behaved beautifully.

A road-construction camp in the middle of nowhere hardly lent itself to making a horseback safari so there were no preparations to make. Even the Italians' delicious food was useless because it was deep frozen and would have melted. We felt sure that we could buy local food in the villages, and since we had never made a journey like this we had no idea what else we might need.

We braided our hair African style, dividing our scalps into eight squares, plaiting the hair and tying the plaits together at the back. We didn't look as elegant as the Nigerian women, in fact Lesley said we looked more like spiders, but it was cool and convenient. Naturally Georgio wanted us to stay on, but seeing that we were restless, he made no attempt to persuade us. Instead, he supported our decision and did everything in his power to help us. The Italians threw a riotous farewell party. We were sad to leave them, and as we rode away in the morning we could still hear them singing their lovely melodious cantos to us.

We set off with the horses into the bush, heading south-east, guided by the sun, in the hope that in a month's time we might reach the highlands of Bamenda (in fact, Bamenda was to the south-west). We didn't have a map or a compass, but then neither did we have a tent, mosquito nets, camping gear, or any provisions. We had draped our sleeping bags over the horses' backs, and took it in turns to ride Cara Mia while Diablo carried the luggage and our waterbottles. The straps of our two back-packs were tied together so the bags hung on each side of his back. We led the horses at a careful walk, stopping to let them rest and eat up every patch of dry grass that we passed. They really seemed to be enjoying themselves, and when we unloaded them at noon they both rolled and rolled in the sand.

Lesley knew nothing at all about horses, and I had forgotten that I was allergic to them and before long I was sneezing myself silly. As a child I had owned a pony, which had lived in a lush green field, and was looked after by the farmer. However, that didn't mean I knew anything about undertaking a ride like this. We didn't have a clue how far the horses could walk in a day, how much they should rest, drink or eat. So we followed our instincts, and it was fortunate that the horses were both very docile.

Endless dry scrubby bushland stretched flatly away to horizons that shimmered in waves of heat haze. We followed tracks and paths which led occasionally through small villages, past clusters of two or three mud huts, but they were all strangely deserted. Sometimes ahead of us we saw a village with people going about their daily tasks, but when we entered the village everyone had vanished, the lanes were empty and there was an eerie silence. It was quite late on the first day when I came upon some young children playing in the sand, so absorbed in their game that they hadn't noticed our approach, but when they did catch sight of us they leapt up screaming with terror and bolted

34

away in a panic. Gradually we began to notice that most of the hut doors in the village were ajar, and in the darkness were many pairs of eyes. Behind every bush and slatted corn-silk fence were more pairs of eyes, but when I waved to them their owners howled with fear, and their mothers dashed out of huts, snatched them up and tore back into the safety of the darkness. Although the people always hid from us we often caught glimpses of them. Many were wearing only bunches of leaves, and we knew that we were in the territory of a primitive tribe known as the Pagans.

On the second day of our journey we tried branching off our path but we inevitably discovered that our way was barred by cliffs and tongues of sharp quartz. After several detours we were forced round in circles and no matter how hard we searched we couldn't find our original path. The day was hot; the flies had converged on us, crawling on our arms and on the horses' faces; the air rang with the chirring of cicadas. We found black and white striped lizards with turquoise tails, and some red velvet beetles, but no paths or villages. The land was still very flat, though in the distance was a hill, so we went there and climbed high up to get a view. We saw only interminable flat plains of bush. However, by narrowing my eyes and staring hard I could make out flickers of movement and tidily thatched roofs concealed among the spiky bushes.

When we arrived near the first village we tethered the horses and went in on foot. The women were gathered in the centre of the village; they were shelling and pounding guinea corn, and were stunned by our appearance, but did not seem to be afraid. We made gestures to indicate that we needed water, which they brought, and when we showed interest in the guinea corn they tried to teach Lesley how to pound it with their big wooden mortar and pestles, while I sat and rested my sore, tired feet.

Each woman was wearing two bunches of leaves hung from a cord round her waist. The front bunch was for modesty, and the back one made a comfortable pad for her to sit on. All the women had bald heads and their entire bodies were covered in

35

rows of raised circular scars. I wanted to ask why, which was rather difficult in sign language, but they finally understood and replied that it was *juju* which prevented them from being killed by spears. They brought us some corn cakes and mangoes, and one of the women went off to fetch some mahogany oil which we wanted to smear on the horses' faces in order to discourage the flies. She returned with a wide calabash full of oil, and we gave her a tiny glass bottle and wondered how she could possibly pour the oil in without spilling it everywhere. Her solution was delightful: she plucked a leaf from her skirt and curled it into a funnel shape. The Africans continually surprised me with their simple but ingenious ways of coping with problems. We thanked the women and moved on.

About six miles later we regretted our decision. The sky turned a yellow colour and the sun disappeared behind a dusty fog which became so dense that we couldn't see more than a few paces ahead of us. Our hair and faces became clogged with dust, and tears streamed from our eyes. I knew that it was the harmattan, the dry dust-laden wind which blew off the Sahara, so dry that the local people covered their skin in thick grease to prevent it cracking open. We had no grease because the harmattan usually blows only in the dry season, and it was now mid-May, which should have been the beginning of the rainy season. The storms were just at breaking point, but the heat had built up to a formidable peak, the air was stifling and taut with electricity and the pressure grew to an agonising degree.

As we rode on the villages became scarcer, and we drank the last of our water. Soon we were no longer able to find people or villages, and for about a week, which seemed an eternity, we found nothing to eat. Within a few days we were plodding list-lessly; we were just putting one foot in front of the other, and staring at the hot stony sand passing underneath us. When we glanced up we saw only the scorched sterile dusty plains; nothing stirred because there was not even the slightest breeze. Our senses seemed to close up and in our numbed state we were hardly aware of the burning heat, the soreness of our limbs, and the blisters on our feet. We lost count of how many days we had been travelling. We could think of nothing but our thirst and hunger.

'I'd love some brandysnaps.'

'Yes, filled with cream.'

'Or some sugared doughnuts.'

'Fudge cake – '

' – and creamy luscious chocolate cake.'

I never normally liked chocolate cake, but now somehow in the desert I yearned for it.

With each day our obsession with food increased. My diary ceased to be a story and became just a long list of foods and imagined meals. On 18 May I wrote: 'I want to eat breakfasts of scrambled egg, tomatoes, sausages and toast; lunches of roast pork, or steak and kidney pie, or fillet steak with ratatouille; teatime snacks of cakes, biscuits and jam tarts. Dinners of palma ham and melon, or stuffed aubergines, or French saucisson, then veal marsala, beef bourguinon, or navarin of lamb, or something simple like cottage pie – then either crème caramel, crêpes suzettes, or fresh fruit salad and ice cream.'

At night as we slept under the stars we dreamed of feasts and banquets. We slept on the sand because there were no trees for our hammocks, and we tied the two long neckropes of the horses together at the ends so that they could wander around foraging for grass. Electric storms zigzagged on the horizon, but although we never felt a drop of rain the showers produced small puddles without which we would not have survived. No doubt there were many ways we could have collected water through condensation and perhaps even find something edible, but we didn't know how or what.

Every day was blazing hot. By mid-morning it was too hot to move, and we had to find shade. If we found a tree it was bliss, otherwise we made shade by throwing a sleeping bag over a thorn bush and crawling in underneath. At 3 p.m. the heat was still intolerable but we had to push on. It was a gruelling test of endurance, but our minds were so busy dreaming of food that we fell deeper into our silent reveries.

'Christina, what are your favourite things to eat?' asked Lesley. It took me the whole afternoon to tell her all of them.

I thought too about how much I would have loved a bath. We were stained dark with dust and sweat, and though we tried to wash in the puddles in the evenings when the temperature cooled a bit, we always ended up more grimy than when we started. We even brushed our teeth in the cleaner water. I shall never forget the sight of Lesley when her toothbrush died – all the bristles fell out and got jammed between her teeth.

The flies were a desperate nuisance: they didn't bite, but they flew in our ears, nose, mouth and eyes. The mahogany oil worked only partially. Thorny twigs don't make the best fly-swats. Once Lesley and I spent the whole of our midday break sitting back to back flapping branches round each other's heads, but the moment we stopped the flies crowded round again. Finally we reached breaking point, leapt up, threw the bags on the horses and ran screaming across the sand. But the flies caught up with us. It was a sultry hot and heavy day, some clouds yellow with dust and rain loomed up from the south, but only one came our way. When it grew closer I could see the rain falling, a small grey smudge over the landscape like a missing piece of a jigsaw. By the time it reached us we were ready for it, our baggage was tucked under plastic, and we stripped off our clothes and danced.

Under these conditions it was not enough just to find water, we also had to take salt. However, we didn't have any salt, and the horses craved for it so badly that they would stand and lick the salty sweat from our arms. Our extreme lethargy was induced in part by our own need for salt.

It was not in our nature to be despondent and miserable, and we knew that pessimism, complaints, and regrets could not alter the situation. I don't know if I had this attitude before I met Lesley. I found it a strange experience to live side by side with her, never apart, and I had rarely lost sight of her since we had left England two months before. There was nothing that either of us did without the other one knowing about it, and nothing we heard or saw which wasn't shared between us. I felt that I was beginning to know her mind better than mine. We never quarrelled: there was simply nothing to fight about. As long as Lesley kept going, I felt I could carry on too. Her physical strength was matched by my stamina; we pushed ourselves to the furthest limit of our endurance; and we gave each other the determination to continue. Sometimes I wondered why we were in the bush, what was happening to us, and I felt as though I was being slowly incinerated. But more often I just sat and stared serenely out over the land which stretched horizontally in every direction as far as the eye could see. I didn't hate this mile after mile of sun-punished wilderness; it was so colourless, immense, and godforsaken. To me it was beautiful even though our throats were parched and our stomachs ached.

By the time we finally reached a village I doubt we could have gone much further. We almost crawled in. We were so hungry, exhausted, sunburnt, that we only felt a vague rather fuzzy sense of relief. My legs began to wobble and my head seemed numb. If our ordeal had ended with the feasts we had savoured in our minds, we would have damaged our shrunken stomachs, but as it happened there was no chance of us eating ourselves sick. This was the leanest time of year as the villagers never stored food to last through the dry season and seemed to rely on yoghurt made from milk, and fresh blood and urine. Nevertheless, they were good to us and gave us what they could. One woman brought a handful of groundnuts, another gave two cobs of maize, a third had some spinach-like leaves. Soon they had collected enough to make a small meal which we ate sitting on a log under a blossoming flame tree. It was one of the most delicious meals I have ever eaten. We didn't stay because the villagers had so little, and also

39

our horses were busily devouring all the scanty grass which they
needed for their herd of emaciated humped cattle.

Over the next two days, though we were still crossing stony
wastelands, we found patches of lush green grass, and papaw and
mango trees which we raided for ripe fruit. Between cliffs of
twisted smooth black rock we discovered a deep clear lake filled
from hot underground springs and as we swam we could feel the
hot and cold currents of water. There were small islands of black
basalt columns eroded into curved lines and scooped into hollows, smooth and silky to touch. Dragonflies skimmed above the
surface of the water, multi-coloured kingfishers hovered and
dived for fish, perching on the branches of leafy green trees
whose roots clasped the rocks overhanging the pool. We floated
lazily, and plunged and wallowed in the water, revelling in its
wetness. Before we left we bought a large catfish from a man who
floated past buoyed up on a gigantic round gourd. I made a fire
while Lesley cleaned the fish which we baked in the ashes and ate
out of its skin since we didn't have any plates. It had a slightly
muddy taste, but we ate it with great relish.

Some local people told us that there was a town ahead, called
Mubi, and they directed us to the road. It was impossible to know
whether to turn right or left along the road, and the only sign
was a maxim scrawled on the side of a bridge. It said: 'Lades and
Gentmen, Knowlej is Powar.'

5
Mubi

We reached Mubi which is a small market town, though to us it looked more like a huge metropolis. Our first stop was at the district vet who said that the horses didn't look too bad. He suggested worm treatment and a tonic, and he also said that Cara Mia was definitely pregnant but could still be ridden for a couple more months. Then we went to a chemist's booth because Lesley told me I needed some cream for my chin. When I asked her what was wrong with my chin she said it looked funny. I wished I had a mirror to look at myself and I could feel that my chin was strangely rough. We remembered to buy a new toothbrush for Lesley, and some anti-histamine pills which she said should control my allergy to the horses.

On our way into Mubi, we had met an Englishman called Steven who had invited us to stay. We continued across town and located his house. We thought that he couldn't really have meant that he wanted two girls invading his home and two horses demolishing his garden, but he assured us that he would enjoy it. Dinner was an enormous meal, we ate until there was nothing left and we were so bloated we could hardly move. There was a spare room which Lesley and I shared, with a large double bed under a white hanging canopy, gathered ornately in the centre, falling in folds to the floor. It hardly classed as a mosquito net. It seemed unreal to have returned to an environment where comfort was normal, fans cooled the air, the fridge was full of ice, and electric lights turned on at the flick of a switch. I noticed a mirror in the bathroom and leaned forward to look at my chin. In horror I peered again at the oozing yellow scaly fungus that had developed all over my chin. I felt ill just looking at it.

'Never mind,' said Lesley, 'I saw far worse things in the Amazon, and I'm sure we'll be able to clear it up.' I relaxed. I had total faith in Lesley's ability as a nurse and knew that I couldn't be in more capable hands.

For two days we did nothing but rest and eat, though we still ate every meal as if we might never see food again. Steven was a lively refreshing person, one of several young English teachers who had come to Mubi as voluntary service workers for two years, but I think he found life rather dull. The weekend promised some excitement, however, as the military governor was scheduled to visit the town and there would be a grand celebration.

On the Saturday morning we went into town to watch the preparations. The air was full of festivity, crowds of different tribes from villages near and far were gathering in the streets, and there were scores of men in white flowing robes mounted on sleek prancing ponies in ceremonial harness with tassels and fringes, flashy trappings round their chests, beads threaded into their long manes, and brightly coloured saddlecloths glittering with gold thread. The governor was not due to arrive until the afternoon, but already processions had started to form and people could hardly contain their excitement.

We wandered over to the chief's house where the displays of dancing were to be held outside. Chairs were being set out, and immediately filled by people who were determined to have a good view. A thrill rippled round as some *alhajis* (wise old men) and chiefs arrived, followed by several trucks full of soldiers; the mounted police were hard at work holding spectators at bay and chasing goats out of the square. The grandstand behind us collapsed, but the yells of people who had fallen were drowned in the braying of ancient trumpet-horns, ringing of bicycle bells, and the arrival of the brass band. Then came the boy scouts all wearing green uniforms with striped yellow kerchiefs; a policeman pulled a duster out of his sleeve to polish his boots; and a storm hung overhead in the sky.

We stood entranced, gazing at men in pink lace gowns with matching pink prayer hats, other men in yellow robes thickly encrusted with gold embroidery, and people dressed in fluorescent orange, puce, crimson, shocking pink, plum and purple. Few were empty-handed. Everyone had brought along the thing they prized most and wanted to show off: a sword, a gun, a radio, a snake, spears, shields, and drums of every description from the traditional 'talking drums' to heavily framed goatskins or carved calabash drums. Above the throng of heads we could see bobbing scarlet berets, sequined headdresses, someone wearing a tea-cosy as a hat, others in paper hats, or plumes of waving feathers. The plumes were worn by men dressed in skins and monkey tails, their chests streaked with white paint.

We followed a man in a costume of cowhide and a black war mask. We wriggled through the crowd to the front and found some chairs which had been reserved for us with the teachers. The noise was a deafening chaos of flutes and pipes wailing tunelessly, bugles and drums, the high trilling ululations and whooping calls of the women, girls with bells in their hair jingling and mingling into the hubub of hundreds of voices, the howl of feedback on the microphone, and the echoing rumbles of thunder. The man standing beside me was blowing a six-foot long horn of intricately engraved silver; the bottom end rested on the ground and curled upwards, and its song was a raucous braying. The houseguards wearing green and red robes took up their positions, and the bodyguards dressed all in scarlet formed lines behind the governor's chair. A hush fell over the crowd and we all waited expectantly. The importance of any African government official is defined by the length of time he keeps people waiting. A clerk tries never to make you hang around, an officer will make you wait half an hour before admittance, even though he may spend

43

the time doodling on his note pad, and a state governor will never appear before he is two hours overdue.

Exactly two hours after the scheduled time of arrival we heard the wailing sirens of the outriders and into the square roared four powerful black and chrome motor-bikes ridden by men in black leather clothes, black helmets and black goggles, looking like monster beetles from outer space. Flashing lights and more sirens heralded the approach of a stream of black Mercedes; men stood around with machine guns, whips, and sticks. The governor was arriving. But the dramatic effect was lost as the cavalcade became a huge beeping traffic jam as all the cars tried to turn round at the same time. Eventually they sorted themselves out, the governor sat down, and the celebration began.

The governor was greeted by the chiefs. Each one in turn galloped up on horseback surrounded by his entourage all carrying long spears and riding wild-eyed ponies flecked with blood, and they jostled, pranced and snorted while the customary salutations were exchanged with tribal cries and the shaking of their spears.

Then it was time for the dancers. First we watched the Ndoro Itchen tribe who had skirts of long wooden beads which leapt to the rhythm of their bodies as they jumped round a masked human-bird-animal disguised in rustling dry reeds who whirled and cavorted in their midst, until they were all chased from the square by the Nyanzi people wielding cutlasses, and they took over with a stomping dance of thudding feet, the jangling of metal anklets and the chanting of their womenfolk. The commentator on the microphone announced the turn of the Gudes, the men in nodding feather plumes and with long fringed chin-straps moved in strong and unrestrained gyrations to the surprisingly euphonious screeching of cowhorns, pipes and bells. They were replaced by the Sardalina, then the Higgi, Mambilla, Margi, and Chamba who did a fantastic war dance and I longed to dance with them. I became so mesmerised that I forgot to take any more notes. Unfortunately the governor had arrived so late

44

that everything had to be cut short and there wasn't time to finish the display. The people didn't seem to care, they continued their festivities throughout the night, and danced all the way home to their villages.

6
Going to Bamenda

We left Mubi the next day having acquired another hammock
and purchased a donkey to carry our luggage so we could ride
both the horses. It was a disastrous start. Lesley fell off Diablo
before we even got out of the garden, so we changed horses and
she took Cara Mia, while I tried to ride Diablo and lead the
donkey. It kept stopping dead. Every time it stopped I was
dragged backwards along Diablo's back, desperately trying to
make him stop as well, but the string reins broke if I tugged too
hard. Diablo bit the donkey. I lengthened the donkey's rope and
Lesley chivvied it forwards in her best cowboy style, but at every
tree the donkey swerved and went round on the opposite side
from Diablo.

It was hard work crossing town. The roads were crowded with
bicycles, carts, an assortment of motor vehicles, and hordes of
people who laughed at the sight of us. On the outskirts of town
we got lost, then came to a muddy open drain which our three
animals obstinately refused to cross. In the chaos of the refusals,
circlings and shyings away, all the ropes got tangled and the
donkey bucked the luggage off into the mud. I found myself
shouting and swearing, and then it would strike me as ludicrous
and I'd start laughing. When the donkey dislodged the baggage
for the third time I screamed so violently that a group of soldiers
jumped to attention. We turned down the first southbound path
that we saw, and fled into the bush at a slow walk. The sun had

already set and it would soon be dark. My hands were scorched with rope-burn and both our tempers were frayed. Neither Lesley nor I dared speak to each other until we had made camp and sent the animals out to graze. Our system of tying together the long neckropes of the two horses had worked quite well before; they had been able to wander around grazing but not run away because the rope would quickly tangle round a bush and force them to stop. So now with the donkey we knotted the ropes in a threesome and hoped it would make them all get used to each other. We tied our hammocks between some small trees, and fell into an exhausted sleep.

Although it was dawn when we rose in the morning, the sun was high by the time we finally moved off, and after Diablo had sneakily managed to kick the donkey she behaved quite nicely. The path wound slowly through the scattered hills and we rode across flat pains of cracked barren earth, and up gentle-sided valleys whose riverbeds were waterless but damp, bordered with glossy green trees, ripening mangoes, bushes in bloom, and wild flowers in bursts of purple and yellow. The path was busy with children walking to school, men on bicycles which they had decorated with dozens of plastic flowers, and there were groups of women on their way to market.

All the people we met stared at us with expressions of amazement, disbelief, or blank incomprehension. No one was ever hostile towards us, and the older people would greet us by clapping their hands slowly together three times. It was an ancient salutation implying great respect, but Lesley said she thought it was because we looked like a travelling circus and all we needed now was a pet monkey.

Some of the women looked entirely different to those we had seen before; they were tall, slim-hipped, fine-boned and very graceful. Though their skin was equally black, their faces were delicate with Hamitic features, and they had tribal markings like stars and arrows. Nose rings were worn by most of them, loops of cowrie shells were threaded up and down the rims of their ears, and their black hair was woolly but very long, often reaching to their shoulders in twenty or thirty tight tassels. They wore ragged leather loin cloths and went bare chested like most other women in the bush – it was only around the towns that women were obliged, or preferred, to cover their breasts. They seemed to be very timid, shy people; they didn't run away when they met us, though their eyes were wide and startled like those of the gazelle we occasionally encountered.

At a village well we stopped for water, and the metal smith trimmed the donkey's hooves for us. We asked him about the women we had seen and he told us they were from a nomadic tribe called the Fulani, who roam around with their herds of cattle to the south wherever the land is tsetse free.

The problem of tsetse fly and the sleeping sickness, which would certainly be fatal to the horses, had not occurred to us before. The semi-desert we had passed through had no tsetse flies, but if we rode into the lusher tropical vegetation and forests we could not avoid crossing their haunts. It seemed likely that the highlands would be tsetse-free, so we decided to push on and try to stay in the same territory as the Fulani and their cattle.

By noon the heat was like a furnace and we rested in the shade of a mighty baobab tree, munching sticks of roasted groundnut, and sharing a pile of mangoes with the horses which loved them and even knew how to spit out the stones. I lay back and looked up through the fat bloated branches of the bulbous grey tree, and watched two white egrets gliding in the blue sky. I realised that I was enjoying Africa more than I had ever dreamed possible, although when my thoughts turned to the future, I felt uneasy. Common sense kept asserting itself and asking me what I thought I was doing. I thought of the security and stability which I had always needed, and found myself now dismissing them as irrelevant. There was no room for those feelings any more, and even thoughts of the past and future were rare because the present moment was always so full, stimulating and wide open. I loved seeing the vastness of the sky which stretched from one far distant horizon that we had already crossed, to the infinite horizons ahead which rose and fell in jagged mountain ranges, each range outlined in a deeper shade of blue against the peaks beyond.

As the horizons drew closer and receded, so the days passed, melting into each other in the same way. We would normally ride for about seven hours, covering perhaps fifteen miles at a leisurely walk, since the donkey still took every opportunity to misbehave. We didn't mind the slowness, it gave us time to scan the plains for herds of antelope, the curly-horned wildebeest, straight-horned hartebeest, giraffe, zebra, tusked bush pigs, and troupes of monkeys which went racing through the bush away from us. But we didn't see much wild life, most of it had been eaten long ago by the local tribes. Our slow pace also gave us time to examine everything we passed. We peered down the shafts of anthills built in the shape of castles with turrets and towers; we admired spiky red caterpillars and thick black centipedes; we started a collection of white stones and red- and yellow-lined quartz; and we gorged ourselves on wild mangoes and spent hours picking the strings out from between our teeth. The countryside was a kaleidoscope of greens with all the bushes and trees unfurling new leaves. It was springtime. In the villages we saw lambs being born, calves wobbling to their feet, day-old muscovy ducklings learning to swim in the puddles, and tiny goats playing crazy butting games with one another.

Once, in a large village, our search for corn led us to an old man who spoke English and who took us to his home. The entrance opened into a square tidily swept courtyard bounded by red mud walls which were decorated with patterns of stones and ornate dollops of mud. In each corner of the yard was a round mud and thatch hut. One hut contained the kitchen with some tin bowls, pottery and gourds, and a smoky wood fire; the other huts were for each of his three wives (he explained to us that he lived with whichever wife was not pregnant at the time). He

49

called them all out to meet us and they brought their children and babies. When the old man noticed I was counting his off-spring he added that he had other wives and children but they were old and lived somewhere else. One of the women made us some *kurnu*, which is hot millet soup, and showed us how she prepared it on a flat block of stone with deep hollows made by untold years of grinding grain.

It was incredibly peaceful sitting in the shady courtyard, closed off from the rest of the village. Weaver birds were plaiting their nests in the branches of the trees, bee-catchers darted about and small birds with long beaks dipped for the nectar in the flowers.

We drank clear sweet rainwater from a huge earthenware pot half-sunk in the ground to keep it cool, and we sat in the shade of a tree while the old man taught us some words of Fulani, like *ndiam* (water), *in a hanya?* (where is the path?), *noi?* (how much is it?), *doodoo* (that is too much!), *miyetti* (thank you), *pootchu* (horse), and *vamde* (donkey). It was obviously a good idea to learn some essential phrases, and I always enjoyed knowing the local greetings and being able to reply to them correctly. The Yoruba salutations had been charming. One was 'I salute you for working', or 'I salute you for being seated', and my favourite was 'I salute you for the expense' which applied whenever someone was wearing fine clothes or had bought a new hat, radio, or a new wife. It reminded me of my family's Nigerian cook years ago asking my father for a rise in salary but then being unable to decide whether to buy a new wife or a bicycle.

The old man took us to the market place to buy corn. We saw many people just sitting with glazed expressions drinking gallons of fermented corn beer while others argued over the price of a cow's head which had been neatly skinned and was still complete with eyes and horns. All the while, unnoticed, a vulture was pecking the eyes out of a live baby goat. The old man said not to interfere, and that we must let nature have its way. We bought our corn and the old man smiled as he warmly said farewell.

One night during a storm the donkey ran away. In many ways it was a relief, and Lesley was positively glad to be rid of her. We put the bags on Cara Mia, and took it in turns to ride Diablo. It seemed we were back to square one.

By chance we found a track that was a well-worn smugglers' trail, which we discovered from the caravans of donkeys that passed at night laden with sacks of groundnuts. In Nigeria the price of groundnuts was controlled, while in Cameroun the price was whatever was asked. We found hiding places where the smugglers camped during the day, and where the sacks were emptied, turned inside-out, refilled and stamped 'Produce of Cameroun'. The land was so wild and rugged that they could never be caught.

The track rose higher into the mountains and as the horses slithered and stumbled up jagged channels, their feet grew very sore and bruised by the sharp stones. We didn't ride either of them, but still they suffered. In many ways their condition had improved since we had owned them, but they were tired and their backs were growing tender. The barren rocky plateau seemed to go on for ever and the sun was scorching hot, but just when we began to think we were doomed again to deserted wastelands, the track plunged sharply. We picked our way down carefully and found ourselves in a valley.

The valley floor was like a meadow thick with grass strewn with tall white daisies, dotted with shady trees, sloping down to a blue lake half-covered in flowering water lilies. The air rang with birdsong. We loosed the horses, watched them rolling in ecstacy, and eating their fill while the white egrets perched on their backs and picked off their ticks. From then on the track descended again, often with parched rocky stretches shimmering with dust and heat haze but always interspersed with valleys which glowed with greenness, and streams whose banks were garlanded with red and white striped lilies.

We crossed the border into Cameroun and the way was again

well marked with villages. Most of the inhabitants of the Fulani villages had been so timid that they never ventured near us, but we had left them on the other side of the mountains and were now back among Negro tribes. We found them a more jovial, outgoing people who often invited us to spend the night in their villages. Sometimes they were afraid to offer us meals because they thought their food would poison us. The staple diet appeared to be cassava, a root crop. Cassava was eaten with one's fingers by rolling some up into a ball and dipping it into a sort of spinach and meat soup. In fact cassava is poisonous and has to be soaked in water for forty-eight hours, then dried and ground into a coarse flour. To cook it the Africans add water and boil until it becomes a heavy lump of stodge which I always found totally tasteless. I once suggested that it would be nicer with some salt, but they replied, 'It is not the custom.' That was a sentence we often heard; it meant that the subject was not open to change or dispute, and that if it was good enough for preceding generations, then it was good enough for present and future ones.

In one village we met a group of young men who were making maracas out of tins filled with stones; they said they were for the party that night in honour of the rain and to draw its attention to the crops which they had finished planting that day. They tied the home-made maracas above their ankles and started to demonstrate how their stamping and feet movements made rhythms. The effect was a compulsive beat, and it was soon joined by some drums, which drew the women from their huts and the air swelled with their chanting. It was not yet sunset, but everyone was ready.

From behind the village came a line of dancers, rippling-muscled bodies led by a figure painted blue and dressed in a raffia skirt and woven raffia mask. He symbolised the good *juju* who looked after the corn and groundnuts. Two attendants sprinkled him with water to keep him cool and content, while the dancing gained heat and momentum. It was wild and free, a running swaying dance with feet that hardly touched the ground, but seemed to undulate on the waves of the throbbing rhythm.

Our friends with the maracas reappeared with feathers and beads in their hair, ropes of beads crossed over their glistening black chests, and snake skins trailing from their hips to the ground. Their movements began with a shaking of their shoulders, and the quiver ran from head to foot. They stamped, and the earth shook. Then they launched themselves forwards in unison into a dance which circled, twisted, shuddered, and seemed to embody the music which was pulsating around us. In the fading twilight their faces shone with pride and arrogance. Evening became night, no torches were brought, but the darkness emphasised the power of the atmosphere. I was aware only of the pounding of the drums, the sharp rattle of maracas, strong chanting, the ground vibrating, blurred outlines leaping and jerking in the blackness, muscle and sinew taut with the effort of the dance. I wanted it to go on for ever.

Everything that begins must come to an end, and that included our journey with the horses. Their feet became increasingly tender and their backs grew too sore for us to ride them. We judged that they had done well, but they should go no further – they deserved a good long rest. Shortly after entering Cameroun we stopped at a big market place, positioned ourselves between the sheep and the goats, and put the horses up for sale.

They were bought by the brother of a local chief and he showed us the stable where they would sleep. He knew Cara Mia was in foal and he was very pleased. We were sure he would look after and value our horses, though he only gave us 9000 CFA (£20) for them both.

We stood in the market place feeling suddenly rather forlorn and lonely, and unable to think about what to do next. We bought a pineapple from a woman who couldn't decide what to charge us and each price she suggested was higher than the last. While we were haggling with her we met a man called Manyjohn, who was a lorry driver, and he offered to drop us at Tibati. We didn't know where that was, but it sounded a good idea.

The lorry was a heavy articulated petrol tanker, so we travelled in the cab with Manyjohn and his truckmate, Tapioca. It was terribly cramped and uncomfortable: some of the seat springs had broken; others had sprung up through the covers; the floor had rusted away so we had to keep our feet on the metal supports underneath; black smoke poured into the cab from the broken exhaust; and the heater was turned on full blast to keep the engine cool. The roads were made of rough dirt and the front wheels of the lorry churned up the dust which also came through the non-existent floor in red clouds and flying slivers of stone. It rained heavily for a short time, which settled the dust, but the water poured in through the missing skylight in the roof. All in all it was not an ideal way to travel. The road became progressively worse, worn down to bare uneven rock over which we bumped and crashed, and even on the best parts we went no faster than a lurching crawl. After six hours the lorry groaned and died. Manyjohn said of course it wasn't dead, but it would take a couple of weeks to get it going again.

We didn't expect to see any traffic for days. The roads were probably only open on alternate days to traffic in one direction, and since a new highway was being constructed down the centre of Cameroun there was no reason for a vehicle to pass here along the western border. But after an hour or two, a bus came up behind us. The driver said the fare was 5 cents per kilometre, so we said we would continue on foot. He offered us half price, and after more bargaining we reached an acceptable figure and climbed aboard.

When the bus stopped for the night at Tibati everyone poured off to arrange places to sleep in the village. The driver, Audu, came up and asked us to take supper with him and said there was a spare room in the other half of his hut. Just before supper he drew me apart, rolled his eyes and said, 'I love your sister.' As we ate supper, I tried to explain to him that one couldn't love someone one didn't even know, but he insisted that he was smitten by her. Lesley hadn't learnt enough French to understand what he was saying, so I sat in between them and translated his words to Lesley and replied for her. Audu was a friendly, helpful person, we liked him and didn't want to be rude (quite apart from the fact he might throw us off the bus which was going in the right direction for Bamenda), so I explained to him that if he wanted to be in love with Lesley he must do it the correct way, according to the traditions of *her* country. He must spend at least two days (the length of the bus trip) just sending her loving smiles, speaking glances, and sighing in a melancholy way.

'Can I sleep with her?'

'No, certainly not. She's a tenderly reared young girl,' I replied firmly. He eventually accepted my words and agreed to woo her according to her custom. I had been cast in the role of chaperone and interpreter.

The proposals that we normally received were not flattering – they came from total strangers. Once I found Lesley standing among a noisy crowd of men. She had received three offers of marriage and was trying to hold an auction! I launched into a speech expounding her qualities and virtues, but no one would bid more than ten goats, three cows and a donkey.

Early next morning we ate a large breakfast of fried doughnuts, cassava and goat's meat, and while the passengers loaded themselves back on the bus we walked down to the lake with Audu to watch the hippos wallowing and the fishermen who used round throw-nets.

On our way to Banyo, we went through four closed rain barriers. A common feature of this part of Africa, they are simply a pole blocking the road. The only vehicles allowed through were buses. Anything else had to wait at the barrier for six hours after a storm. If it rained again during that time they would have to wait another six hours. Audu said that sometimes they waited two or three months. The mud was deep and we frequently sank up to the axles, and all the men jumped out and pushed. The downhill slopes were a bit alarming as the bus slid sideways down every one, but Audu was an excellent driver and took good care of his precious cargo. Though Lesley was a fairly hefty girl Audu regarded her as fragile and delicate.

The bus reached Banyo, its final destination, and Audu suggested we three spend the afternoon climbing the highest mountain in these parts. We had grown very fond of him and were happy to spend more time together.

The ascent was easy, although every time I thought we were almost at the top some higher peak would appear. Audu solemnly helped Lesley over the rocks, clucking like a mother hen if she ventured to jump a crevice without his approval, while I was left to stumble along in the rear, never letting them out of my sight and playing my part of chaperone.

There were some ruined fortifications on the summit which Audu said had been German lookout posts; the view was breathtaking, stretching across a sea of mountains. We scrambled around the top among the smooth giant boulders. We discovered a clear running spring, some caves, and Audu pointed out varieties of plants which the *juju* men used in their cures. Predictably, when we wanted to start the descent none of us could remember which way we had come and every side of the mountain appeared to be sheer cliffs. We checked everywhere, but there was absolutely no way down. There were several deep pits and holes leading down the joins between rocks; one of the holes was a nearly vertical chimney about twenty foot deep with daylight at the bottom. We lowered ourselves gingerly down by moving our feet and keeping our backs pressed hard against the opposite wall and came out on another platform above more cliffs. We climbed down tree roots which were clinging to the outside of the cliffs, then we swung across narrow ravines, Tarzan style, using hanging vines, and leapt from rock to rock above dizzy heights. We beat our way through thick undergrowth, crashing, stumbling and sliding down. Audu had long ago put aside his chivalry and let Lesley fend for herself because it was safer like that. I nearly came to disaster when I toppled over a cliff, but luckily it was only a short fall and I landed on some fairly soft springy bushes.

I stopped to rest a moment. Far below was a village, the smoke of the fires was spiralling lazily upwards, a woman was pounding corn. The sound travelled so slowly that the thuds I heard were lagging way behind her actions. I listened to the harmony of the rhythmic thuds blending with the strange twanging song of the tree frogs, wood pigeons cooing, and the rising-falling notes of the cicadas.

We ate cassava and goat meat for supper and spent the evening talking. When Audu heard that we were intending to go to Bamenda and walk around the highlands there his face fell into a worried frown. He warned us that those mountains were the home of the Bamileke who were a fierce tribe known to attack. In the past many foot travellers had been molested and robbed, cars were ambushed with falling trees, and the victims were often killed. However, despite any fears we were determined to go to Bamenda.

Bamenda was more civilised than we had imagined, with electricity, and many white faces. The climate was so pleasantly cool that all the church missions had chosen it as their headquarters. The town was filled with churches, church schools, bible schools, teacher training schools, hospitals, farming and agricultural schemes, peace corps, and everyone out to do good work.

We decided to stay at the Presbyterian mission in Bamenda, but they were so cold and businesslike that we moved over to the Baptists who were much friendlier. As we went upstairs to bed I noticed that their calendar said 16 June. Time was certainly flying past, but I didn't feel it was passing us by. I already felt a good deal older than the kid who had left England three months before.

7
Walking Around the Highlands

Bamenda disappointed us, so we set out almost immediately on foot to walk around the highlands. Despite Audu's warnings, we took no weapon of any kind. A ring-road of some two hundred miles encircles the highlands, and we followed this most of the way. At first we travelled through thick steamy rain forest with huge shaggy trees, moss hanging in curtains from their branches, giant ferns growing in a jungle of bamboo mixed with palm and trees of cactus. Waterfalls thundered down vertical rocky valleys, producing clouds of spray and sweaty humidity.

We walked at a good speed, covering about twenty miles a day. Our rucksacks were light and we felt fit and strong. At nights we stopped in villages and slept in thatched huts on beds of palm and dried leaves. The Bamileke were certainly not the barbaric savages that Audu had warned us about. It was true that they did look very primitive: they were squat and heavily built, with jet black skins. Their faces could seem fierce because they had protruding foreheads, woolly eyebrows, very thick lips, and noses which were so flared and flat that you could see *down* their nostrils. But by nature they were courteous and compassionate. We spent happy evenings roasting maize cobs on their fires and listening to the music of instruments made of calabashes and waxed fibre strings which produced sounds like an acoustic guitar.

We stopped to visit the chief or *fon* of each region. At Bafut the *fon* had recently died, but one of his sons offered to show us round the palace where the old *fon* had lived with his two hundred wives. The central building was a square hall fifty feet high, made out of intricately laced palm stalks and held up by tall pillars of palm tree trunks. The inside was black with accumulated years of soot from a fire which was kept permanently burning to keep away the white ants which ate the palm, and to smoke dry the palace meat supply. The steps which led into the hall were immense hexagonal basalt rocks which our guide said had been carried there on people's heads. The hall was surrounded by a maze of small walled courtyards, the odd tree, and groups of men in extraordinary hats made of elephant hair. Some were curled and clipped, others dishevelled and wild.

The palace was just a relic of the past. Our guide explained that with the death of the old *fon* the tradition had lost its significance. The new *fon*, the third son of the 150th wife, was still at college. He had taken one wife, a European girl, who was a teacher in Bamenda, and they lived outside the palace in a guest house. At Wum the *fon* now made his living embroidering robes because he had no riches left in his palace.

The land became more open. The track had risen slowly above the forests and was winding among the grassy mountains. The only traffic was an occasional man cantering past on horseback and one astonishing bicycle made entirely of wood, even the wheels. The further we continued, the more Fulani people we noticed, with their herds of cattle grazing on the hillsides.

Suddenly a man stepped out into our path and said, 'Welcome. So you have come to see the lake.' He took us first to meet his family and sign his visitors' book. When the family assembled we shook hands with all twenty-one of them, three wives and eighteen children. This marvellous man was called Lucas Beer Nerah, and the visitors' book had records of his family history. None of the birthdates were known. On the marriage of his daughter

Lucy Bin was the entry: 'Received dowry 7500 C F A' (£17) – for them a lot of money.

Then he put our rucksacks in one of the huts and sent us off up the mountain to see the lake. The mountain was an extinct volcano. We walked down to the lip of the crater where the last flow of lava must have poured out. There were flat rocks shelving deep into a fathomless blue lake encircled by sheer cliffs. We stripped off and swam – the water was warm.

Lesley set off to swim the whole way round the lake. I climbed out and went to gather some avocados and then perched myself on some high rocks. It was early evening, the clouds were beginning to creep up the valleys from the lowlands. They rolled imperceptibly forwards, flooding slowly over the mountain passes, rearing up on the horizon, hitting against far-away cliffs and spraying up, spilling over like waves in slow motion.

On the neighbouring hillsides cowbells and the sharp whistles of herdboys echoed – the Fulani were herding their cattle home for the night. Down below me I could hear the occasional splash of Lesley swimming. The ripples washed across the glassy smooth lake tinged with the copper and gold light of the setting sun. Our volcano was still sunny and cloudless, but ahead of me a swelling cumulus drifted higher up the valley, leaving a trail like forest fire. It crawled forwards engulfing the hills, coming closer, billowing and thick, densely white, blotting out the land leaving only the mountain peaks like islands in a tumultuous sea. Tendrils of cloud surged upwards hugging the ground, surrounding the crater, pouring over the lip and wisping out over the water. The ocean of clouds was lit up with glowing red and orange, dying slowly and fading to iron grey. All I could see were the black peaks floating in the sky. The evening star appeared and a fork of lightning flashed in the hills. I shivered with cold, ran down into the clouds and round the crater lip to where Lesley had just finished dressing.

On the fifth day we walked a long, long way. We saw no one at all, not even any huts, only the hills scattered with boulders of ancient volcanic eruptions, a few herds of antelope, and some waterfalls from icy streams which we lay down in to cool off. The day was hot and unpredictable with storm clouds. In the late afternoon we saw a strange flashing light several hills away. It turned out to be a big hut made entirely of shiny new corrugated tin and, as we approached, it stopped flashing in the sun, the sky went dark and rain bucketed down on us. Within seconds we were drenched. We dashed up the hill to the hut, knocked frantically on the door. Someone opened it and we nipped inside.

Our host turned out to be a game ranger. We had been walking through a game reserve, but the ranger told us we were quite safe. Any animals we met would be far more frightened of us than we need be of them. The rain hammered so loudly on the tin roof that we had to shout to be heard. In fact it rained so heavily that in the morning the rain gauge measured ten inches. We breakfasted on meat and plantain (savoury boiled banana which tasted rather like potato), then Lesley and I set off again through the reserve. The track wound upwards all day among open grassy hills. We stopped to swim in passing streams and at a village market to buy some red-coloured sweet bananas and another fistful of local tobacco for a penny.

We noticed some large insect bites which had swollen up round our ankles. They itched desperately. Lesley thought they were caused by jigger fleas which laid their eggs under the skin. I suspected tumbo flies – they live near fruit trees and lay their eggs on damp clothes hung to dry in the sun. If you iron your clothes, the eggs are scorched dead, but if you don't, then they hatch, burrow into your skin, and develop into a maggot. In Nkambé we found a small hospital so we went to ask the Camerounian doctor what insect had given us the bites. He said he didn't know, we must wait and see.

He invited us to stay and I was intrigued to see the way that European-style hospitals failed to work in west Africa. I had assumed that if a hospital was built, the sick would go there to be cured. But it was generally not so. When a person was ill he went to the witchdoctor, and when everything had been tried and failed, then as a last resort he would go to the hospital. But usually he came too late, and died. So it was now common knowledge that if you went to hospital you would die. Of course, this wasn't always the case. There were people who didn't die, but they seldom got better either. When women were given medicine they hid it in their beds. It was hopeless to discharge a woman with medicines to take at home because no matter how many times the doctor told her that her health depended on it, she would throw the medicine away. When she fell ill again she returned to the witchdoctor because she believed in him. Hospitals were far more successful with menfolk. They would crowd round asking for pills and injections. They didn't care what they were for and would claim any sickness in order to get them.

The doctor warned us that all the streams, rivers and crater lakes in Cameroun were infested with bilharzia, a minute parasite which causes irreparable damage to the human system. It is difficult to detect and cure, and very painful.

By daylight Nkambé and its district were the epitome of how I had imagined the highlands. We left the village, out past the chief's hut with its border of grinning masks and spider designs in woven bamboo, and we followed the road over sprawling hills covered in braken, grass, distant herds of cattle and horses, the red flash of flame lilies, bushes studded with gaudy yellow flowers, budlia trees (like lilac) in blossom, poinsettia, and red bluebells. We trudged up hills and went running down the other sides; the morning was sunny and crisp.

We were already halfway round the ring road and apart from a few blisters we still felt strong. A lightweight rucksack was easier to carry than a handbag, and we didn't look out of place because the local people, the Neu tribe, also carried their loads on their backs. It struck me as delightfully logical that the custom of head-loads prevailed in the flat lands, while back-baskets were traditional in the mountains.

62

Slowly the huts became more sophisticated, the valleys more cultivated and the hillsides covered in pine and fir trees. Ndu is situated in the highest part of the highlands, at 6500 feet. We learnt that there were some white people called MacNicol running a tea plantation there. We had not seen any white people since we had started walking so we decided to drop in and say hello. The steward answered the door. He told us the MacNicols were out but as we turned to walk away he invited us in and bustled off to make some coffee. Then he lit the log fire, ran us each a hot bath, and then disappeared into the kitchen to prepare a steak and kidney pie. Feeling rather like Goldilocks we guiltily sat down to dinner, wishing that the MacNicols would return. They were not back by bedtime, but just as I was dozing off I heard the front door slam. I wanted to hide. But the bedroom door opened and a voice said, 'I'm terribly sorry we're so late. I hope the steward looked after you. I'm so pleased you're here. See you in the morning.' And that was our introduction to Margot MacNicol, one of the merriest and most generous people we met in Africa. Her hospitality was to grow into a lasting friendship.

On the rest of our walking tour back to Bamenda we were surprised at the advanced development of the local tribes. This was not the wilds of Africa. The land was cultivated, huts were made of cement bricks, traffic ran along the dirt road and we were within easy reach of facilities. We were rather disappointed. We joked about Audu's fearsome warnings and concluded that his information was many years out of date. We were in for a shock.

Stopping in a village one night we suddenly found ourselves standing beside a thick pole in the centre of a ring of men who were dancing in a tramping jog-trot and whooping with glee as they circled round us. A spear came twanging into the ground at my feet. It was over six feet long and decorated with bands of white horse tail. The men continued to circle us, chanting now as their dance grew more excited. Then one of them whirled into the centre, leant forwards and hissed at us with a long drawn-out snake-like hiss. In one deft movement he plucked the spear out of the ground and sprang high in the air with it. As he landed he plunged the spear back into the ground only inches from my toes. Lesley and I both moved closer to the pole. A second man swooped forward and took the spear. He feigned some thrusts at us, then he bounded outwards, kicked the ground and jumped, vaulting clear over the heads of the other dancers. He ran weaving among them as they circled and then he lunged towards us and stabbed the spear back into the earth. I was mesmerised by the way the spear shaft vibrated with the impact and how it swayed backwards and forwards like a pendulum. Before it had slowed to a stop a third man pounced and grabbed it. Each man in turn took the spear and danced, while the others continued round in a short heavy gait, keeping time with each other and singing in a compulsive sonorous chant which rose spasmodically into waves of triumph and jubilance.

Lesley's fixed smile had fallen from her face.

'I wish we hadn't got into this,' she muttered.

I tried to look on the brighter side and whispered back, 'But isn't it wonderful music. Doesn't it make you want to dance?'

'Christina, if you want to dance, then you go ahead and dance,' she snapped. So I did.

My dance bore no comparison to the spectacular performances of the men, but it was enough to bring the circle to a halt. Faces broke into smiles, we shook everybody's hand, and left rather hurriedly.

That seemed to mark the end of our walking tour – not because the dance had disturbed us, after all it was only a game – but because we felt we had completed a full circle of surprises. There was nothing to add. Anything else would be superfluous. There was also a second circle which I had turned in my mind: I had assumed that I was moving forwards, growing and expanding; soon I would know everything. But instead I discovered that I was back where I had started – the only thing I had learnt was that one could never assume anything.

The only unfinished circle was the ring road. We hitch-hiked back to Bamenda, collected our passports, and then went off to see what the rest of Cameroun held in store for us.

8
Cameroun

It was in Ngaoundere, a town in the Adamoua range of mountains in the middle of Cameroun, that we acquired the bicycles. It was a spontaneous idea and the bicycles were borrowed from an obliging storekeeper. They were rather old and tatty, but each was adorned with a selection of bright plastic flowers growing on long wire stems attached to the handlebars and mudguards. The bicycles turned out to be one of the most hair-raising methods of transport I ever experienced. The corrugations on the rough dirt roads made us bounce and hop like drunken kangaroos.

Our first port of call was at the palace to pay our respects to the chief. He was a Fulfulbé chief, from a northern tribe with similar looks to the Fulani. The chief had over fifty wives, most of whom were inherited from the previous chief who died aged 100. The chief also inherited the riches of the palace, thought to consist of chambers full of gold, chests of jewels, and rooms lined with weapons. The work of the palace was done by slaves; the chief had a massive entourage of bodyguards, and he had a private army of men dressed in colourful flowing robes, with long swords in leather scabbards. We met a massive bodyguard with deep scars in his bald head who kindly offered to show us around.

Men sat resting in the corridors and brown clay cloisters, leaning against thick sculpted pillars, or lying in the shade of long fringed grass roofs which shone like neatly brushed hair. Many of the men were from various other tribes; some looked almost

66

Negro-oriental with slit eyes and high cheekbones, others had huge hooked noses, some seemed ferocious, while others had soft gentle expressions.

Our guide told us that Cameroun has a hundred separate tribes, with fifty different languages. Cameroun encompasses a wide variety of peoples as it does climates, from the Sahara and Lake Chad in the north, the high mountains of the south-west, the coastal belt, to the thick equatorial forests of the south. He described these forests as a dark mysterious place where tribes fight constantly against each other, men eat other men, huge gorillas beat their chests, and when outsiders venture in they seldom return. Then he took us to the front gate where the chief had arrived to hold council. Throughout the session the drummers drummed, the trumpeters brayed, and an old man chanted songs of the chief's greatness.

We left Ngaoundere and set out on a mystery tour. It was a beautiful day, the sky was navy blue with thunderclouds; lightning flashed sporadically; some rain fell which cooled the air and made the earth glow red. The road was bordered with thick-leafed damp smelling trees and plants in profusion. I swerved sharply to avoid some baboons which ran out into my path. The babies were being carried along clinging to their mothers' chests; the males barked at us and advanced rather angrily, so we pedalled on.

We turned off the road along a track which led up an ancient black lava flow. It was rough so we pushed the bikes; the rock was pitted, brittle and lightweight like pumice – we could throw boulders around. From the crest of the hill we saw an enchanting crater lake set in cliffs overhung by palm forest. The water was a clear deep black colour. We plunged in and swam among shoals of tiny black and white striped fish. As we climbed out we remembered the warning about bilharzia, but it was too late to worry. We both had a fatalistic attitude towards diseases, we weren't prepared to let the fear of them spoil our pleasures. However we didn't drink or swim downstream from villages, or in shallow slow water, and we knew that fast running or very deep flowing water had filtered itself and was fairly pure.

Later as we sat in a village eating our customary meal of rice and beans we met a local man who insisted that we shared his bottle of neat gin. He told us about a river which apparently jumped over another river, so we bicycled off to look for it, but instead we found a funeral where all the women had painted their faces white, and a village with a craftsman who was making a brass statue of a rearing horse. He was using the lost-wax method of casting. I had always been interested in handcrafts, and in the past had taught myself to work with leather, wood, plaster, and also metal.

The craftsman said he would show me the process from the beginning; we shook hands, and he introduced himself as Toolo. He dived into his hut to fetch stools for us to sit on. His hut looked more like a round haystack, its long-fringed thatch almost reached the ground, but at the apex of the roof the grass was plaited into an ornate topknot. Toolo came out with a three-legged stool and a folding wooden chair which he said had been carved out of one single piece of wood, and he also brought some wax and clay. We sat in the shade of a tree beside a smouldering fire. I leant forwards, took a twig from the fire, lit the tobacco in my pipe, and sat down to watch.

He began by modelling the shape of the rearing horse out of wax. He worked it skilfully between his long supple fingers and its rough shape soon became a proud horse with muscled chest and flanks some three feet high. The final details of the head, mane and tail were fashioned with rapid knife-strokes. When it was ready Toolo covered it thickly with clay, leaving some ducts opening through to the wax. He glanced at the fire, moved the smouldering logs into the centre and asked me to pump the bellows. The bellows were two bags of soft goatskin connected to a joined line of old tin cans leading into the fire. I took hold of one bag in each hand, pulled them upwards and pushed them down. Clouds of ash shot out of the air-holes at the top; Toolo guffawed with laughter, and came round to show me how they worked. He held the bags open as he drew them up, then closed them between his fingers and thumbs and pumped them down with his fists. He got the fire going and my uncoordinated efforts fanned the flames.

The next stage was to put the mould on the fire, and as the clay became hot the wax melted out through the ducts. Toolo took over the bellows again, turned the fire into a roaring furnace, melted a ladleful of brass, and poured it quickly into the mould through the ducts. He moved the clay mould vigorously around, explaining that he must be sure to disperse the brass so that it would coat the inside of the mould evenly. When the brass finally set, the clay mould could be broken off. Then Toolo would file off the rough edges and decorate it using a hammer and chisel.

The heat of the fire had made me thirsty. Toolo said I would find a jar of fresh rainwater in his hut so I went inside. It took a couple of minutes for my eyes to adjust, and while I waited I noticed an unusual fragrant smell like blossom. It seemed to arise from all around. I drank a canful of water and went outside to ask Toolo about the smell. He grinned broadly and replied that it was an experiment from a recipe he had learnt when he was a boy. He had blended some coconut oil, juice from fruits, sap and gum from trees, and mixed this with crushed charcoal and wood cinders, then he used the concoction to plaster the inside walls of his hut and since that day his hut had been scented. I clapped my hands and said it was a brilliant idea. If his skin had not been black I'm sure I would have seen him blush.

A week later we visited Foumban, a town that seemed filled with craftsmen. Outside every hut were men sitting carving tall wooden statues of primitive beasts with round blazing eyes, distorted elephants, sheep and goats. Some men were metalsmiths casting masks and statues or working with hammer and anvil to create wrought iron; potters were busy moulding clay; weavers were hard at work on their looms making cloth embellished with the traditional Bafoum symbol of a two-headed snake; leather was being stitched with beads and cowrie shells; and straw mats and baskets were being decoratively plaited. I sat down to watch a man chiselling figures onto a wood screen depicting hunting scenes; the man's hut was supported by wooden pillars carved like totem poles of men mixed up with lizards.

None of the workmanship was at all like that which we had seen in Nigeria, and by comparison the art of Foumban was far more sophisticated and finely finished. Foumban dates back to AD 1200 when the Bamoun dynasty was established, and in about 1300 their culture reached such an advanced level that they created a written language. Many of their rulers were women, although they also had sultans (one had 900 wives). The palace was a beautiful four-story building, every stair of the staircase was carved, but we were allowed no further than the throne room because all the wooden floors had rotted and were unsafe.

We returned our bicycles to Ngaoundere, and resumed our hitch-hiking. We found a lorry which was going to Victoria, carrying a load of oxyacetaline cylinders, dried fish and a goat. The driver was a Bamileke and spoke English. He said that the journey would take thirty-six hours and we were welcome to ride on the back. He was called James Bond, which was rather appropriate since it turned into a thriller-type trip with us spending a whole day hiding half under the dried fish, concealed in the fold of the tarpaulin, while at every checkpoint police boarded the lorry to search for passengers. We held our breath, but they didn't find us. It was apparently illegal for the lorries to carry passengers, although it wouldn't have been too serious if we had been caught – we would have had to pay a fine which we could ill-afford. When the lorry was moving we threw back the tarpaulin and gasped the fresh air, and frantic hand signals from James Bond would send us scurrying for cover as the next road block approached. The third passenger was a Bamoun girl with a superb hair style that reminded me of a sputnik. Her scalp was divided into twelve squares, each section was bound in shiny black thread, the braids stuck straight out two inches long and fluffed into pompoms at the ends.

Victoria was a shadow of its past when it had been the central hub of a great plantation area. We saw big German-built houses with their shutters hanging off the windows, peeling paint, wide cracks in the walls, falling into ruin; an abandoned harbour where rusty boats were still anchored, but half-submerged and sunken; the overgrown airstrip with an old broken aeroplane; the plantation railway system with warped twisted rails that criss-crossed the roads and vanished into dense undergrowth; and we saw an ancient steam engine dating to early 1900 that someone had preserved. On our way back through the town we bought some English airmail newspapers. They told us that the date was 5 July; that London was in the throes of IRA bomb attacks; that Britain had said yes to the Common Market; that the weather was cold and rainy; that there were rail strikes, industrial unrest, the pound sterling was plummeting, and prices were skyrocketing. It depressed us.

The beaches in Victoria were small and crowded, and the sand was a dirty yellow colour. We decided to go off on foot heading west along the beach towards Calabar, Nigeria. We had no intention of actually going that far, all we wanted was to walk beside the ocean for a while. We packed a few things, and made ready to leave the next morning.

The first day we walked fast, passing many fishing villages, and the further we went the more streaky and dark the sand became. It wasn't until the second day, when the villages were behind us, that the sandy beach became a pure colour. Black – mile after deserted mile of jet black sand glittering with specks of mica – it was stunningly beautiful. The beach was bordered by groves of shady almond trees laden with nuts, and every few miles a freshwater stream flowed out into the ocean. We frolicked and

71

romped, surfed and dived, and played fighting games with the thundering waves. I loved to wrestle with the cascading foam and to pit my strength against the power of the ocean. Just behind us to the north-east sat Mount Cameroon. Often when we glanced above the trees we saw nothing, it was obliterated in cloud, but other times when we looked back we saw it towering majestically 12 000 feet into the sky.

We wandered for days along the glittering black beach, spending as much time in the sea as we did walking, or running through shallow water jumping the ripples. In the sunset we surfed on waves tipped with fire; in the evenings we ran chasing the crabs which came out to feed at low tide; in the moonlight we swam catching the lights of phosphorescence to decorate our hair; and at dawn we surfed as the fishing canoes went home from their night's work.

The coast was deserted but we eventually reached the village of Idenau which contained a palm-oil mill. We went to the manager's house but he was out. The cook said we should leave our bags there, and he called someone to show us round the mill. It was so old that the outbuildings still had the metal rings for tethering the slaves. The machinery was turned by an immense system of interlocking cog-wheels and rubber bands, all powered by a fire which fed on the husks of the palm nuts. As we scrambled up slippery vertical iron ladders to the top of the building among the cogs and pulleys I felt like a mouse inside a grandfather clock. Down below us were huge vats of thick red palm oil covered in yellow froth.

Jim Wilkie, the English Manager, made us tremendously welcome; he said he was bored with being the only white person in Idenau, and our visit was an excuse to go adventuring. He took us exploring by dugout canoe up the lagoons and creeks which led far inland, through bewitching swamps of mangrove whose roots grew down from their branches so profusely that there were more roots than trees.

Down at waterlevel we looked through tangled tunnels which
merged into perfect symmetry with their reflections and echoed
with birdsongs. We pottered along a labyrinth of channels, pushing aside curtains of white-flowering creeper, and stopped to fish
in a wide pool encompassed by thick forest with orchids hanging
from the trees, monkeys chattering, and flocks of red and grey
parrots winging overhead.

Jim also drove us for miles along overgrown tracks in the hot
damp forest of oil palms.

'Can you see it yet?' he asked, 'It's somewhere in that direction.' Looking hard and far away between the trees I could just
make out a darker grey against the dark misty grey background.
We stopped and plunged on foot into the wet undergrowth. We
found the ruins of an impressive German mansion, with grand
halls, balconies and ornate balustrades. Everything was covered
in moss and lichen; ferns and grass poured out of the cracks;
trees grew straddling the top of twenty-foot walls, their gnarled,
twisted roots gripped firm to the stone, cascading in trailing patterns down to the ground. Sunlight filtered through the leaves
still dripping rain and the earth sweated steamily.

Some distance away Jim showed us more ruined buildings
which were German plantation offices. At the back was a concealed courtyard and in it someone had hidden a car, one of the first
Mercedes ever built. It was probably owned by a German who
fled Cameroun, and since he was unable to take his car he decided that no one else should have it; maybe he hoped to come
back for it after the war had ended. The car was still there, its
long nose, bulbous wings, running boards, untouched by people,
but destroyed by time. If you were to touch it, it would disinte-
grate; it was pure rust. The powerful six-cylinder engine had
fallen through the chassis; grass and flowers grew up through
the floor; the leather and woodwork had rotted into thin air.

We went back to Jim's house for a superb dinner, which
started with crabs and wine, and ended with pudding and
liqueurs, and spine chilling ghost stories. Thoughts of grisly

deaths and spirits wandering forever in limbo made us feel so morbid that we dashed down to the sea for a swim. The night was dark and the water was warm. I plunged in among the ragged roaring waves and surfed until my throat and eyes burned with salt. Then I swam out beyond the breakers. The ocean gleamed like molten lead beneath a sky overflowing with stars. I felt totally content.

9
Bureaucratic Barriers

We had noticed in our passports that our Cameroun visas were due to expire in five days, and although we could have extended them again we thought we ought to move on. We decided to go to Kenya, and once there we could stop, rest, and work. Since our money was running a bit short we chose to hitch-hike there, going through Central African Republic via Bangui to collect our mail, and immediately on through southern Sudan to Kenya. The route which went through Zaire would have been more interesting, but we were determined to go fast, not to make detours, and anyway the Zaire borders had been officially closed since before we left England, so it was out of the question.

Fast cars, slow lorries, a ride on a tractor, punctuated by stops to see a rubber factory and a rock cruncher. Rides which were slow, but felt fast, because all the needles had fallen off the gauges. A boneshaking jeep, and a chauffeur-driven Peugeot whose mission was so urgent that the chauffeur bribed the guards at every closed rain barrier to let us past – while at a level-crossing where a train was stopped, he ordered the train to move on. The speed, style and mood of different rides melted over each day in patterns. Patterns set to the music of the forest passing overhead. Some Dutch peace-corps volunteers moving house had let us ride on top of their truck, the top being a large comfortable mattress. I lay back and listened to the rhythmic swishing sounds as we drove beneath branches. Each note varied according to the description of branches and their broadleaf foliage. Forest closing overhead, against a stormy grey sky, backed by the muddy splashings of the truck trundling along the road. Frequent rainstorms, so frequent that sometimes there was no interval between them. We didn't mind that our next lift was in the rear of a covered lorry. We used old bottletops to play backgammon. At the bottom of a hill the lorry stopped. I looked out only to find a traffic jam that stretched farther than the eye could see. We put on our rucksacks, climbed out of our lorry, thanked the driver, and started walking up the hill.

It was a chaotic traffic jam: most of the lorries were stuck in mud two feet deep. They were all over the road and intermingled with lorries facing the other way which couldn't get past and had also become glued down in the mud. Five miles later we arrived at the front of the traffic jam and the closed rain barrier. We managed to climb aboard the very first lorry in the queue. We left that lorry at the frontier, Garaoua-Boulai, because it was going north and we were going east. The customs officials stamped our passports, 17 July. The only problem was that the entry permits to CAR were valid for just two days.

Our next three days were spent trudging on foot down a deserted and very muddy road. Every rain barrier was closed and there was not a single vehicle to be seen. On the fourth day a bus came along from behind us, stopped, and the driver called at us to get in. One glance inside was enough to convince me that there was absolutely no room. I looked up at the roof, the full-length roof rack was laden ten feet high with boxes, bundles and suitcases, but there was a small empty space at the front. We scrambled up the iron rungs onto the roof, tucked our rucksacks securely under some ropes, and edged round to the front. The roof rack had a narrow ledge which we could just about sit on and our feet reached down onto the roof of the cab. I tapped on the roof to indicate when we were settled and the bus sprang forwards.

I have never been more frightened in my entire life. The roof rack swayed independently and in the opposite direction to the bus; we had nothing to hold on to except the boxes and bundles which were themselves attached to nothing, and the driver drove like the devil. The bus went downhill like a rocket so that it gained sufficient momentum to take it up the next hill, the road was littered with rocks and potholes, and at the bottom of each valley were narrow wooden plank bridges and patches of deep mud. The bus bounced, leapt and swayed down the road, and whenever it hit a rock or hole all the passengers inside shrieked and yelled at the driver.

I forced myself to stop looking at the rushing rutted road, and looked up at the sky and the rolling verdant hills with gaping red mud ravines carved by countless rainy seasons. The view was fantastic and the speed and the wind were exhilarating. The terror that numbed me was transformed into a strange, awesome feeling. It was glorious.

The bus stopped in a small thatched village and some people alighted. The driver shouted up to us that there was now room inside the bus, but we replied that we were happy up on top. The bus carried us for sixteen hours. At a deep muddy patch it became bogged down, all the men jumped out to push and throw branches under the wheels, and we stayed on top while they struggled until it was freed. When it began to rain we pulled a tarpaulin over us, and when night fell we put on our dark glasses to prevent the flying insects from blinding us.

Late at night we stopped in a village and an instant market sprang up to sell fried maize cakes and kebabs to the passengers. Seventy hungry passengers were fed and space was found in huts for everyone. Lesley and I shared a bed made of wooden slats, in a hut with eight other people. At 4 a.m. we set off again, and rocketed downhill, descending into the hot lowlands, to Bangui which was situated on the bank of a wide river.

We tumbled off the bus in Bangui with only two ideas in mind: to collect our mail and to eat a huge meal. The post office was packed with people all tightly squashed pressing forwards, the heat rising from them in visible waves. Lesley started aiming for the counter marked *post retante*, while I queued for stamps. It wasn't quite a queue, it was a mob, all waving bits of paper and trying to reach the counters. I elbowed my way into the mêlée; it took me an hour to reach a counter marked stamps, and the clerk wouldn't speak to me until it was my turn. Everyone always knew when their turn had come, except me, so I let three go ahead and then asked for stamps.

'No, no stamps here, try No. 12.' I reached No. 12, gasping for air, but No. 12 had run out of stamps, and told me to try No. 4. At No. 4 I was successful. Lesley was still at the *post restante* counter, and she had just discovered that the clerk would not give us our mail until we paid him 1800 CFA (£4); he said there was a charge of 30 CFA (10p) for each letter. That meant we had to go to the bank.

The bank was crowded and stank of stale sweat. When our turn finally came I handed the clerk a cheque and my passport. He paged through my passport to the end, stopping to examine all the different visas. We were longing to collect our mail and eat, so I asked him if he would kindly hurry. He began turning the pages backwards even more slowly, and when he reached the beginning he stopped, looked up and said, 'I cannot change any money for you.' I asked why not. He pointed to the passport expiry date, and said, 'Because it is not yet 1984.' I tried to explain his mistake, but he became very angry.

'Are you telling me how to do my job?' he shouted.

We left, went to another bank, and after a long delay we received our money. The post office was still full of people, but this time we managed to get our letters. We were determined not to start opening them until we were installed with food at one of the tables in the market place. Here (for the first and only time in our whole relationship) Lesley and I nearly came to blows, because every cafe had only rice and meat and I wanted rice and beans. Lesley was so hungry that she didn't care what she ate and I was so hungry that I became difficult. Finally I realised that I was not being reasonable, and so we settled down with bowls of rice and meat.

In the afternoon we intended to go to the Sudanese Embassy for visas to cross southern Sudan to Kenya, in the hope of leaving Bangui straight away. But the Sudanese Embassy was closed all afternoon. So we looked for somewhere to stay.

Bangui was a modern city, the hotel prices were extortionate and even the church mission wanted 2700 CFA (£6) from us per night. We found another mission on the outskirts of town who offered us a flat space of concrete on their garage floor for 350 CFA (75p). Obviously even concrete was considered a luxury, though we didn't think so, and Lesley suggested that we spend the evening at a nightclub and keep dancing until we were so tired that we wouldn't notice the discomfort of our bed.

The liveliest nightclub in town was at the Rock Hotel, a sky-scraper building overlooking the river. It was impersonal, and in the foyer was a stuffed freak antelope with eight legs. The night-club was westernised with flashing lights, a rich decor, discreet tables in alcoves, and a discotheque playing British rock music and French love songs. Most of the people there were African, all dressed in highly fashionable and flamboyant European clothes, though the girls had done their hair in the African styles of short shiny black braids. There were about a dozen white people. Lesley and I had chosen a table at the far end, and all sorts of people asked us to dance, though the general rule seemed to be that you didn't need a partner – when you wanted to dance, you just got up and danced. The music blared, the lights flashed and, in contrast to the sounds of the bush, I felt dazed.

We met a talkative American who was one of a team working in Bangui under contract to engineer the installation of a new telephone network. Lesley and I kept thinking of our hard con-crete floor, and having another drink. Lou had a bottle of Johnnie Walker whisky on the table which we helped him drink; he drove us home to our concrete floor and arranged to collect us the next day for a quick jaunt out to Boali waterfalls.

In the morning we set off with Lou to drive to the waterfall, but at the police road block on the edge of the city we were turned back for not having an exit permit. We went to the office in town which handled exit permits but they pointed out that our entry permits to C A R had expired, we couldn't go out until we were officially in, and we also needed an entry stamp to be in Bangui itself. We asked them for an entry stamp and they directed us to a different office three miles away. On arrival at the office they said they only dealt with immigration, and that we must go to yet another office. So we went there, but they had run out of the correct forms and told us to wait. After an hour we decided to leave, but that was not permitted and we were ordered to stay and wait properly. Obviously our waiting was not up to some kind of standard. Finally the bureau closed, they said we could go home, but must return at 8 a.m. sharp the next morning. The day was over.

At 8 a.m. sharp we presented ourselves back at the office; the forms were ready, we completed them and were told to wait yet again. Two hours later the clerk returned with the forms, said they were fine, but now we must take them to another office to be stamped. I wondered why it was all such a difficult and lengthy process, they were acting as though they had never issued a visa before. The official stamps cost us £10, the visas were only valid for ten days, and if we wanted an extension we would have to repeat the whole performance. We inquired about the exit permit to leave the city, and they directed us to a bureau four miles away, so we left and went to the Sudanese Embassy instead. The Sudanese official was very nice, but he explained that southern Sudan was swampy, that it was now the height of their wet season, that all the routes would be impassable and it would take us many months to hitch-hike across to Kenya.

It was rather a shock to have our plans terminated so suddenly. We sat down, looked at each other, and began to laugh. Neither of us actually minded that we couldn't go to Kenya, it had just been an idea, that was all; there were plenty of other places where we could go. There was a big map of Africa hanging on the opposite wall. We were now almost in the centre, which was perhaps not an advantage because it made it impossible for us to decide where to go. We sat back to think and I pulled out my tobacco pouch to fill my pipe. I used three matches before it was properly lit and noticed there were only seven matches left. Yes, that's the answer, I thought, and emptied the matches into my hand. We marked each match in biro with the name of a different country. We chose at random – Chad, Egypt, Ghana, Senegal, Gabon, Angola and Botswana. The Sudanese official watched curiously while I shook the box and Lesley picked a match. It said: Go to Gabon. We had never heard of Gabon before that day, and we looked at it again on the map. It was a thousand miles to the south-west, on the coast just below the bulge.

It was only one mile to the Gabonese Embassy, so we went there and applied for visas. We were told that visas would be ready in a week, which would be at the end of July. We didn't mind the delay and we prepared to wait. There was no longer any hurry so we moved into the house which Lou shared with three fellow Americans.

They were a lunatic bunch of men and great fun to be with. They taught us the principles of atomic energy, the constitution of electricity, theory of heat generation, vacuum spaces, how telephones transmit voices, and one of them called Mark tried to explain to me how to build a flying saucer. I liked Mark especially; we had a common interest in our fascination with insects and together we kept an aviary of flies, bees and anything that flew. We also had a cage whose first occupant was a cricket and when Cricket grew lonely I caught another one and named it Company. They fed on grass and leaves, and when they ate the whole of their red and green patterned faces would go chomping up and down.

Lesley and I found ourselves living a totally American lifestyle. Almost every meal was hamburgers; no one touched African food. The Americans shopped at the big modern supermarket where the arrays of imported meats, vegetables and fruits made my mind boggle. I would just wander up and down between the tall rows looking at everything in amazement. The prices were very high and I calculated that goods were costing about four times as much as they had done in England.

Meals were unscheduled, and tended to happen at all hours. Sometimes we got up at 2 a.m., sat down to a meal which was neither dinner nor breakfast, then went off to dance at the Rock nightclub until 7 a.m., slept until mid-morning, ate cereal and hamburgers, and climbed back into the day. In the bush we had lived our days from sunrise to sunset, and we were stunned by the impact of this new topsy-turvy life, though not less so than by the vast amounts of whisky we all consumed. Each man drank a bottle of Johnnie Walker per twenty-four hours, and they changed us from virtual tee-totallers to averaging a bottle between us per night.

We often strolled around town during the day but our walks were frustrated by the police who frequently stopped us and demanded to see our passports. Unfortunately it didn't end there. When they could find no fault with our passports they started pushing us around, jabbing their elbows in our ribs – doing everything they could think of to make us lose our tempers. We asked the Americans what was the matter with the police and they told us that the men had not been paid for four months, their families were hungry and they needed to buy food. The only way they could obtain money was in the form of bribes, so they prowled the streets looking for quarrels. One hasty word was sufficient to lock you in prison, unless you gave them money.

Aware of our frustrations, Mark invited Lesley and me to join him on a short trip up north near the Chad border. The president of CAR had a palace at Ndele and he wanted a radio telephone installed there. Mark was going to drive up in a big American land-cruiser and he suggested we make it into a camping holiday. His idea of camping was very different from ours. Into the back of the land-cruiser was loaded a large deep freeze full of ice, bottles of whisky, beer and a small box of hamburgers.

The road led north-east through rich flat grasslands where the Bororo people grazed their herds of cattle, and the villages of square huts had many walls painted with life-size murals of men hunting buffalo and elephant. The forest began to close in over the grasslands, rain made deep red puddles and deep red mud, which sprayed out from our wheels onto the newly washed green verges. We camped the night in a forest glade where there were red lilies and some remarkable anthills shaped like giant mushrooms two feet high.

Mark's business in Ndele necessitated a visit to the presidential park, where we found the president entertaining the president of Senegal; a large celebration with feasting and dancing was planned for the evening. We thought we would be asked to stay for it, but instead we were thrown out under military escort. President Bocassa was known for his idiosyncrasies; I gathered that he had dismissed all his ministers from government and taken personal charge of every ministry. His titles included: 'Saviour of the Republic' and 'Central African St Christopher'.

Like Idi Amin of Uganda, Bocassa was obsessed with medals of which he wanted more than any other man in the world. We were told that when the French refused him a medal of honour because he hadn't deserved it, Bocassa had been very upset. In the ensuing quarrel France had declared that she would withdraw her embassy from Bangui, and Bocassa was so outraged that he dealt a historic political blow – he nationalised the French Embassy.

Although it was good to be out in the bush, I couldn't relax. City life had made me tense and our present style of camping with all the sophisticated equipment seemed artificial. Lesley and I yearned to get back to our own way of experiencing Africa at first hand.

It was 1 August, but our visas for Gabon had not yet arrived.

They said it would only take a couple more days. Lesley and I decided it was time to think about the future again. Walking back through town we stopped at a modern stationery shop and bought a map of Africa, and as soon as we arrived at the house we spread the map out on the dining table. First we located Bangui, then Gabon.

'There's not much in the way of roads,' Lesley commented. 'We will have to go back through Cameroun and down.'

'Umm,' I said absent-mindedly. I was looking at the river which went past Bangui. It flowed south, joined the Congo river and continued south-west past Brazzaville and to the sea. 'It's a pity we can't hitch-hike down the river. If we could go to Brazzaville then Gabon would only be a few hundred miles to our north.'

We were still staring at the river when the Americans came in from their morning's work. They all leant over our map, asked what we were thinking, and when I indicated the river to Brazzaville Mark joked, 'Why don't you paddle down in a dugout?' Everyone roared with laughter.

I turned to Lesley. 'Well, how about it?' and she replied instantly, 'Yes.'

We spent a busy afternoon at the river's edge trying to buy a dugout. Nobody wanted to sell a dugout, or else they asked absurd prices. When word was passed around that we were looking for a dugout then we saw scores – all were either too big, too small, or too dilapidated. Someone assured us that we would find a good selection at a fishing village called Poco.

Among the Africans it was considered polite to say 'Yes', and it was rude to answer 'No'. So when we asked 'Is this the way to Poco?' they would all say 'Yes', and the actual direction of Poco was irrelevant. When we asked, 'Is Poco this way or that way?' they also answered 'Yes'.

We walked up to a group of men.

'Excuse me, which way is Poco?'

'This way,' and they pointed in three different directions.

It was also considered rude to say that they didn't know – one must always give an answer to a question. All this could be very confusing, but it was never intended to mislead you; it stemmed from an overwhelming desire to please, to tell you what you wanted to hear so that you would be happy. So we walked for hours but we never found Poco.

Next morning we returned to the riverside, and a fisherman took us across to a village on an island. There we bought a dugout. We were thrilled – it was a superb dugout with definite character. It looked like a hollowed-out tree; it was long and thin with warped gnarled sides and a funny kink in the middle. Both inside and out were a slimy green colour, there were three holes which leaked, and the front end had a long crack. We knew that no African would pay more than £5 for it, but prices for Africans and prices for Europeans were very different things. They wouldn't sell it to us for less than £20, which included two spear-shaped paddles, and since that was the exact amount of money which we had received from the sale of our horses, we agreed to it. Some young boys offered to paddle us in the dugout over to the main wharf, which was lucky as the river suddenly looked awfully swift and wide, and we had discovered that neither of us knew anything about paddling or boating.

We tied our dugout to a barge, and raced back to the house to tell the Americans our good news. After lunch we all assembled on the fishing wharf, with swarms of inquisitive onlookers. Work started immediately. We scrubbed and hosed the slime off the wood, filled the holes and cracks with clay, and patched them with some offcuts of tin which we found on a rubbish dump. I unearthed an old iron bar and picked up a plank of wood to make into a tiller and rudder; Lesley dug around and produced a tattered tarpaulin and some discarded tent poles which we could use to make a rain canopy, and a rather rusty tin trunk for stowing our belongings. Then we returned to the house to spend the evening making lists of things to do and to buy. Lesley and I shuddered at the thought of extensive plans and preparations, we knew that they made no difference to what would actually happen.

I was convinced that our voyage was a perfectly normal undertaking for tourists. We had no idea how long it would take us to reach Brazzaville, but we guessed it wouldn't take more than two months. According to the map the distance by river was roughly 900 miles, probably 1000 miles with all the meanderings, and it led through the heart of the rain forest. This was an exciting prospect because we knew nothing about rivers or forests. African rain forest is never called jungle, it is called forest. Jungle is not an African name – though without doubt Africa's forest constituted one of the deepest and darkest jungles in the world.

Early the following morning we rushed down to the workshop, and found Mark, Lou and their entire staff working furiously on our boat. Mark was making an anchor out of long bolts welded together, Lou was tearing up some old freight boxes. The polystyrene packing became buoyancy bags and the wood of the box was hammered down over the bags producing a flat, slightly raised area at the back of the dugout. Someone was using oxyacetaline equipment to cut a piece of wide-bore pipe which he then bolted to the stern, making a swivel point for the tiller arm. Someone else was hammering wooden blocks in place, and drilling holes through them so we would be able to insert the tent poles for mosquito nets or rain canopy. Another man was washing out a six-gallon plastic jar, destined to hold our fresh water supply, the office clerk was splicing ropes and the watchman was scraping the rust off the tin trunk. We helped everybody and got in their way, so they sent us off to town to do our last-minute shopping.

In the market we bought an assortment of fishing hooks and many yards of nylon line, a length of chain and two padlocks for the tin trunk, two large enamel mugs for us, and a saucepan (no plates, we decided we would use disposable banana leaves instead). Then we went to the European-style shops in the city centre and bought two mosquito nets, lots of plastic bags, and an enlarged map of the area between Bangui and Brazzaville which wasn't very detailed (twelve miles to the inch) – but then there wasn't much to detail, just endless forest with some rivers wriggling through it.

Our provisions were a small tin of coffee, a jar of jam, and five loaves of bread. Admittedly that wasn't going to feed us for very long, but we were sure that the river would be full of fish and there would be fishing villages where we could buy local food; and also we felt that we weren't really experiencing Africa if we lived on canned and imported things.

Next stop was the post office to check the *post restante*, to leave a forwarding address to Brazzaville, and to send our last letters home. In the letter that I posted to my parents I hadn't mentioned the river until the last paragraph, where I wrote: 'Please don't expect to hear from me for several months as we're going by boat to Brazzaville and it's very slow.'

I had begun to be slightly less confident that the voyage would be as easy as I had at first assumed. We had asked many people for advice and every single one of them had said that it was impossible and we were insane to try it. I didn't call that advice, I called that being negative.

'Why is it impossible?' I asked,
'Because it's a dangerous journey, you'll be killed.'
'Why?'
'You'll get lost.'

But Lesley and I couldn't see that it made any difference whether or not we knew where we were, and anyway how could we get lost if we were following the river? They warned us of a hundred unlikely and absurd factors, such as sirens which would lure us onto rocks, hurricanes, or thick fog. But nobody ever mentioned the whirlpools.

10
La Pirogue

I woke up. It was 7 a.m., 4 August – the Great Day had arrived. Lesley and I drank beer with a huge breakfast, put our luggage in the car, filled the storage jar with fresh water, and went down to the dugout.

It certainly was a funny looking craft, but the patched holes hadn't leaked overnight and the inside was dry. The dugout was twenty-five feet (including the pointed ends) by one foot six inches. The sundeck at the stern, which hid the polystyrene buoyancy packing, was five feet long and raised several inches above the curved floor of the dugout. An old iron bar which was attached to the wood plank rudder extended from the point of the stern to the back of the sundeck. The tin trunk fitted neatly lengthwise in a less crooked part of the front end; we put the ropes and the anchor at the point of the prow and there was plenty of space in the middle for the water jar and our rucksacks. We didn't dare admit that we had no idea how to paddle.

All the American team came to see us off. A bottle of champagne and glasses appeared, and we used the dregs to christen the dugout *La Pirogue*, meaning dugout in French. Champagne finished, farewells said, we picked up our short spear-shaped paddles, hopped aboard, waved frantically, and we were off. Although it was the middle of the rainy season, the morning was sunny and the river was calm. Lesley, acting as lookout and chief paddler, was up front perched on the old tin trunk. I was perfectly happy to find myself at the back, and was therefore in charge of the tiller, navigation, and a paddle. I sat on the sundeck with my legs outstretched; the dugout was just wide enough to fit into comfortably, and it rode so low in the water that its rim was only eight inches above the surface of the river.

Bangui disappeared from sight. Now we were on our own and I felt an overwhelming sense of freedom. There was no going back, even if we wanted to we couldn't paddle upstream against the strong current. We had left the security of Bangui and were now out in the big African world of giant trees with roots gone crazy and pale trunks against the black depths of the rain forest.

At this point the river was about a mile wide, with occasional long islands covered in forest but sandy at the ends. We paddled slowly past a fishing village set in a large clearing where men were repairing their nets and women were pounding corn outside their thatched huts. Everyone shouted greetings in French and a man in a dugout paddled over to throw some fish to us. The fish landed on the sundeck. I had considerable difficulty in holding the squirming wet fish while keeping a smiling face. I put them down by my feet and they lay still.

Suddenly ten minutes later one leapt flapping onto my legs. I yelled and jumped, the dugout skewed sideways, hit a half-submerged tree, and Lesley fell off the tin trunk into the river. The dugout straightened up and sailed merrily on as I shouted, 'Stop, stop.' I pointed the front towards the river bank, but it went even faster downstream and no closer to the shore. I paddled desperately towards a bush which grew over the river, grabbed some branches and hung on grimly. They were full of red ants which ran down onto my hands and arms and bit me furiously. Lesley swam alongside, hauled herself aboard and I let go. We shot forwards and found ourselves hopelessly entangled in some reeds along the bank. It was going to be a long way to Brazzaville.

Keeping close to the shore was fraught with problems; the currents constantly pushed us around and we got caught in all the eddying pools with little power to choose our direction. We invariably ended up in the reeds. Many trees had fallen out across the water where the river had undermined the banks, and trying to dodge their sturdy far-reaching branches made me feel as though we were on an obstacle course.

By noon our muscles were aching and we were very hungry so we decided to stop and cook the fish. The shores were densely overgrown so we aimed for the sandy tip of an island. We paddled hard, but the river was stronger and we missed the island completely. Spurred on by our hunger we paddled more fiercely towards the next, but hit the shore at an angle and shipped a lot of water. While Lesley bailed it out I went to gather wood and started the fire. Two branches balanced on forked sticks made a good grill for roasting the fish. We ate a loaf of bread and four fish, which looked like perch, were very filling and tasty, but rather full of sand. Having eaten, we rested in the shade until a long black snake slid past us and into the river, swimming with its head above the water and a rat in its mouth. It was time to move on.

We spent the afternoon mid river, where the current was much stronger, though the only danger seemed to be from the clumps of water hyacinth which came spinning downstream. They wound themselves round the rudder making steering impossible. Legend said that the hyacinth was introduced at the source of the Congo by a Belgian missionary's wife who thought it was such a pretty flower. It was also the fastest spreading weed in the world, and could not be destroyed or used. It grew and multiplied on the surface of the water, with hairy roots, strange bulbous stems, attractive diamond-shaped leaves and delightful purple flowers. I picked some of the flowers and arranged them in my bailing can.

As clumps of hyacinth went past us, we had the impression we were going backwards. Lesley's clock had been soaked in one of the morning's accidents – it stopped working and we moved into a state of timelessness (I had sold my watch in Kano). When it was nearly sunset we found a parking space between overhanging trees alongside a low cliff of sand.

With blissful ignorance we set up camp, rigging our mosquito nets over the old tent poles in the central section of the dugout which was long enough for both of us to lie in comfortably. I lay down contentedly to listen to the night noises, but the only sound was a strange, loud humming, like mosquitoes. The noise was so loud that Lesley and I had to shout to make ourselves heard. I found some mosquitoes inside my net, and some more, so I assumed the net must be torn. I sat up and started looking for the tear, but couldn't find it. I looked again, but there were more and more mosquitoes inside. Then I realised what was happening, and I stared with fascination and horror.

The outside of the net was thickly coated in small mosquitoes, small enough to simply fold back their wings and crawl through the netting. Within five minutes I counted over three hundred mosquitoes in my net, and the number kept growing. They bit viciously and repeatedly, even stinging through a layer of cloth, so I threw on more coverings, until they couldn't bite that deep. I didn't dare move a muscle in case the padding slipped. It was a hot equatorial night and I became slimy with sweat. There was not a breath of wind and inside the dugout the air was still and close. Underneath all my coverings I felt claustrophobic. I wanted to scream and scream and scream. The high pitched howling of the mosquitoes made me feel twisted with loathing; my stomach felt knotted; and my fists were clenched tight. I pleaded with the night to end quickly while the sweat continued to pour off me until my bedding was soaked. I wrapped a towel around my head and face, leaving only a tiny slit for breathing. The mosquitoes crept through the crack and stung my nose, lips, tongue and all round the inside of my mouth. In exhaustion I dozed off, but I woke up choking with my head under water. A torrential rainstorm. 'Lesley,' I yelled. She leapt up sleepily, overbalanced, fell in the river and was swirled away. The cliff of sand beside our parking space became waterlogged and collapsed forwards onto the dugout, which started to sink. I sat down, put my head in my hands, and began to laugh.

Lesley somehow reappeared, and in the dark we bailed out the sand and water while the mosquitoes feasted on us. All our clothes, everything we had was wringing wet. The night seemed interminable. We huddled silently together wrapped in a sodden sleeping bag, shivering, constantly looking up to the sky for any sign that the night was ending, and praying that dawn would come soon.

The sky lightened, and the blood red sun rose slowly above the forest horizon. The horror of the night faded quickly in the beauty of the day. The howling mosquitoes had gone. We heard instead the cries of monkeys, the splash of pied kingfishers diving for fish, and the whirring wings of flocks of red and grey parrots flying overhead.

Our reverie was interrupted as a cross current flung the dugout head first into the reeds. We pushed through them to the bank, it was a good opportunity to stop, find dry firewood, make coffee, and rummage in the tin trunk for the nivaquine pills. Over the past month we had been taking one pill every day, but because there were so many mosquitoes we doubled the dose to two pills daily. At the bottom of the tin trunk we found a lovely surprise. It was a bottle of whisky which the Americans had hidden there and marked: 'For use on rainy days.' Next we re-erected the tent poles, strung a washing line from the front to the back of the dugout, and hung all our clothes and gear out to dry while we floated on down the middle of the river. We passed some local fishermen in a dugout. When they caught sight of us they stood up, their mouths hanging open and their eyes bulging. I suppose we must have made a strange picture: to them it would look like nothing on earth, to me we looked rather like a floating Chinese laundry.

Our day was heaven. It was peaceful drifting along in the gentle current, and every now and then when I had nothing better to do I would paddle lazily, listening to the riot of jungle noises, and watching clouds of large yellow and black butterflies against a sunny blue sky.

At dusk we moored *La Pirogue* to a fallen tree. It was another horrific night of mosquitoes and the darkness rang with their evil blood-frenzied song. This time I didn't use thick coverings, I climbed into my sleeping bag, but the sweat bath was just as bad and somehow the mosquitoes found a way inside the sleeping bag. I screamed a long anguished howl. Lesley didn't go to sleep, she sat up inside her mosquito net and used the torch to spot the mosquitoes, clapping her hands on five or six at a time and announcing the death toll in a monotonous voice all night long, while far away we could hear pounding drums of people celebrating in the forest. We opened the whisky bottle but took only a small drink, knowing that there would be many more nights when we would need it again.

As the sun rose we floated off downriver. Dawn in an iridescent world, hushed as the inner wall of a shell. Mist floating suspended in a never-ending sky, vulnerable as all beautiful things. The water was like glass; purple flowering hyacinth cast reflections as true as life; we drifted silently; it was not for us to disturb the tranquillity. The wide flat river went snaking through dense tangled mighty forest; trees tall and majestic, roped together with knotted vines, strung with white flowering creeper; branches hung shaggy with green trailing lichen, and enshrouded in cobweb; straight trees with pale luminous pinky-yellow bark, short squat trees with leaves like fans, or feathers; trees with leaves the size of umbrellas; gnarled old and crooked trees; immense trees 100 feet tall with roots like the fins of rocket ships; impenetrable dark undergrowth; monkeys fighting and thunder rumbling; parrots and hornbills flying overhead; hot and sultry sun; the smell of sweating earth in the forest, and the perfume of flowers hanging heavily in the air.

I caught sight of a movement on the water; it was a dugout going across the river to an island where there was a group of six small round huts. The dugout was paddled by a woman returning from her vegetable garden; she came over to look at us, steering close alongside. She sold us twenty maize cobs and a branch of plantain bananas for 50 CFA (11p), although what she really wanted in exchange was *La Pirogue*'s rudder.

I really enjoyed being helmsman and learning how to handle our dugout. There was a variety of factors which affected our course and every change in each small element altered our direction. I had to take into account the river currents, the breeze, what clothes were hanging up to dry, which side Lesley was paddling, and how strongly we were paddling. When we both paddled powerfully the dugout responded far more quickly to the rudder and was much easier to control. The kink in the middle of *La Pirogue* meant that it always looked as if it were moving crabwise. Navigation was no problem; we either aimed for the furthest river horizon between the islands, or else we chose a particularly beautiful water hyacinth and followed wherever it went.

We reached the junction of three countries, Central African Republic and Congo on our right, and Zaire on our left. It was about noon so we stopped on an island, made fire, roasted some corn and plantain, and finished off the fish from the previous day. We dug under the trees looking for worms to bait our fishing lines. Our tackle was rather primitive, just hooks tied onto nylon thread and wound round bits of wood, but then our fishing wasn't very skilful either. Generally I just dropped the hooks overboard and looped the lines through my toes.

Lesley fell asleep in the sand, she hadn't slept at all the previous night, and I went off to chase big colourful butterflies. A swarm of flies appeared which didn't bite but tried to crawl into my ears, eyes, nose and mouth. They had also besieged Lesley, so we jumped into the dugout and fled. One island that we paddled past produced an echo, and we started clapping, tapping and drumming on the sides of the dugout, the rhythm resounding back and forth punctuated by the screeches of the monkeys and the haunting song of the hornbills which sounded like the ringing of a crystal wine glass when you run a damp finger fast round its brim. Our melody ended with the hiss of rain which swept upriver, made the water bubble and drenched us. We tried to take shelter under the tarpaulin, but it was full of holes and totally porous.

As the day drew to a close I started thinking about the night ahead and I shuddered with fear. The dugout was too wet to sleep in, the river banks were sheer clay cliffs topped by thick forest, there was nowhere to stop, and we hadn't seen any villages or huts since early morning. We kept moving, hoping to find a stopping place; sunset became twilight, and the night arrived, but we still hadn't found anywhere, and then it was too dark to see. We knew that if we went along near to the shore the current would push us onto rocks and half-submerged trees, so we pulled further out into the river. In the dim moonlight and with the aid of our torch we could just make out the line of the cliffs; the torch batteries were failing, so we put in new batteries, but they didn't work. Obviously we weren't going to be able to spot a camping place. A couple of miles later Lesley called out that she had seen distant flickering light and our hopes soared: the flickers of light turned out to be moonlight glinting on waves, white waves; soon we could hear the roaring noise of fast-rushing water, though we couldn't see what was happening. Time stood still, and we kept moving.

The noise grew louder, and my eyes ached from straining to see in the darkness. The river became choppy, then it was churning and foaming, as we both paddled desperately; the dugout veered to the left and began to swing round; I pushed the tiller out against the current, a wave flooded in over my legs, the dugout responded, and we slid into calm water. Whatever it was back there, we had missed it. I was terrified.

It started to rain, and the miles stretched on. Then we heard voices, real voices, somewhere on the Congo shore ahead of us. We shouted to them, 'Help, help, please get us off this river,' and we kept yelling until we were hoarse. Lamps appeared, and we were guided to the bank by the light. We tied the dugout to a tree, staggered up the rough clay steps hewn in the cliff, and into a small clearing with a *campement* of three huts. Five people wearing grass skirts stood in the lamplight staring at us in astonishment. We shook hands with them all and when we smiled they beamed back at us with their old and wrinkled faces.

The language of the river tribes was Likouala. It was a harshsounding tongue but easy to understand from tones and expressions, and some of the words were derived from French. Many of the local fishing folk we had met spoke simple French, but here they only spoke Likouala.

'What are they?' one asked.

An old woman replied something to the effect of, 'I think they are girls.' Whatever it was she had said, the other disagreed and they took us to the fire to observe us more closely. We sat down by the fire. Since we couldn't converse with them in French we drew some pictures instead. They were delighted with the pictures and put them proudly in their huts. They gave us supper of highly peppered fish, which was so hot that I felt as though I was breathing flames. We slept on mats on the floor; more rain cooled the night, but the mosquitoes still tormented us.

A sore-throated rooster woke us at dawn. We thanked the people for their kindness and as we clambered into our dugout we found that they had put a pile of fish and cassava there as a present to us.

We drifted and paddled leisurely onwards, ran up against a submerged sandbank, climbed out and pushed, glided on, then hit another sandbank, climbed out and pushed again, but every inch only wedged the dugout tighter and higher on the sand. Soon it was stuck firm. The water was only a few inches deep. We pushed and pulled and dug away the sand from underneath, but got nowhere. A strong fisherman paddled up, gave our dugout a hearty shove, refloated it, and handed us another fish.

In a short time, we were out of the sandbanks and onto a fast

La Pirogue

straight stretch of river. We raced along feeling elated with the
wind blowing through our hair as we sped the paddles in short
rapid strokes through the water. We zigzagged among the clumps
of hyacinth which floated spinning lazily in the swirling movement of the current. Then the surface of the river suddenly
erupted and we shot head-on into the bank. The surface of the
river could change abruptly; one moment the water would be
flowing strongly but placidly, and the next instant it became a
raging, bubbling mass of wide circles which spun with uplifted
edges. I presumed that they must have been caused by the powerful underwater currents hitting rocks or shoals on the riverbed,
and as the current veered to a specific angle, so the surface
erupted in turmoil. The local people called them whirlpools.
Many were permanent whirlpools, like the ones round every
headland, some were small and weak, others were very large and
very strong. Being caught in them produced a feeling similar to
driving a car on ice; suddenly you were out of control, skidding
and sliding weightlessly.

To begin with we were not very good at managing the dugout;
we spent a lot of time hurtling downriver broadside or backwards, both shouting instructions to each other that neither
could hear. We were growing expert at spreading out our soaked
belongings to dry in the sun. The tarpaulin was constantly wet
because it lay in the bottom of the dugout, and as soon as we
dried it, something unfortunate would happen. Accidents such as
once when Lesley was carying the freshly dried tarpaulin down
to *La Pirogue*, which had moved out slightly from the shore.
Lesley took two paces in ankle deep water, and at the third step
she fell up to her neck in the river. The tarpaulin was soaked
again, and we laughed until we cried.

Nights were less horrifying after Lesley suggested that we try
sleeping on the shore in the breeze and not too close to the
water's edge. The first night we tried that we found a riverside
glade on the Zaire bank and made camp there. Within half an
hour three men arrived in a dugout, and one, who claimed he was

97

a member of the militia, came ashore. He wanted to see our papers and examine our boat. We were rather anxious because we didn't have visas for Zaire, but we needn't have worried – he didn't know how to read. After looking intently at the pictures he turned to *La Pirogue*, started pulling all our gear out of the tin trunk and ordered us to tell him what it was for. We knew from experience that if we explained the items then every time he saw something he fancied he would demand it. So we offered him coffee and sat chatting with him instead. He was very pleasant and he left after dark. We dug the tent poles into the ground, draped our mosquito nets over them, and settled down to sleep. The mosquitoes invaded us but it was not as bad as before. Then it started to rain so we got up to pull the tarpaulin over the dugout. The rain was followed by the noise of monkeys fighting, squealing in anger and throwing nuts at each other which landed on us. Finally, there was peace and quiet, except for the eerie howling of a wildcat hunting nearby in the forest.

In the middle of the night the militia man returned. This time it was a social call – he had brought a huge smoked catfish to eat as a midnight feast. It was delicious, but the man showed no signs of going away. I had an inspiration. I started to scratch. I scratched my arms and legs and head as though I was thick with fleas; Lesley joined in. It had a potent psychological effect and after five minutes the militia man bade us goodnight.

Our second visit to Zaire was more fun. We stopped at a village to refill our giant water container which was almost empty and we found that the local water supply was of course the river. The river was a muddy brown colour from the rains which were falling here and to the north, but if the villagers could drink it then so could we. A huge crowd had gathered round us the moment we stepped ashore, the atmosphere was friendly, but they stared and stared. The bolder ones spoke to us in simple French and asked if they could touch our hair, exclaiming with wonder at its softness. Others peered curiously at the colour of our skin, assuming that the whiteness was due to a disease. Several people wanted to know if we were girls. Then they brought out two stools, sat us down, and stared at us for a long time. I was equally curious about them. Most of the people wore grass skirts, and I noticed some remarkable tribal brands, including many narrowly-spaced parallel lines which gave their faces a weird stripey look. At first I felt embarrassed about wanting to stare at Africans, I had always considered it impolite. But in Africa it is not rude to stare and by tradition a newcomer was usually expected to sit or squat while he was scrutinised for half an hour. When the people were satisfied having looked at his appearance, they would formally demand to know his tribe and destination.

'What tribe are you?' asked a big man standing at the front.

'English,' I answered.

'Where are you going?'

'To Brazzaville.'

A murmur ran through the crowd, and the big man who was obviously their chief observed (in all seriousness) that we would not reach Brazzaville before nightfall, so we had better stay the night in his village.

They were gregarious affable people; they wanted to know about the countries we came from and why we were paddling down the river. Lesley noticed a young girl with some infected sores on her arms and aked if she could help her. Our medical kit consisted only of aspirin, nivaquine and a tube of antibiotic cream, but Lesley couldn't bear to see untreated injuries or people in pain. The girl took us to her parents' hut where we boiled some water and someone brought a piece of cloth to tear into bandages. Then someone else came and requested Lesley to go and look at his sick father, and several people turned up who seemed to have malaria, so Lesley dispensed some nivaquine to them. Quinine was the only cure for malaria; I was surprised to learn that quinine trees did not grow in Africa. For white people malaria could be a killer, but it seemed that the Africans had adapted to some extent and only suffered from a mild form of it.

99

A tiny man whose chin only reached to the height of my waist asked in gestures for Lesley to come and attend to someone who had been wounded by an elephant. It was quite a long walk, inland from the river on a small path through the forest which was very overgrown with vines and creeper that wrapped itself round our necks and ankles. Every plant had thorns. Many of the trees had claws like large rose bushes which grew all over their trunks and branches. Other trees had spikes; the vines had thorns, the bushes had barbed prickles, the undergrowth was a tangle of brambles, briars and thistles. The little pygmy man slipped through the forest as though it was silk, but Lesley and I got lassoed, tripped up, and clawed by every plant we passed.

He took us to a pygmy village where huts were simple grass shelters in contrast to the mud and thatch of those of the river tribes. Pygmies seemed to live a hunter-gatherer style of existence, moving from place to place in search of a fresh supply of food. Six pygmies were standing beside one of the shelters, the tallest of them was about four feet high. They weren't dwarfs – but they looked like miniature people. They were wearing loin cloths and a couple had quivers of arrows slung over their shoulders, but all six of them vanished off among the trees when they saw us.

The man who had been hit by the elephant was lying in the shelter; he had a deep gash in one leg, but Lesley said it wasn't serious. He watched her every move as she cleaned and bandaged the wound, and when she finished he smiled and chanted a sing song speech. The forest was quiet. No one was going to return to the settlement while we were there, and since it was probably getting late we hurried back to the river village. The chief welcomed us back, and sat us on stools outside his hut. The crowd gathered to watch what we did. I felt like an animal on display and wished that I could perform tricks for them. My only trick was to fill and smoke my pipe, which startled them as effectively as if I had done a series of cartwheels.

During a supper of hot peppered fish and spinach, I asked the chief about the pygmy tribe. He told me they seldom came to the river (none of the pygmies were river people) and they never inter-married with other tribes. Other tribes considered the pygmies equivalent to animals. He added that we would see a few more of them in the morning because it was market day and they would bring dried antelope to trade in the village. Lesley and I shared a wooden bedstead in our hut; it wasn't sprung but the mattress was made of bundles of rushes and was very comfortable.

The morning market was a good time for us to stock up our food supplies which had dwindled to half a loaf of bread, jam and three maize cobs. It was not a busy market – it was more a village social gathering. We walked around chatting to people as we tried to decide what to buy. There was no need to buy anything because all the villagers came up to say thank you to Lesley for helping their sick families, and they gave us presents of plantain and sweet bananas, maize, smoked fish, cassava and papaw in such quantity that the centre section of the dugout was too full for us to move from front to back unless we balanced on all fours and clambered along the rim of the sides. We shook hands with everyone and just as we were casting off the little pygmy man came running down to give us a chunk of antelope. Then we set off and the people lined the bank to wave goodbye.

I enjoyed our stopovers in villages, but most of all I loved the free feeling of being alone with our dugout floating downriver, watching the day roll past, and threading our way at random among the islands. By now I had realised that I was wrong in assuming that tourists always paddled dugouts to Brazzaville. My original mistake was in thinking that there were other tourists, for as Lesley pointed out, Central African Republic was hardly an attractive resort. The astounded reactions of the fishing folk made it obvious that they had never seen white girls before and the nature of the river made it clear that this was not to be an easy jaunt. Lesley said she had known this all along.

'Then why didn't you tell me?' I asked.

'Because I didn't think you'd listen,' she replied.

Neither of us had any wish to change our mind, not that it would have made any difference if we had as we couldn't go back. The thought crossed my mind that this was certainly a good way to learn about taking responsibility for one's actions. We didn't regret our impulsive undertaking, not even at nights when we suffocated in sweat baths tortured by the mosquitoes, and when the ants tunnelled inside our mosquito nets, and when we were drenched by rainstorms, or during the day when we stopped on fly-infested islands, and when crocodiles plunged from the shores into the river where we had just been swimming.

The river was now a couple of miles wide, and every day it provided us with a fresh challenge. It alternated from glassy calm to raging roughness in storms that whipped up out of the blue in a matter of seconds, and it took us to extremes of paradise, hell, exhilaration and fear.

With the heavy rainfall upstream the water level in the Oubangui and Congo basins rose, releasing acres of previously trapped hyacinth weed. Some of the hyacinth floated in single plants, each with its decorative purple flower; sometimes it came in clumps which were the size of small islands. Some days there was little hyacinth, while on other days such as this one the surface of the river was thickly coated in it. I deduced that the daily quantity of weed was equivalent to the amount of rainfall upriver; I smiled at its simple logic, then turned to stretch my arm down to the rudder and disentangle a clump of weed which had become wound around it. A gust of wind blew more hyacinth against one side of the dugout and I had no sooner freed the rudder than it became entangled again. The wind that had blown the weed against the dugout was still blowing and pushing both the weed and the dugout over into the main current, but we could do nothing to prevent it because the harder we pushed away from the build-up of weed the further we moved into the fast main channel. More weed jostled against the dugout and when a large clump bumped into the stern the dugout swung broadside. Everything happened very rapidly. The dugout was heavier and floated more slowly than the weed, so the weed quickly accumulated against the upriver side, pushing hard, trying to force its way underneath, and the dugout began to tip.

'It's going to roll us over,' screamed Lesley. We both threw our weight to counterbalance it and tore at the plants with our hands. We grabbed them to throw them aside but they slipped through our fingers in sludgy disintegration, and every moment more weed was massing up against us. It was moving so fast that the already tightly packed plants doubled up and wedges of hyacinth cascaded into the dugout. The dugout had become a barrage and was creating a backwash of water that roared underneath it from the free side, and it needed only one more push to flip it upsidedown. The danger girded us into a desperate balancing act on the upper rim of the dugout and with frantic efforts we bailed out the slimy plants. But we knew we didn't stand a chance of freeing the dugout from the wall of weed that mounted steadily higher over it. I glanced forwards and noticed that the river was swinging into a bend; the current swung wide round the curve digging the bend deeper into the forest; it had eroded under the banks and many of the giant trees had fallen out across the river. We smashed through the branches of the first. They ripped us to shreds but we didn't stop, our wall of weed pushed us through and on, sweeping us under the low-lying trunk of another tree which I hadn't seen. It knocked me flat and passed within an inch of my head. Then there was the grinding splintering of wood followed by oaths from Lesley. The dugout halted and I looked up to find that we were firmly stuck in the middle of a tree. The weed was left behind lodged against a strong branch in a monstrous bulwark of green foliage. The current was still forcing us on under low branches and in the pandemonium of swirling water and cracking wood we hacked our way forward, chopping at smaller branches with our paddles. In a last desperate effort we freed *La Pirogue*, drifted into a quiet cove, and came to a gentle stop on the sand.

Several sharp lessons were necessary before we learnt how to cope with the hyacinth. By paddling hard we could travel at the same speed as the hyacinth; we found we could keep control, and where shallow backwaters were choked with the weed, we cut down a sapling to use as a punt pole.

One afternoon as we floated lazily downriver, resting and sunbathing in the sweltering heat, I heard a noise that sounded like a series of grunts. There, sticking up above the water was a pair of ears. Then a hippo surfaced, and a second one, a third, fourth. The dugout jolted abruptly and seemed to bounce backwards. Neither of us had noticed the hippo in our path and now we had forced ourselves on his attention. He turned, remarkably swiftly for such a bulky animal, opened his massive jaws, showed an amazing display of tusklike teeth, and went for us. We backpaddled frantically, steered hard right, and raced for the other side of the river. A storm broke overhead. We reached the shore, sheltered between the roots of a tree, and watched the hippos. The rain poured on and on, but we got tired of waiting, so we decided that if we ignored the weather it might give up and go away.

At sunset the sky cleared, and the river turned to molten gold. We made camp on a small sandbank with one tree, sat contemplating the beauty of the endless river horizons between the islands, and drank some more of the whisky. Lesley was so tipsy that when she went to fetch her mosquito net from the dugout she fell overboard.

We had spent exactly one week on the river.

11
A Celebration in Impfondo

The eighth day of our voyage marked a change. The river was crowded with dugouts scurrying around, and some were so crammed with people that they had to stand up in a row to fit inside. The passengers were wearing their best grass skirts, in addition to a selection of coloured or shiny pieces of cloth which they tied round their arms and legs, and garlands of flowers in their hair. There was excitement and laughter in the air. Everyone was going to a place called Impfondo for a grand celebration with music and dancing. I pulled our map out of its plastic bag and located Impfondo. It looked as though it must be a town, but there were no roads leading to it through the forest.

Two young men in an overweighted dugout offered to come aboard *La Pirogue* to help us paddle faster. Their tribal markings were a dramatic three-forked Y on their chests and backs, and their faces were covered in crosses and zigzags. We were very grateful for their help as the river traffic was too chaotic for us to negotiate on our own.

Rows upon rows of dugouts were parked along the village riverbank and there were queues trying to navigate into the creeks. One of our young men suggested we try the dugout-park which looked rather full but they nosed *La Pirogue* in among the others and tied it to the one in front.

We joined the thronging crowd of people heading for the celebration which was being held on a flat area above the river cliffs. Our men left us because they had to go and get ready to dance. The drummers had already started and had apparently been warming up since early morning. We wandered around chatting with people and stopping at various makeshift bar booths to drink the local beer. We met the headmaster of the primary school, many friendly people, and to our absolute amazement we caught sight of three white men. The headmaster said they were French engineers organising the construction of a new airstrip.

We walked over to the dancing area, the drumming grew more vigorous, the music swelled with rattles of tins filled with stones, jingling of metal scraps strung on cords and a cow horn trumpet. Anything that could make a noise was added to the rhythm. The womenfolk began to dance, starting in a shuffling line, swaying together in a long undulating movement. Their eyes were glazed and they flowed with the music as they formed into a wide circle. On the outside of the circle were smaller bands of dancers, each with their own drummers, creating a medley of contrasting rhythms for the different tribal dances. There was a group of pygmies, but as I edged my way over to them my attention was caught by the action in the main central circle of dancers.

Twenty men wearing kilts of leather strips tied round their hips with monkey tails ran into the circle. They divided into pairs and began to wrestle with each other; as one opponent was thrown to the ground the victor roared with triumph, the crowd roared back, and the loser was carted off. Then victor fought victor in a process of elimination, until only two were left. The drum beat intensified, the men circled each other, stealthy, controlled and powerful, bodies glistening with sweat, every movement in time with the rhythm. As they fought, the ring of women urged them on with whoops and ululations, moving round in waves of pulsating bodies, flickering hips, combining into one entity with the atmosphere, noise and turmoil. The warriors fought on, each seeking a firm grip on each other's black and slippery body, tussling, wrestling, writhing free and leaping to attack. The fight reached its climax; one held the other high in the air, then let him fall to the ground like a stone. The crowd rushed forward and the champion was carried on their shoulders in a march of triumph. A group of very well-dressed men congratulated him, and I asked someone who they were.

'That is His Excellency the President of the Republic of Congo. Do you want to meet him?'

I wondered what on earth the president was doing here in the middle of the forest, and was told that he had come officially to open the airstrip that the French people had engineered. Neither Lesley nor I had ever met a president before and when we were introduced we didn't know whether to shake hands or curtsey. We shook hands. The president was charming and we were invited to attend the party in his honour that evening. During the party we met Albert, a very likeable Congolese man from Brazzaville who said that he lived in the African market but that we were most welcome to come and stay when we arrived in Brazzaville.

At midnight Lesley and I retired and went to an empty school teacher's house which the headmaster had kindly said we could use. He had given us a key and warned us to lock the door securely. Just as we were falling asleep another key turned in the lock from outside, the door opened, and in marched the chief of police.

'You do not have my permission to be here,' he said in clipped speech.

'The headmaster said we could use this house,' I replied.

'No you can't. It's illegal,' and he proceeded to inform us that it was illegal for us to sleep anywhere in the district unless we had permission from the police. As to the problem of obtaining permission he was sure he could help us. He went into the adjoining room and we heard some shuffling sounds, then he ordered us to come there. He had laid out a very rat-eaten mattress on the bathroom floor.

'Right, which one of you wants to be first?' he said, undoing his trousers.

The absurdity of the situation was too much for us, Lesley and I both pointed at each other and said, 'You.' Then we started to have a mock argument while we pondered how to get out of this. As we argued we walked back through our bedroom and out of the front door. The police chief caught up with us outside and demanded to know where we were going; he was furious when we replied that we were going to see the president, and although he could do little to stop us, he persisted in trying to bully us. We deliberately misunderstood everything he said. It was a tricky situation as we didn't want to be insolent or imply any disrespect.

'Don't you understand, as chief of police I am the man with the power to allow you to sleep in that house.'

'Thank you.' We strode back into the house, barricaded the door, and went back to bed. There were no mosquitoes, the night wasn't too hot, and we slept soundly in peace.

On the following day while walking to the market, Michel, the boss of the French team, drove up and invited us to lunch. Their camp was five miles from the town and consisted of eight little plywood bungalows, which looked like cardboard boxes and reminded us of the Italian road camp in Nigeria. The inside of Michel's bungalow didn't remind us of anywhere we had ever been – there were luxurious shaggy carpets, raw silk curtains, stained glass lamps, rich Chinese hangings, paintings and scrolls of rice paper etchings, and air conditioning powered by a generator. Lunch was a seven-course meal, with a different wine for each course. I think their supplies had come directly from France and were brought to Impfondo by plane.

We had intended to continue paddling downriver that afternoon, but we were too bloated and sleepy from the wine. Michel said there was a spare bungalow which we could have, and in the morning our departure was postponed because I found a butterfly net which I was determined to try out. We spent the day dashing along forest paths chasing butterflies which flew faster than I could run, and just as I lunged at them with the net they would flick their wings and vanish high among the trees. There were large and incredible butterflies; many had a wingspan of four inches, and on some the secondary wings tailed into long points. They were every colour imaginable from plain metallic silver, to reds, blues, greens, yellows, and spotted striped or patterned. We leapt and cavorted after them all day, while they fluttered around us stopping to rest on our arms, hands, and on the net. We collected the most beautiful and pressed them like wild flowers in a book.

Dinner was another splendid seven-course affair, so lavish that even the cheeseboard had varieties from goat, sheep and cow. Michel was our host, but the other four Frenchmen also wanted to entertain us. They planned a barbecue for the following evening, so we delayed our departure yet another day. During the morning we received a message that the police in town wanted to see our passports. We went directly there and reported to them. The police chief made us sit and wait for an hour before we were shown into his office. It took him another hour to read our passports from cover to cover, then he wrote our details on some forms. My name was entered as Ibadan Designer (birthplace and profession), but I didn't want to tell him his mistake.

The evening barbecue was lovely. I had expected them to buy and slaughter a local goat, but they didn't. They went to their supply shed and brought out enormous, juicy fillet steaks. As we sat talking the Frenchmen begged us to stay longer in Impfondo; I sensed that they felt isolated and tired of each other's company. They were all married men, but their wives had not been able to face the isolation and physical discomforts of living in Africa and had returned to France. They were not the sort of men to harass us sexually and we knew that they genuinely enjoyed having feminine company, chatting, joking and showing us things they had found in the forest, or photographs of their families in France.

On the fifth day Michel tried to put pressure on us to stay, so we decided that it was time we left. The date was now 17 August – I smiled when I thought of everyone back home taking their organised summer holidays. Lesley and I spread out our map, and using some cotton thread we measured that we had already come 250 miles. That distance had taken us seven days, we had covered roughly thirty-six miles per day, travelling an average of eight hours per day, at about 4½ mph. We concluded that Brazzaville was still 650 miles away. According to our calculations it would take us another three weeks.

12
Down the Congo

We were once more on our own with the river. We felt full, and
rather drunk, from the farewell lunch party. We paddled into the
roughest water we could find, seeking out the waves and turbulence, laughing our way along eddying currents. We didn't mind
if we were soaked – it was bound to happen soon anyway. Late
afternoon the river became calm, the forest echoed with song, the
sun jabbed multi-coloured daggers through the trees and
reflected golden paths for us to paddle along. We stopped for the
night in a sandy bay, built a fire, roasted our very dry maize
and a fish which Lesley had caught. We had gone from the
sublime to the ridiculous, but weren't sure which was which.

Dawn, and we set off meandering down tranquil backwaters behind the islands. They were narrow, shallow waterways
with grasses growing up through the surface midstream and
herons wading around. Heavy curtains of creeper hung out
across the water from thick branches of trees intertwined so
densely that they appeared to be growing out of each other. In
amongst the greens were bursts of bright orange, yellow and
scarlet red leaves. Everything in the forest seemed back to
front: the trees sprouted their new spring leaves in all the
colours of autumn, and worked backwards until they became
green. Other trees were bearing fruit or clusters of berries; we
often heard the crack of seed pods exploding and I wondered
if perhaps they would soon be in flower. This was a land

where we were travelling backwards in time from the middle of the rainy season in Bangui to the early rains in Impfondo, and soon we would be at the beginning of the dry season which we had already experienced. It was an upside-down world, where reflection was as real as the actual thing. We sat on a sandbank eating our lunch of rice and jam and felt as though we had stepped straight into Alice in Wonderland.

Mid-afternoon we came to a fork in the stream, one side went on through peace and idleness, the other would link into the main river. Oh decisions! I yawned, and opted for some action. The river was boisterously pleased to see us and we realised that now we must concentrate. The sound of rushing water turned into rushing water; there were patches of deadly calm bordered by waves surging in confusion; we hesitated and went through. Lesley was singing, 'Che sera sera, whatever will be will be, the future's not ours to see, what will be will be.' A wave poured into the boat, I began to bail it out and thought how this would have terrified us at the beginning of the voyage. We didn't shrink back at the sight of white waves anymore. In fact, we had started rather to enjoy them and, to prove to ourselves that we were no longer amateurs, we spent the rest of the afternoon racing slalem between the clumps of water hyacinth, ducking through the arches and roots of half-submerged trees, and dashing across the small whirlpools that we found after each headland.

At dawn, after a very bad night of mosquitoes, Lesley cast the dugout off from a tree. Unfortunately, she gripped a caterpillar on a branch and its poisoned black spines broke off in her hand. As we drifted downriver, I sat on the prow with Lesley and plucked the spines out, one by one, with my nails.

A wispy mist lay over the glassy smooth river, hyacinth floated past, and the sky reverberated with thunder. The islands were swampy, smelling of stagnant water mixed with the fragrance of orchids that festooned the trees and the lilies that adorned the marshes. Black and white pied kingfishers hovered in the air and flocks of brilliantly coloured butterflies settled on the dugout.

We tiptoed unnoticed past the red flag of a village police post, because we knew that, if we allowed every village to stamp our passports, they would soon be full, and we couldn't get new passports in the Congo since there was no British Embassy.

We stopped on a large, sandy island with palm trees that rustled in the gentle breeze. I stretched out in the sun and watched an eagle high overhead being attacked by two glossy, black starlings. I could almost feel the wind in my feathers as I soared with them. The afternoon was heaven, every shore was a pure white sandy beach, the sun blazed down, the river was calm and we jumped overboard and swam for hours leaving the dugout to drift on its own. The breeze blew towards Zaire, so we went with it. We liked sleeping on the Zaire bank because it faced west and the twilight lasted much longer. At dusk we built a veritable fortress on the shore, using every piece of mosquito netting, linen, towels, long skirts that we carried, determined as we were that it wouldn't fail. We slept soundly and overslept the dawn.

The riverfolk were curiously funny about the opposite sides of the river. The Congolese would point to Zaire and say in hushed tones, 'Don't go over there. Over there they eat people.' The Zairois would point at the Congo and say, 'Beware, those men are cannibals.' We were not alarmed and it never occurred to us that anyone should want to hurt us, let alone kill and eat us.

Human sacrifice and cannibalism are known as *bouiti*. It is not murder; it is simply the traditional and established method of reversing bad luck or appeasing the anger of the spirits. Many tribes believe that something or someone is responsible for every disaster. If lightning strikes a hut and the occupants are killed, the villagers are convinced that someone in that tribe has offended their ancestors. It could be anyone, even someone who was not present in the village. Whoever is declared guilty cannot argue or plead their innocence. The victims of *bouiti* are chosen by the tribe's witchdoctor who is in charge of the physical and spiritual welfare of the people. Generally, he will nominate people whom he dislikes or those whom he considers have not given him enough favours. The whole ritual and process of sacrifice is wrapped in superstition and tradition and, although there are variations from tribe to tribe, *bouiti* usually takes place after the accidental death of someone important. On such occasions, a child is sacrificed to pacify the ancestral spirits.

One evening I fell into conversation with a group of young men whose teeth were all sharpened to V points. They invited us to a party the following evening and we spent the day in between rambling in the forest with them. They showed us how to extract a waxy resin from a tree; when dried and mixed with oily fibres, the resin burns as a torch for twenty-four hours, and gives off a smell like incense. They took us to some crocodile pools and one, who was called Heko, explained a simple method of catching crocodiles.

We returned to their village and sat chatting round the fire. I noticed something in the ashes. The longer I stared at it, the more it looked like a burnt-out, half-chewed hand. There were several of them, some charred out of recognition, but some had unmistakeable fingers. I wasn't disgusted or even disturbed by the implications, I was simply curious. I picked up a stick, twitched one of the hands out of the ashes, and asked Heko what it was. He roared with laughter, slapped me heartily on the back and spoke rapidly to the others in their own dialect. They all fell around laughing. Lesley and I were not sure if we should laugh too, or if the joke was on us.

'Don't worry,' Heko said, 'we don't eat white people.' In fact, we never did worry and I trusted these Africans implicitly. When Heko asked if our tribe ate people, I replied that for us it was taboo.

A lot of what followed that night was unclear to me, but I do know that we didn't eat human meat. In fact, Heko brought us a dead monkey and said, 'You may cook this for tonight's feast. You must start now or it will not be ready in time. We will help you.' First, we put it on the fire, to singe off all the fur. It looked such a sweet baby-faced monkey, but, as it burned, the skin shrivelled and its face changed from a sleeping baby into a grotesque snarl. Then, we washed it and the men left us to cut it up. I gulped, but Lesley, practical as always, said, 'Here, pull its legs straight Christina, I want to cut off the feet; and its arms, too, we don't want to eat the hands.' She severed them off at the wrists, and I added: 'What about its head? Do you think they'll mind if we chuck that away too?' So we hacked off the head. The rest we dissected like a chicken.

Palm oil is generally used for frying but, on this occasion, our companions brought over a pan full of grasshoppers. They put it on the fire and soon there was a puddle of fat which had dripped out of the insects.

'You can use this to fry the monkey; brown it until it's crisp, you'll like it that way.'

'We never skin a monkey – same with humans – the skin doesn't come off easily,' said Heko as he chopped up some onions and pimentos and threw them into the pot. He told us that we should mix in some water, then leave it all to cook for as long as possible so the meat would grow loose from the bones. He added that the problem with monkey, and especially with human flesh, was that the meat tended to cling to the bones. That was why his tribe sharpened their teeth, so that it was easier to gnaw and tear the meat off the bone. He grinned at me, showing both upper and lower sets of needle-sharp points.

I liked Heko tremendously. He spoke slowly in French and was very frank and open. It was rare to meet an African who was as entertaining as he; he knew what would amuse and interest us. Most of the Africans who had enough education to speak French had also learned to look down on their culture and be ashamed of its primitiveness. To those people, I could not speak on equal terms because they regarded themselves as inferior. Heko and his friends were different. They did not see themselves as primitive; they were proud people, who saw themselves as the living embodiment of an ancient heritage. The question of equality, superiority or inferiority never arose in our conversation; we were from another tribe, another world.

We had a terrific evening; the monkey was delicious, but a bit strong and tough, and tasted like a cross between pork and mutton. Heko tried to teach me to play bongo drums, and we chanted and danced until we were exhausted.

Early morning we shook hands with every person in the village and set off again.

The river was calm and silky. I hung my legs over the side in the water, while little fish nibbled at my toes. The day was gentle and blissful. We didn't cover many miles and our overall progress seemed to be growing slower and slower, but we weren't in any hurry. *La Pirogue* ran aground on sandbanks innumerable times and at noon we headed for a beautiful group of sandy islands. The islands were paradise; nothing but white sand, a few trees and a couple of bushes hung with seed pods like lanterns.

'What's for lunch?' asked Lesley, and we decided to try something different. Taking the old mosquito nets, we plunged into the shallow water, scooped up a netfull of tiddlers, and fried them like whitebait. Since there were no broadleaf trees, we couldn't pick leaves to use as plates, so we improvised and made plates from some twelve-inch squares of flat tin which we had brought from Bangui to use for patching leaks and holes in the dugout.

Our staple diet was rice and jam, plus the occasional fish that we caught – until the day we found the pumpkin patch. We had stopped to brew up coffee beside the ruins of some huts; the forest had regrown over the clearing; the huts were half-buried under creeper and, when I went behind them to have a closer look at some red and yellow flowers with sprays of long, fluffy stamens, I discovered that I was in an overgrown vegetable garden and that the logs I was tripping over were, in fact, huge, long pumpkins. Many of them were rotten, which proved that nobody else was interested in them and, anyway, there were enough ripe ones to fill twenty dugouts. There were also pawpaw trees laden with fruit, some maize, and cassava, whose roots and leaves are both edible. We filled the dugout to capacity and, for several days, we were in danger of sinking, so we ate like mad to lighten the load. They were glorious days; we saw no one, not even local fishermen, just birds, butterflies, islands of white sand and the full moon at night.

The river seemed to be losing itself in a maze of sandbanks and water hyacinth, in every direction we could see a river horizon and we decided that the river must be turning a wide corner. It occurred to us that it might even be the junction of the Oubangui and Congo rivers, and when the Zaire bank loomed ahead of us we knew that we had guessed right. It meant that we were on the wrong side of the junction; we didn't want to be hurled out into the focal point of their confluence, we wanted to slide smoothly in, following close to the western shore.

Since it was almost sunset, we camped on the Zaire shore. We were woken by shouting voices and stamping feet. I inched my mosquito net up and peered out. Against the moonlight I could see a line of men stomping around us; their heads jerked backwards and forwards with each footstep. The shouting was coming from a group of five who stood to one side chanting in chorus. After each chorus the leader stepped forward and shouted, 'Come out. Come out. We want to see you. Come out, we've come to get you.' More chorus and stamping.

Lesley suggested that they didn't mean us, and she went back to sleep.

The next verse made my blood boil. 'Wake up. Come out. We're taking your dugout, you'd better come out.'

That was going too far. My temper snapped, I flung a wrapper to cover myself, and emerged from the tent spitting with rage like a wildcat, snarling and screaming violent abuse at the dancers – who took to their heels and fled. Then I rounded menacingly on the chorus, who trembled and took a pace backwards, but their leader stood firm and demanded to see our identity and to know our purpose there.

'We're tourists, and we're asleep,' I screeched at the top of my voice, growing shriller with every word. 'You can look at us in the morning. Now go away.' I shook my fists at them and they scarpered off into the darkness.

It took me a while to calm down enough to go back to sleep, then I thought I heard a noise, so I got up and checked around. Nothing. With a sudden shock I remembered that I was afraid of the dark, but now wasn't the right time to dwell on that. It occurred to me that I was constantly having to deny all my inbred reactions to situations, they were no longer appropriate. Every shred of my old character was being re-evaluated, but not by myself; it was circumstances which now governed me. The most profound change was in my lifelong craving for security which was turning into a love of the unpredictable. I told myself not to interfere or question the changes.

I checked that the dugout was still there and realised that we shouldn't leave it in full view in case the men came back. So I climbed aboard, paddled it into a creek and hid it there. I had to swim back. I crawled wearily under the net and flopped down to sleep; but the night was full of strange noises; even the cry of an owl sounded sinister. The Africans said that an owl was a vampire and they dreaded hearing them.

In the morning, we made an early start out across the river, determined to reach the Congo bank before the junction of the rivers. The Congo shore was not visible, there were so many islands in the rather marshy delta, but we knew that we would get there if we took a diagonal route across to the west. It took us three days — three very long days — to reach the Congo side.

During this time we were attacked by tsetse flies — big, squat, grey flies which are carriers of sleeping sickness. We were bitten by so many that we couldn't paddle, all we could do was scratch fiercely, and with each hour of each day the flies got worse. They crucified us. Though they were big flies, we could never feel them sitting on our skin, but we felt their sharp stings and the bites and the itching were no less aggravating than the frustration of not being able to kill them. We experimented by wearing different colours, thinking there might be a colour which would repulse them, but there wasn't. So then we invented a new method of paddling: we attached sets of twigs to our paddles, and each stroke was a combination of swat-paddle-swat; unfortunately though it didn't stop the tsetse flies from biting the soles of our feet. We tied twigs everywhere, so every movement made us rustle like scarecrows, but the tsetse weren't afraid. They simply flew in and hid under the leaves to bite us.

To make matters worse, the current was sluggish and the dugout responded slowly to the tiller. We then got drenched by a storm. Emerald green bushes grew thickly out from the islands over the water and concealed the banks. The bushes would have made excellent shelter, but we knew from bitter experience that they hid a million evil things. By evening we were miserable. To our great relief, the solid line of bushes ended and a sandbank came into view. We stopped there for the night. There was no dry firewood. We were wet, cold, sore and exhausted.

Two more days of tsetse torture passed before we felt a fresh breeze and saw the sun sparkling on the choppy backwash which marked the end of the delta. The current picked up speed; soon we were racing along, and we launched out onto the Congo river, into the roughest waves we had yet encountered. It was exhilarating as the dugout surfed along, while the currents merged, tossing us around. When we tried to cut the corner, we ran straight into a vast whirlpool. *La Pirogue* skewed sideways, shipped a lot of water, hit some rocks and somehow ended up still hurtling downriver.

As we looked up, we saw the red flag of the Congolese police post at Liranga village. There were several men watching our performance from the bank, so we knew we must go and report in for passport examination. It took several hours for them to read all the fine print of all the previous and expired visas, which was a good opportunity for us to catch up on sewing and mending. The police were good-natured people and they kindly gave me some grease to loosen the tiller pivot which had gone rusty. While Lesley attended to a man with a cut on his head, I went into the village to trade some of our pumpkins for yams and sugar-cane. When I asked for tobacco, they looked at me blankly. I asked everyone and, eventually, found a young boy who understood my request. He set off down a path which led through a maize garden, back into a forest, until we arrived in a clearing where there was one solitary hut – with tobacco plants growing beside the mud walls. The owner was a very old woman; the boy said she was not allowed to live in the village, but he wouldn't tell me why. The old woman cackled with delight, clapped her hands with glee, and broke off many huge tobacco leaves to give to me. I gave her some money, but she didn't know what it was. She pointed to my sandals; I tempted her with pencils, matches and everything else in my handbag, but she made it absolutely clear that she wanted the sandals. So I gave them to her and returned barefoot. Lesley had finished coping with sick people and was fixing up the broken wing of a lovely falcon which the police had shot by mistake. Finally, we were ready to go and all the policemen turned out to wave goodbye to us.

They made us promise that we would stay close to the shore, and we did intend to, but the dugout floundered in the swells and the currents pushed us onto rocks where the waves broke and tumbled. We decided to try going farther out, and soon we were so far out that the land was just a thin line in the distance. The dugout rose up the crests of the waves and crashed down into the troughs. We paddled swiftly and spray flew in the wind. The river was muddy brown and now about six miles wide. *La Pirogue* rode so low in the water that often we could see only the swelling waves though, from the crests, we caught sight of some large islands. Occasionally, one of the islands had a *campement* of a few fishermen's huts, but the majority were deserted isles of white sand and dark green forest. Very far in the distance we could see the spiralling smoke of a forest fire.

The following day we realised that it was a colossal fire, and it was directly ahead along the river. The sun was blurred behind clouds of smoke, ash and cinders floated down in the air and we heard the crackling of the flames. As we drew nearer the smoke thickened; I hung my tobacco leaves from the washing line to absorb the smoky flavour and steered a course down a relatively calm current a hundred yards from the Congo mainland. Far ahead of us the fire was moving rapidly down the river bank; the trees were tinder dry because the rains had not yet started here. The fire hadn't left much – a black smouldering landscape, wisps of smoke, and stark black skeletons of trees. We camped in a flat, burnt-out glade; the ground was still hot and my bare feet began to feel scorched. The day turned into an eerie pink and, at night, the sky was dramatically lit with glowing orange clouds while on the horizon flickered the crackling red tongues of the fire.

Dawn and away. We soon caught up with the fire and found that the mainland and many of the islands were ablaze. We paddled down channels between banks of flames. It looked unearthly; the sun was visible overhead as a flat red disc and I wondered if hell could possibly be as beautiful. The heat was like a furnace, and the crackling was deafening. Sparks showered, hissing into the water. Burnt grasses and leaves rained constantly from the sky.

I didn't understand why the islands were burning; perhaps someone had deliberately set them alight. We passed some fishermen, so I asked them about the fire. One said it was the villagers who were clearing the forest to plant their patches of corn; another said it was to facilitate wild-pig hunting; and the third said it was because, when the river rose and the islands became submerged, the fish would not be able to hide in the vegetation so would easily be caught in the fishermen's traps.

At Lukelela we didn't stop to offer our passports to the police, but someone must have seen us passing. They alerted the army, who came out searching for us, caught us and dragged us ten miles back upriver in their motorised dugout. The next major stop was Mossaka, a river port and regional headquarters. It was a town in the same sense that Impfondo had been – there were no roads to it or in it – and Mossaka didn't even appear to have an airstrip, nor any white people. However, to us it seemed to be the height of civilisation. We stayed in a house and we each had a bed. We relaxed on the terrace, drank bottled beer, ate a late dinner and went dancing to modern Congolese music in a cement-floored bar-disco.

In the morning, we were called to the police post. So far no one had noticed that our visas for Congo had expired, which was not really our fault and also the Congolese Embassy in Bangui had told us that, since the river was international water, we didn't need visas at all (provided that we didn't land anywhere on the way). Anyhow, our visas were not a problem, the only thing that interested the police was our age and marital status.

On the river after Mossaka we saw a cargo boat with a big paddle-wheel propelling it from the rear. We watched a few passengers disembark – by simply jumping into the river and swimming about a mile to the shore. A dugout full of people went racing out towards the cargo boat and, although the boat didn't slacken its pace, the people caught hold of its railings and hauled themselves aboard.

Lesley and I agreed that it looked an interesting manoeuvre. We decided to try it for ourselves, so when the next boat came along we paddled into its path. Despite some small mistakes, we latched on successfully and many hands came to help us aboard. It was a scruffy old tug, pushing four barges laden with mahogany. The main deck was a hive of activity: women were pounding cassava and cooking on open wood fires on the deck, stoking their fires with chips of mahogany from the barges; there was a live crocodile tied to a post and someone had made a smoky fire in an old oil drum and was smoke-drying fish on top. Between the drum and the crocodile post was balanced a plank on which an old man was ironing a pair of trousers; his young son was filling the spare iron with redhot charcoal. Everyone was talking loudly while they worked. The captain was a friendly soul to whom we gave a pumpkin and he, in exchange, let us take over the steering wheel. The tug travelled at 5 mph which was hardly faster than our dugout, but it was a lot heavier to handle. The captain gave us a turtle, which the women on deck showed us how to cook. First it had to be boiled in water so that the meat wouldn't stink, then it was roasted upside-down in the fire. It cooked quickly and, when they agreed it was ready, they chopped off the bottom of the shell and we carried it up to the bridge to share with the captain. Most of the insides were its stomach which we didn't eat, but there was some lovely tender white meat thickly lining the shell. We peeled the skin off its legs and found they were also soft, white meat, not at all fibrous, tasting rather like shellfish. After lunch we said lots of goodbyes, hopped back into our dugout and the captain slowed the tug as we cast off so we wouldn't be swamped by the wash.

Many of the local people on the tug had warned us that this was one of the most dangerous stretches of river, but I had forgotten to ask why. The wind blew strongly upriver against the current, creating white-capped waves, but that was nothing new. The river had broadened to an overall width of about ten miles; it was a labyrinth of channels and lagoons among galaxies of swaying papyrus reeds and hundreds of flat, sandy islands, only just above waterlevel. They were covered in grass, ferns and flowers, with an occasional solitary baobab tree. I could see for miles and it was breathtakingly beautiful. The wind slackened and the waves became calm. All afternoon we threaded our way randomly, exploring the more devious and distant ways between the myriad islands. We saw not a single person or any huts. Even the night was heaven – there were no mosquitoes – and we lay under the stars listening to the song of the bullfrogs and watching the fireflies flitting amongst the grasses.

We spent the next day plunging deeper still into the watery

wilderness. During that morning Lesley started acting strangely; at noon she was distant and uncoordinated; in the afternoon she was very peculiar, she seemed to be afraid of sirens (the kind which lured ships onto rocks), so she stuffed her ears full of leaves. The river became rough and turbulent and Lesley, paddling backwards, couldn't hear me yelling because her ears were blocked with leaves. It was impossible to control the dugout on my own; we got tangled in a fallen tree, emerged the other side, but Lesley wouldn't let go of the branches and the dugout swung round the wrong way – then she let go. She did help paddle to the shore, in fact she kept on paddling even while I tied up the boat and for half an hour afterwards, paddling gently, pensively, in the air while I wondered what to do. I took the paddle away, then emptied her ears, laid her down and asked what was wrong.

'The grass is tickling me.' She began to giggle but ended up shivering and groaning for an alarming length of time. She suddenly sat bolt upright, spoke lucidly, told me that she had malaria and discussed the correct dosages of nivaquine to give herself. Then she lapsed back into delirium and alternated between hot and cold sweats.

Malaria is an unpleasant fever. It usually lasts about five days, it can be shorter and mild, or it can be very severe and result in permanent brain damage – but people rarely die of it. We were still taking two nivaquine daily, though it seemed that the mosquitoes were more powerful. I thought Lesley should probably be in hospital, but, of course, that was out of the question. Then I started to consider our options: I might be able to find a witch-doctor, but I couldn't go by dugout since I wouldn't stand a chance against the waves here. I would have to go on foot and swim until I reached a village, which would probably take days, and I certainly wouldn't be able to find my way back again, and, of course, I'd have to tie Lesley to a tree in case she tried to wander off. I regret to say that I found the whole situation so ludicrous that I began to laugh. I could only do my very best for her and, of course, I was worried, but our predicament definitely had its funny side. I tried to make Lesley be quiet, but she was in the middle of a long monologue and when I interrupted she got very angry. She was telling me the correct way to fold up the tarpaulin, explaining each fold in great detail and embellishing her words with hand signals. Hardly pausing for breath, she then started explaining how to fold up a dugout so that it would fit in one's pocket. Remarkable idea.

A few months earlier, Lesley had had her first bout of malaria and we thought it was concussion, so we didn't treat it. I had been teaching her to dive off a spring-board. She practised all day and must have done a hundred dives, so when, a couple of days later, she had complained of violent headaches, we naturally assumed that the repeated impact of water on her skull had concussed her. She slept for four days and, looking back, I think she was probably unconscious. It turned out that it had been cerebral malaria.

I got up to make some coffee while Lesley continued talking. In the hours before dawn she covered subjects like how to fold a dead man into the boot of a car, milking a cow (I listened to that, one never knew when it would come in useful), and how to make rat soufflé (which I already knew). Pills again, she was in another cold sweat, so I bathed her face and she fell into an exhausted sleep.

I must have slept the whole day without stirring because when I woke up the sky was in a foggy twilight. I roused Lesley, gave her more pills and she went back to sleep. So did I. It was daylight when I next awoke, the sun was low and I judged it must be about 8 a.m. I pottered around, made fire, brewed coffee and tried out the first of the dry tobacco leaves, shredding part of them and filling the pipe. I inhaled deeply. It tasted exactly like tobacco and was not half as rough as the local tobacco I had bought in various markets. The day became darker; I glanced at the sun – it was sitting on the horizon. I was baffled. It must now be evening, but I had only just got up. Time flies. No. More likely, I was going mad. Maybe malaria was infectious. I looked suspiciously at the tobacco, but it was just plain, ordinary tobacco.

I was ravenously hungry. In the dugout I found a choice of either pumpkins and jam, or cassava and smoked fish. I opted for the latter, took them back to our camp, and then went over to a nearby gnarled baobab tree. I threw stones to knock down a large seed pod. Inside the hard-shelled pod were edible, white, mushy seeds which tasted like cream of tartar sauce and went excellently with the smoked fish. The young leaves could be boiled and eaten as a vegetable and, in fact, the seeds could also be roasted and ground to make coffee. It was less easy to make cassava appetising, though Lesley had shown me a south American method of roasting it – the smell was so good that Lesley woke up, said she was completely recovered and felt hungry. She asked how long she had been ill and I told her about the strange foggy half light which must have been day. Then it stirred a chord in my memory; one of the people in Bangui who had called us mad had also spoken about a fog, but we had dismissed it as a joke.

The next morning was sunny; we set out again among the islands, the wind blew and the waves crested white. The afternoon was different. The fog descended; flat, grey river met flat, grey sky without horizon or definition. Land appeared and vanished in the mist. It was deceptive the way the current moved down slow channels which led deeper and deeper into papyrus marshes, so that every time we thought we were in a main stream we ended up in a swamp. We pushed our own path across the swamp. There was complete silence except for the eerie swish as the misty forest of green stalks parted to let us through.

Our food supplies were getting low and we were hopeless at catching fish, so we consulted our map and decided to call in and stock up at Mongolo. We arrived there one evening, spent a long time trying to park because there were so many other dugouts in the way, a large crowd gathered to watch us and, when we finally stepped ashore, we were greeted by the chief of the village. He called some prisoners to carry our luggage, installed it in a spare hut and invited us into his own hut for refreshment. As we entered through the low doorway, my hairpins got caught in the woven grass doorfringe and I had to call Lesley to disentangle me from it. The chief clapped his hands and said this was a wonderful omen. The grass fringe was part of a magic spell that should make his wife bear twins, and my unorthodox entry was doubtless a sign that all was well. Locally ground coffee was served and we sat with the chief, talking late into the night about the river tribes and the legends of their ancestors.

Our visit was well timed for obtaining more supplies because the next day was the occasion of a special monthly market for fish and game, and people would be coming from far and wide to trade their wares. Everyone was up and about shortly after dawn, and when I stepped outside our hut I found a mass of people who had come to check the truth of a rumour they had heard about white people in their village. They had been waiting noisily, but that was nothing compared to their shrieks and hoots of laughter when they saw me. I knew it was just their way of expressing surprise and pleasure, but I still hadn't got used to it.

We ate breakfast of yams and fish soup with the chief and then went to the market. On the way we stopped off at *La Pirogue* to collect our own wares for trading. We selected six pumpkins (which was all we could manage to carry) and took them to the market-place. Wooden bench stalls had been set up and were already piled with smoked fish of every shape and size up to six feet long. Everywhere we looked there were more piles of smoked fish, heaped high on rush mats on the ground, and hanging in huge woven baskets from the low branches of the mango trees. Turtles were the second most plentiful item. They were all alive, and because live turtles didn't sit still they were joined into bunches of five with twine threaded through a hole in each one's shell. There were also stacks of boxes filled with live turtles packed in wet mud – they could be stored for months like that and would stay alive and fresh until they were wanted. Rows of open baskets were filled with dried or smoked monkey, antelope and small game; the air was full of voices arguing shrilly and haggling, or simply chattering.

The people were so intent on their business that Lesley and I were free to stroll around unnoticed. It was a rowdy, colourful crowd, not colourful in colours since they mostly wore dark, ragged cloth wrappers – their colour was in the animation of their faces, howls of protest at high prices, or the satisfied gleam of striking a good bargain. Many of the women had tribal markings all over their backs, chests and arms consisting of wartlike bumps in diamond patterns, and their faces were decorated in lines of bumps from the forehead to the tip of the nose. I had watched the scars being applied in a village earlier; it didn't look painful, the skin was broken with a sliver of bamboo and a mixture of ash dirt and herbs was rubbed into the incisions to form the correct type of scar.

We swopped our pumpkins for a pile of smoked fish and half a dried monkey. Goodbyes had been said earlier that morning when we had stowed our nightgear back in the dugout, so now we were ready to go; all we had to do was to find our dugout. Scores of other dugouts had arrived and, as we walked to the parking-lot, we wondered if we would ever be able to recognise ours.

We needn't have worried, for we spotted *La Pirogue* instantly. All the other dugouts were nicely made, square-hollowed with straight and even sides, while ours was just a poorly hollowed-out log trunk. We had noticed that every region of the river had its own traditional design and style of craftsmanship. A foreign dugout could easily be recognised and identified, though people didn't know where on earth *La Pirogue* had originated, and often our boat attracted as much curiosity as we did. The inhabitants of the calmer stretches of river made lightweight, speedy dugouts, and they didn't sit and paddle, they stood up and used a heavy oar in a fishtail movement through the water. The tribes of the rough river required a rounded exterior to their crafts so that the waves would flow along more smoothly; some used paddles shaped like big ping-pong bats, others like spears. Sea-going dugouts were another style altogether, much shorter, heavier and taller sided. It was remarkable how every tribe had adapted the same idea to suit their environment. Dugouts were made from a variety of trees, though here the forest white-wood was the most popular because it couldn't sink, and many of the dugouts were decoratively carved, or inscribed with spells for successful fishing or safe journeys.

The nature of the river had begun to change again; flat horizons gave way to hills, craggy and barren, tumbling down grassy slopes to groves of mango trees in russet blossom; along the shore-line were scattered palm trees, headlands of red rock, and coves of silver sand. The river itself was about to converge from a lazy, vastly wide watercourse into a tight rocky gorge, and would continue very fast and narrow for over a hundred miles until it broadened out once more at Stanleypool.

I steered us into the fastest lane mid-river, then relaxed in the sun. There was a fair amount of hyacinth, but it was no longer a problem to us; it still often tangled around the rudder, but whenever it threatened to mass up against the dugout we would take evasive action and wriggle free. We entered the river bottle-neck; we shot through the backwash and went slithering over the maelstrom patterns. The central current raced along in a swirling confusion of waves too rough for our liking, so we moved over towards the Congo shore where the current was less turbulent, although we found that there were rather a lot of sharp rocks showing above the waves. It was quite hard work paddling because, although the current was going downriver, the wind and the waves were coming upriver and we had to battle to make progress. We hit a couple of rocks, shipped a large quantity of water and retired to a sandy bay where we spent the remainder of the afternoon building sandcastles and spring-cleaning the dugout.

Travels with Fortune

We cooked some monkey for supper and sat playing backgammon with flowers and stones (luckily we did have dice), while the sun sank crimson red among the western hills. It felt wonderful to be free of the mosquitoes and the rains, and when we were tired we lay back and slept in the sand.

The next day, we again tried to keep close to the shore, but the river was a foaming mass of jagged rocks. We didn't know what course would be easiest; the least rocky was mid-river, but the current there was so wild we reckoned we'd be crazy to try it. While we discussed it, shouting at the top of our voices over the roaring water, an old man paddled up in a dugout. He spoke to us in Likouala and it was only after a few sentences that I began to understand his urgent and frantic arm gestures.

'What's going on?' yelled Lesley.

'He says we're about to run onto some rocks and we must move out to the middle of the river,' I shouted back.

The man accompanied us, herding us along like a sheepdog, bumping our dugout with his own until we were on the right track, shepherding us on a zigzag course through a bad patch of rocks and down the middle where the waves were at their fiercest, spraying up around us in fast-surging turmoil. Without the old man we would not have ventured out like that, but he knew exactly what he was doing and had probably lived all his life on this part of the river. He herded us for several exciting miles, then on to a *campement* of three huts, where he moored the dugouts and ordered his family to catch a chicken for us. Various wives and children joined in the chase and one wife even brought out a long fishing net to trap the hen. Another wife was sent to fetch home-brewed beer, and while we rested the old man chatted to us in Likouala. He was a charming old man, with curly, white hair and black skin weathered with wrinkles. When we left, he presented us with a bowl he had carved out of ebony, and told us that if we followed the river we would arrive in Brazzaville.

130

Many local fishermen warned us of death and danger, but our attitude towards the river was never serious: we weren't trying to achieve anything; there was nothing we needed to prove to ourselves or anyone else; we were light-hearted and carefree; we enjoyed just being part of the river and going wherever it went. We had learnt to handle our dugout and, though we looked totally unprofessional, we were astonished by the precision of our manoeuvres, our exact timing and perfect coordination.

This stretch of the river could have been paradise, were it not for the swarms of flies, so tiny that they were almost invisible. Their wicked bites became large, itchy, red welts; my hands and feet swelled up to the size of balloons; one eye was so swollen that I couldn't open it and the other eye had only a narrow crack to peep through. Lesley suggested that they were the flies which carried river blindness; I suggested that we opened the whisky bottle again. The flies were only in evidence during the day in places which were sheltered from the wind; we were safe on beaches in howling gales, and when the wind dropped and the flies attacked we would pack up in a hurry, run to the dugout and paddle downriver. The flies never pursued us over the water.

The effect of an afternoon spent playing drums with some men who insisted that we drank a bowlful of fermented cassava juice was somewhat strong. By the time we paddled away, I was so blind drunk that I couldn't differentiate the river from the land. I didn't come to my senses again until the next day when we reached the police post at Ngabé. Just beyond Ngabé, the river turned a sharp S-bend between cliffs, and the two whirlpool areas were reputed to be the most dangerous on the Congo. From three miles away we could see the cliffs and feel the dugout swinging from side to side as the currents battled against each other. We were hugging the shore, keeping well clear of the main stream and chewing twigs of a special tree which the police had said would give us extra strength. The sap must have been some kind of stimulant, but it tasted foully bitter.

To paddle round the outer edge of the bend would have taken

all day, so Lesley suggested that we make a short-cut straight across the middle. After a last minute check that all the baggage was tied secure, we altered course.

Keeping a steady course was difficult because the current was churning and the dugout was rocking and veering madly around. We entered the bend. I was tense and very alert. My ears were straining to catch the roaring of whirlpools, but I could hear only the waves, the ringing of the bush and the lyrical calls of some parrots in the sky. My eyes scanned the water for some kind of warning and I saw only that we were far from the shore. We were paddling fast and forcefully, determined to sustain the necessary speed to keep control of the dugout.

A whirlpool spun to our right, another ahead, and another and another; the river all around us was boiling and heaving. The dugout lunged sideways, bucked and plunged, while we paddled furiously, weaving among and through the whirlpools, dodging, spinning, shrieking with excitement, forcing the dugout free, only to skate head-first onto the biggest whirlpool we had ever seen. I hauled the tiller round and leant far out; it took all my strength to hold it firm. The dugout shuddered under the strain, then responded and flung itself over the outer rim. But, the force of circling water pulled us backwards. 'Paddle, paddle harder,' we screamed to each other, and we paddled more desperately than we had ever paddled before. Then I threw my paddle down and leant again with both hands and all my weight against the tiller. The dugout catapulted out and we went racing forwards at a crazy speed, swerved through a series of smaller whirlpools, spun again, shot out and tumbled down some rocky rapids. The river went roaring on in a confusion of rocks and spray. Lesley pointed sharp right and we swung neatly round between the rocks and came to rest in a tiny, calm inlet under the cliffs. We were both grinning from ear to ear.

I lay down on a flat rock and stretched out my aching arms. We relaxed, rested and ate an enormous lunch of smoked fish and stewed green mangoes mixed with jam. Then we climbed down into the dugout and moved to the mouth of the inlet. The river outside was a raging, whirling torrent. We paused – not in hesitation – more like an actor waiting in the wings for his cue, or a dancer standing motionless attending to the beat before he begins to dance.

We plunged out into the tumult, heading for the fastest current, racing, twisting and weaving among the rocks and spinning eddies. There were still large clumps of hyacinth weed which were a menace, but it was now battered and dying. It had come a long way.

The pattern of our days on this section of the Congo river was dictated by the wind. When we woke up with the first light of dawn, the air was still; then swarms of tiny flies appeared and we leapt around, slapping ourselves, while we brewed a pot of coffee which we took with us into the dugout and filled our mugs as we floated along at sunrise. The air in the dry season was always rather hazy, much thicker than English air. It blurred the outlines, and the sun would rise over the mountains as a red globe against a blue sky with never a cloud in sight. At times of little wind, the river was glassy smooth and, though its course was narrow, it was about a mile wide. Dawn was a peaceful time of day. Fish eagles sat loftily in the branches of dead trees, yellow and black weaver birds plaited their nests in the trees, and large hornbills flew overhead, their wings whirring as they flapped fast, their flight dipping up and down as they pedalled and free-wheeled, and their songs echoing like rubbed crystal.

Sometimes, the wind rose early, blowing aggressively upstream, creating high, white-crested breakers and upsetting the currents so that the river became, once more, a frenzied, whirling mass of foam and spray. If the wind was not strong enough to blow the flies into hiding then we breakfasted in the dugout. Food was passed from front to back by putting it in a bailing can and floating it in the river for me to pick up as I passed. It never failed. The only time we lost something was when Lesley floated a banana leaf carrying some pawpaw, which rolled off and sank before I could grab it.

The river shores became more mountainous, with tall, red-coloured cliffs, wide-mouthed caves and banks of palm forest. There was a growing amount of river traffic: women with babies tied on their backs, paddling dugouts to market; children paddling to and from school; families going to visit friends and relations. Most of the dugouts travelling upstream had hoisted wide, square sails made from a patchwork of old cloth; the wind propelled them forwards at a good speed; and there was also a river bus service, in rusty motorboats with small outboard engines. As the river grew more populated, we lost our privacy; everyone who caught sight of us came to stare. We seemed to collect an armada of male admirers, who paddled alongside to offer us their bodies, saying politely that, since we didn't have a man with us, we must surely be desiring satisfaction. However, to discourage their advances, we would sit up stiffly, look straight ahead with blank eyes, paddle slowly in unison and hum dirges or the funeral march. They found that very frightening and they left us alone.

One morning, as we sped along mid-river, we saw rocks showing above the water in the main channel and a warning beacon for boat traffic. We passed rather too close to the beacon and we ran into a seething mass of whirlpools. The dugout reared up over the lashing waves and smashed down onto a rock. It made a sickening thud, but the wood was so thick that the hole didn't puncture right through.

We rode through the whirlpools, but we couldn't cope with the waves. They washed over us, pouring into the dugout, and when it was full it started to sink. We bailed the water out so fast that our arms went like windmills in a gale. The shore was far away and the breakers ahead of us looked formidable. I felt rather pleased that we had discovered our limitations; it was good to know that all was not possible and that there were times when we couldn't win. Using a technique called 'paddle-bail-paddle-bail' (similar to paddle-swat of the tsetse fly days) we surfed and floundered our way forwards. In every trough floods of water gushed into the dugout; we scrunched onto more rocks, but stayed afloat and clawed our way to the shore. It took about half an hour to reach the shore. We pulled the dugout up on the sand and flopped down laughing and gasping with fatigue. Then we rolled *La Pirogue* sideways to empty out the water and see what damage the rocks had done. There were four deep gashes and some minor scrapes, but the wood still looked fairly solid and, anyway, Brazzaville couldn't be much farther.

The land was changing again: the cliffs had flattened down and the river had grown wider. As we continued, it became wider still until it turned into hundreds of small, meandering channels among a jigsaw of sandflats. We realised that we had arrived in Stanleypool. It didn't take us long to run aground. We didn't leap out and push. We beached the dugout on the sand, lay down and went to sleep.

When I awoke it was afternoon. I stood up and stretched. The sky stretched too, in a flat empty circular horizon which shimmered in the heat-haze. There was nothing growing anywhere, not even a blade of grass. I noticed that there was something outlined against the sky, far beyond the sandflats and the heat-haze. I splashed water on my face and looked again. Yes, far, far away I could see the towering skyscrapers of a city.

Over that day and the next we wove slowly towards the city. Having been almost seven weeks on the river we were in no hurry. It wasn't difficult to go slowly, as the dugout continually ran aground on sandbars which were submerged a few inches under the water. We walked alongside pushing it, then, as the water grew deep, we jumped back in the dugout, paddled a few yards and ran aground again. We walked and pushed the dugout for several miles as the city of skyscrapers loomed closer.

A local fisherman told us that we were on the wrong side of the river and pointed at the opposite side, to a distant bank of greenery with two or three buildings, which he said was Brazzaville. So we had to cross over the river. At this point, where Stanley-pool ended, the river once again became narrow and extremely powerful, with the whole of its force in one single torrent. Thirteen sets of rapids began one mile downstream from Brazzaville, and among them were rapids that no craft had ever come out of alive. Lesley and I looked at each other and sighed. It was sunset. We had to hurry. I don't know how long it took us to paddle across, but I do know that we had never in the whole voyage paddled so grimly or with such determination.

When we arrived on the opposite shore it was dark, our arms were shaking like jelly and our minds were quiet and sad.

And so we reached Brazzaville.

Part Two

West and Southern Africa

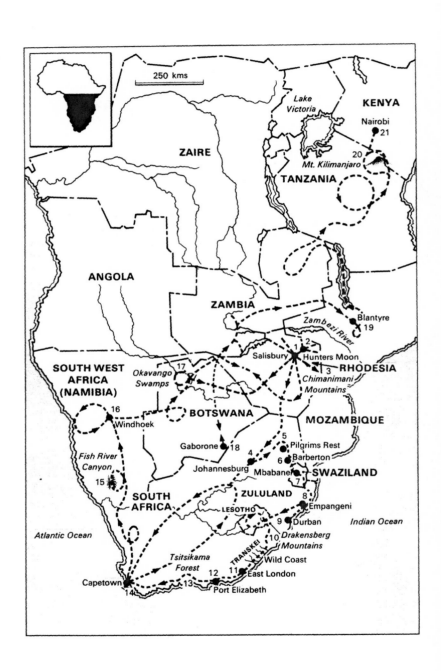

250 kms

Lake Victoria

KENYA

Nairobi
21

ZAIRE

20
Mt. Kilimanjaro

TANZANIA

ANGOLA

ZAMBIA

Zambezi River

Blantyre
19

Salisbury   1   2
Hunters Moon

SOUTH WEST
AFRICA
(NAMIBIA)

Okavango
Swamps   17

3   RHODESIA

Chimanimani
Mountains

16
Windhoek

BOTSWANA

MOZAMBIQUE

Fish River
Canyon

Gaborone   18

5
Pilgrims Rest

4

Johannesburg

6   Barberton

Mbabane

7

SWAZILAND

15

SOUTH
AFRICA

ZULULAND

LESOTHO

8

Empangeni

9   Durban

Indian Ocean

Atlantic Ocean

10   Drakensberg
Mountains

TRANSKEI

Wild Coast

Tsitsikama
Forest

12   11

East London

Capetown
14

13

Port Elizabeth

13
The Forests of the Congo

On the morning after our arrival we were arrested and accused of being 'white female spies'. The port immigration authorities said we couldn't have come by dugout because it was impossible. Lesley was hussled away in one direction, and four soldiers came forward for me.

Ordering the soldiers to accompany me, I told the chief inspector that we were just going to the wharf to see the dugout as proof of our story. Lesley was still in sight, so I collected her and we marched at our fastest walk with the soldiers trotting to keep up and unsure whether or not they were meant to shoot us for trying to escape. But at the wharf, we found that *La Pirogue* had disappeared. We immediately encouraged the senior officer to exert his authority by organising a search for our dugout.

They located it a mile away, in the public dugout parking lot, so we went there and all the soldiers climbed aboard. They were fascinated by its shape and style, and they insisted on going for a ride in it.

Afterwards we returned to the immigration building for further interrogation. Despite the obvious truth of our story it was a very tough interrogation. Lesley forgot all her French, and the inspector kept trying to trap me into contradicting myself. I fell into every trap, and Lesley started to giggle, but hid her face and pretended to cough. Eventually he agreed to let us go, although he insisted on keeping our passports while we stayed in Brazzaville.

Feeling relieved, we walked to the city centre and strolled down the main street window-shopping. There were perfume shops, haute couture centres, beauty parlours, ice cream vendors, confectioners, all selling goods imported from France, and everywhere were chic French ladies. All the white people looked identical. It was a shock to be in a city again and we were terrified of crossing the roads. As we stood trying to make up our minds which pavement café looked most inviting, a car pulled up beside us.

'Are you Christina and Lesley?' the driver asked. He introduced himself as a friend of Lou in Bangui, who had told him he would recognise us by our deep suntans and long skirts. He invited us out to lunch and took us to a modern French bistro, where the menu was so long that it took me half an hour to choose. I finally settled for smoked salmon, but couldn't decide between *steak au poivre* or *Lobster thermidore* so I had them both, and finished off with two helpings of chocolate and cream profiteroles.

Our new friend, Chimu, lived in Kenya and was in Brazzaville for a few days to negotiate an ivory deal. He lent us his car for the afternoon, and as the driver I found it was a far more terrifying experience than the worst whirlpools on the rockiest river headlands. However, we accomplished calls at the post office, the bank, and we even got to the Gabonese Embassy to collect our visas. Predictably, they said they knew nothing about them, that we must apply again and the delay would be two months. At that moment the ambassador arrived. He was most helpful and offered to telephone Libreville for immediate clearance. Our intention was still to go to Gabon, and settle there for a few months of work, and have that long rest which we had been needing since Cameroun. We still had the address of a German man whom we had met in Bangui; he lived in Moanda, south-western Gabon; he had promised us interesting jobs with his company and assured us we would love Moanda. We had decided to take him up on his offer.

After the embassy we returned the car to Chimu and he drove us out to look at *La Pirogue* and see if there were any potential buyers. Not a single person showed any interest in buying our dugout and many laughed at it very unkindly.

On arrival at Brazzaville we had gone to stay with Albert, the Congolese man whom we had met in Impfondo. He lived in the market quarter of the city and installed us in his spare room. His house was small, just three rooms; the cooking was done outside on a charcoal burner and there was also an outside loo, which was quite a rarity — most other market dwellers shared a communal one. It was a friendly place, everyone who knew Albert wandered in to say hello, to teach us a new song, to show us some novel thing, or to try and improve Lesley's French. After a few days, however, we felt that we were disrupting Albert's life and Chimu intervened. He went and booked (and paid for) a suite for Lesley and myself in the most luxurious hotel in Brazzaville for a week.

Hotel Mistral was run by a powerful big French lady called Madame Solange. She hugged us warmly to her ample bosom, told me to straighten my eyebrows, change my hairstyle, and she issued us both with eye make-up kits which we dabbed around our eyes before we went into the hotel and washed off when we went out.

Lesley, Chimu and I spent some good times together. We lunched in every restaurant in Brazzaville and danced every night until 4 or 5 a.m. at the trendy French nightclubs. I enjoyed the informality of being in a threesome, and I was adamant that I would not go out without Lesley. Chimu asked how I would feel when Lesley and I finally split up. The thought of parting was unbearable. I felt that it would never happen, and if it did I would have been ripped apart with grief and desolation.

I valued Lesley's friendship more highly than I had ever valued a girl's friendship. There was nothing physical in our relationship, but it reached an ultimate in partnership that I had never dreamt existed. I had had friends, but I had never even begun to imagine the real quality of companionship, the true meaning of sharing, or the incredible closeness that was possible between two people.

It was known throughout the African section of town that we were the girls who had arrived by dugout, and the news had spread quickly round the whole city. When we walked around many people would point at us, or rush over to shake our hands. To our surprise, Congolese television asked to make a film of us for the news, then they interviewed us on television for an hour. They announced that our dugout trip from Bangui to Brazzaville had made history, that it was rare for anyone to attempt the voyage, certainly it had never been undertaken by two girls, and that 90 per cent of the men who did try were forced to give up because of disaster or exhaustion. Lesley reckoned that she couldn't speak enough French so she refused to say a word; I could only manage to talk in the present tense, but we both waved our arms dramatically, and it seemed to go off very well. We also did a radio broadcast. The newspapers and journals of the Congo and the whole of French Equatorial Africa heralded us as 'intrepid explorers' and described our trip as an 'extraordinary odyssey'. Suddenly we were famous.

All the ambassadors started giving parties in our honour, inviting us to stay in their guest houses, and the Spanish ambassador offered us seats on his private plane to Rwanda the following day. Government ministers also entertained us and the press crowded in for interviews. After two weeks the social whirl became too much for us; none of it felt real and we longed to go back into the forest. We gave up waiting for a reasonable price for *La Pirogue* and we sold it to a fisherman for £2.

As soon as there was a lull in the round of entertainment, Lesley and I put on our rucksacks, walked out of Brazzaville, and returned to the dark depths of the forest. I felt like laughing and crying with happiness as we went back into the forest; it was wonderful to be free again. Our plans were forgotten, and we spent the next three months roaming randomly through the jungles of Congo and Gabon.

We travelled by foot on forest paths and tracks, though if we saw a vehicle we would flag a lift, and when we found a railway line running across Congo we hitch-hiked a ride on a rail buggy. The driver was very startled to see us standing in the middle of nowhere, in a clearing where a red mud track crossed the railway line. We waved at him to stop and he jammed on the brakes. The buggy was a small open wagon with wooden benches, and was used for collecting railway workers from their villages. We rode with it for about fifty miles. The railway led through dark green tunnels of forest; between immense trees with vast tangled roots; dank munificent moss; ferns growing ten feet tall; giant leaves like variations of aspidistra; vines and creeper covered in flowers; jasmine, purple convolvulus; large turquoise butterflies. We passed white-leaved flag trees and circular finger-leaf patterns of umbrella trees whose fruit was a favourite of the gorillas – the railway line was littered with the fruit skins and branches which they had torn down and hurled aside. The buggy slowed to cross areas where the swamps were deep and stagnant-smelling, and slowed again where the forested hillsides were traversed by marvellously eroded canyons of red laterite, and finally it stopped at its destination – a village where we stayed and dined on crocodile stew. Crocodile is one of the nicest things I have ever eaten; the meat is white, tender, and has the texture and taste of lobster. Huge fillet steaks of lobster. The man who had caught the crocodile said it was a young one, no more than five feet long, and that the section we had eaten was from the tail which was always regarded as a delicacy.

Our best achievement in hitch-hiking was when we flagged a passing aeroplane down out of the sky. It had all started a week earlier when we were at a foresters' camp and we overheard the French forester saying, 'Yes, there are caves. Jean discovered them, and he came here full of excitement intending to organise things and go back to explore them properly, but the next day he was dead.' Lesley and I exchanged glances. We both knew without speaking that in the morning we would set off to search for the caves. We asked the men if they had any idea where we could look, and they said they didn't really know, it would probably be about two hundred miles to the north-west of us, but we would find no traffic and would have to walk.

So we walked, and on the way we met a group of villagers on an elephant hunt. They had borrowed a Landrover and Lesley and I rode in the back squashed between hunks of raw meat. Another stroke of luck was meeting some men who knew the location of the caves and they pointed us in the right direction. Finally we reached a deserted logging site and unfortunately we could go no farther. The next stage had to be by river, but there was no dugout, no possibility of finding one, no villages, no way along the overgrown marshy riverbanks, and no way round as even the grassy areas were impenetrable. The grass was sharp and spiked with poison sap, and when we tried to walk through it, it hooked onto us and tore our our clothing and skin. While we were walking around looking for other possible routes we saw more snakes than I had seen in the whole time I'd been in Africa. So we stomped around heavily and beat the undergrowth with sticks because snakes only bite if they are taken by surprise or trodden on.

The next obstacle was a herd of buffalo, which didn't run away, but looked at us very meanly and a big male at the back started coming towards us. We retreated hastily. So that was that. We obviously weren't going to get to the caves. We were a bit disappointed, but the most annoying factor was that there was no other track away from the camp except the one which had led us here and that meant we were in for another long hot walk.

We rested a day. I was lying in the shade watching a fight between an ant and a worm when I heard a motor. Good grief, a motor! I sat up eagerly and looked to see what it could be. The noise came closer, then I saw a speck in the sky, it was a little twin-engined aircraft and it was on course to fly overhead. As it approached I grabbed my bright yellow and orange shirt and waved it in the air. The pilot must have noticed it, because he circled, and circled again lower. He landed the plane on the old airstrip which had served the camp; the grass had grown so tall that the propellers mowed deep furrows through it, and the buffalo and antelope stampeded in fright. The pilot was a charming Frenchman who was flying supplies to various camps; he was on his way to a Polish mechanical engineering project in southern Congo and he asked if we would like a lift.

After that we frequently hitch-hiked aeroplanes, but only the ones waiting on the ground. We often emerged from the forest at a mission or foreign aid project, where there was always an airstrip for supplies to arrive by plane, and when we found an aircraft there we would ask the pilots for a lift. The pilots were terribly kind and if they had space they would take us free of charge wherever they were going.

The diversity of foreign projects in Congo astonished us. We saw Chinese chalk and cement factories, Russians mining for gold, a Rumanian agricultural scheme growing cotton, a Bulgarian cane-sugar refinery, a Polish fertiliser factory, and a Czechoslovakian manioc industry. Each foreign project was an isolated and self-contained community and they were not friendly to outsiders. Their white employees were not encouraged to leave the compound, or to speak (other than to give orders) to the Africans. In the Chinese hydroelectric scheme at La Bouenza in central-southern Congo we were told that it was forbidden for the Chinese to learn French, speak to any non-Chinese, and the place was surrounded by high wire fences. Apparently the workers were all Chinese political prisoners who had been sent to the Congo to serve sentence. One thing that all the foreign projects had in common was the knowledge that as soon as their task was completed and they left, their scheme would cease to run efficiently, grind to a halt and fall apart.

People often quoted us the example of the Rumanian team who set up a cattle ranch in the north. They worked for three years to make it run efficiently, and when they left they handed the fully stocked ranch over to the Congolese who sat down and ate all the animals within a month.

From La Bouenza and its Chinese prisoners we moved sixty miles south to visit the monastery at Le Briz. The Catholic father was a good and kind man, as were all the French missionaries and foresters that we met. They were the old-timers, men who had lived in remote parts of the forest for the past twenty to thirty years, and they knew the ways of the land and its people.

Loubomo was an important place in our travels – it was where the road to Gabon branched off from the road to Pointe-Noire on the Congo coast. We decided to stop overnight and think about our choice. A friend in Brazzaville had given us an introduction to a Frenchman called Marcel Regnier who ran a sawmill in Loubomo, so we went to see him. He installed us in a suite in the town hotel. The hotel was a remarkable place and seemed totally incongruous in this setting. It had been built in the grand manner of French colonialism, with an old-fashioned bar and saloon-type dancehall, and I expected at any moment to see a troupe of Tiller girls doing the cancan in black lacy suspenders and frills.

Instead we had dinner with Monsieur Regnier, who was a genial and gentlemanly person. He too had heard about our exploit with the dugout, congratulated us, and assumed that of course we had hired some Africans to paddle for us. When we told him that we had been alone he said that such a feat was impossible.

Early morning when we breakfasted on croissants and fresh coffee we felt no closer to having decided which direction to go, so we spun a knife to decide. It came slowly to a halt pointing west towards Pointe-Noire. Monsieur Regnier called in to give us a picnic lunch and arranged for us to travel onwards with one of his timber lorries.

We arrived that evening in Pointe-Noire. The French Ambassador had kindly offered us the use of his guest house there and we enjoyed our short stay. We met many rough and disreputable sailors and oil-rig workers, and one who was quiet and sincere. He drove us down the coast to the Cabinda border. The beaches were of golden sand backed by palm trees and we stopped every few miles to swim and surf in the ocean. I collected some heavy clusters of oyster shells in beautiful multi-scalloped patterns.

When we had had our fill of Pointe-Noire we packed our bags and set out down the road. A Frenchman in a Peugeot 404-pickup stopped to offer us a lift. We slung our bags into the rear and climbed in front. The driver, Phillippe, was a young forester with an engaging smile and a great love of the forest and we liked him immediately. He didn't ask us where we were going and we didn't ask him – we didn't want to know because that would have made the journey too predictable and logical. The road followed the coast leading north and after about fifteen miles Phillippe swerved off the road, we bumped along a track, and arrived at a magnificent place. We were on high cliffs above an enormous deep hole which was several miles wide and made of bruise-coloured red and purple rock weirdly eroded into gorges, knife-like ridges, and needle-sharp pinnacles.

Farther along the coast the road ended and we sped along the sandy beach between the ocean and the lagoons, charging across the shallow waves washing over the beach, sending out clouds of spray which the wind blew back all over us. We stopped at a small village and he parked the pickup under some palm trees and transferred our rucksacks into an old speedboat which was moored in the lagoon. We clambered in too and Phillippe steered the boat inland along the network of creeks through the mangrove swamps. We came to a river and turned upstream between banks of thick forest. Lesley and I were beginning to grow curious, but that made us even more determined not to ask where we were going. Phillippe opened the throttle wide, the boat leapt

147

forwards, the speed and spray were exhilarating, and tears streamed down our faces from the force of the wind.

At midday the boat reached a logging yard and our luggage was moved to a Landrover. Late afternoon we came to a river; we were bundled into a dugout with outboard motor, and hurtled off upstream again. The sun set in streaks of red and gold; the twilight was followed by moonless darkness. The dugout raced onwards. Later we transferred into another 404-pickup, continuing still deeper into the forest. In the beam of the headlights we saw our first gorilla. It was standing on the track ahead of us, then it shook its head and lumbered off among the trees. It didn't scamper on all fours like an ape; it ran almost upright. It was large, with long thick-muscled arms, and its chest was incredibly broad. Phillippe said it was not yet full grown, but to me it was an awe-inspiring sight. What a fabulous day it had been; I stretched and yawned, the forester smiled and assured us we were nearly there. Finally we stopped in a large clearing, and there on the edge of a stream was a wooden bungalow with welcoming oil-lamps burning brightly at the windows. Servants came running to take our luggage and, exhausted, we stumbled through the front door.

In the morning we breakfasted on lobsters that Phillippe had brought from Pointe-Noire and spent the day prowling with him on foot in the dim greenish light of the dark primordial forest. He pointed out the different species of trees, talked about their characteristics, and explained that he was looking for trees of a particular size and age, and when he found what he required then they would be felled by the African woodmen, hauled to the river by bulldozer, and floated to the logging yard. The timber market had virtually closed down in recent months because of the rocketing price of wood and cheap availability of plastics. The only demand now was for the trees which could be made into plywood.

We spent two blissfully happy days with Phillippe. He was a strange man, with fascinating charm and an air of savage restlessness, but underneath that it was as if he were haunted or living under a curse. I would have liked to stay longer, but was suffering from agonising stomach cramps and pains for which Lesley said the only cure was a starvation diet. How could I ever refuse the dishes heaped with prawns and crayfish that the cook prepared for every meal – it was unthinkable. I would have to starve myself as we travelled onwards.

Slowly the vegetation grew less dense: dank-smelling forest gave way to savannah and finally we came out on the road to Gabon. The road was deserted and we followed it across a flat plain which was blackened and burnt out by a recent fire. In the middle was a group of cone-shaped hills, perfectly symmetrical, like high, rounded pyramids. The whole landscape was charred black and the clouds lay low in heavy shades of grey. There was complete silence. Even the wind was still. The only movement was our walking and the ash which exploded in noiseless smoky puffs under our feet.

After the hills the road became just a straight line across the plain. It passed through some villages and everyone we met inquired if we were on our way to visit Alphonse. We asked who he was and they replied that he was a Dutch Catholic father living twenty miles up the road at Makabana on the edge of the forest of Niari. However, Lesley and I still felt that it was an intrusion to visit people who hadn't invited us. But a truck came along behind us, offered us a lift to Makabana, and without consulting us he dropped us outside the Catholic mission. Hoping that we might be offered a cup of coffee, we knocked on the mission door. It was opened by a tall dignified grey-haired European who looked at us in surprise, then said joyfully, 'Welcome, welcome. You have had a long journey. What would you prefer first, some coffee or a drink? – Ah there you are Ignau, we have some visitors, please prepare lunch for three and make up the spare beds.' Our protests were brushed aside.

Our host, Père Alphonse, had lived for twenty-five years in this region. He was a gifted man and he had translated the Bible into eight of the local dialects. One of the tribes didn't have a written language and so he had created one for them. In addition to all the local tongues he spoke six European languages, including very fluent English (although he had not spoken English since 1946). He was addressed by everyone as '*mon père*'; he thought of all the people as his children. He would sigh when they broke into his house to steal from him and shake his head sadly when they took every ripe mango off his trees.

The church service at the mission on Sunday was boisterous and merry. Hymns were sung to the accompaniment of tom toms, and rhythmic handclapping, interspersed with ululations and whoops of glee. The choir master danced as he conducted the choir and the lessons which were read by Africans reminded me more of acts from Shakespeare – with booming voices, wringing of hands, and sweeping arm gestures. Père Alphonse stood watching the congregation; his expression was gentle and happy.

After the service Père Alphonse drove us out to see where the altar stones had been hewn out of a rock cliff beside a river. On the Blue River, so called because the water was cerulean blue and clear, we found an old dugout. Lesley and I punted upstream while Père Alphonse sat missionary-style at the back. There were water lilies growing on the river and cornflowers growing on the banks. We left the father drifting slowly while we swam in the river and swung in the trees over-hanging it.

Lesley and I both adored Père Alphonse and I know he enjoyed our company. He often took pictures of us. We had forgotten that things like cameras existed; ours was somewhere buried deep in our luggage and we seldom used it. It no longer worked properly because of the dust which had crept inside and the films had suffered badly from the heat and humidity. We couldn't photograph the more unusual tribes we had seen because they didn't know about cameras. To them it was an instrument with an eye which if pointed at them could have disastrous consequences. Our presence was accepted on terms of trust; if we had brought out a camera that trust could have been shattered.

During the five days that we spent with Père Alphonse we trundled in his 404-pickup all around the forests of Niari visiting his remote village parishes. Everyone was thrilled to see him. The people had interesting features; very flat wide noses and round woolly-looking faces. Few of them had tribal markings, though I saw one very striking man whose forehead was decorated in patterns of flames. The women's faces were very hard; except when they laughed their expressions fell naturally into an angry sneer. Many of the women were smoking rolled-up tobacco leaves with the lighted end inside their mouths because they claimed it tasted stronger like that.

Père Alphonse was due to visit the father and sisters at Mossendjo which was fifty miles along the road to Gabon, so we decided that we would accompany him and then continue north. We were all miserable that it was time to part. I gave *mon père* my treasured oyster-shell clusters, which I had carried faithfully since Pointe-Noire, and he gave me a decorated brass tobacco pipe from Arabia, the same shape as the one Moktar had given me in the Sahara.

From Mossendjo to the border should have been a straight road and easy hitch-hiking, but one of the river ferries had sunk, so the road was closed. Lesley and I detoured down the forest tracks, found a few rides on timber lorries, and got so lost that we couldn't tell if we were going forwards or backwards.

At one stage when we were on foot we left the track and went chasing after a particularly pretty green shiny butterfly. After half an hour we lost the butterfly, and we couldn't find the track again. The forest was so dense that it was impossible to check our bearings by the sun. We tried to retrace our footsteps but the undergrowth showed no signs of our passage and was soon so thick that the only way we could continue was on hands and knees. We crawled slowly along the moist leafy floor of the primeval forest, under the massive tangles of its roots and thorny vines. The thought occurred to me that people who got lost in the forest generally never returned. They stood a chance if other people knew they were missing and could raise the alarm; the villages could signal by pounding their drums to guide the lost people to safety. I wondered if perhaps the situation was a little serious – but the sight of Lesley crawling along on all fours ahead of me struck me as very amusing.

The forest smelt dank, an occasional shaft of sunlight pierced through the trees, and my attention was constantly being distracted by flickers of movement from antelope only one foot high to the strange and interesting insects which abounded in the foliage. We didn't stand upright again until we reached a glade. The sun was behind us. We continued forwards, bent double, forcing our way through dense thickets, pushing aside the creeper which caught round our necks, shouting and stamping at a python to make it move out of our way, climbing over barricades of roots, and squeezing through a spinney of saplings. I could see a gap in the forest ahead. It turned out to be the road.

We realised that we had been lucky and decided that it was high time we settled down to a respectable life of regular work and a steady roof over our heads.

14
Gabon

At the end of October we crossed the border into Gabon and finally arrived in Moanda. We went specifically to work for our German acquaintance, but we discovered that he had moved to Koulamoutou, a hundred miles away. We decided to stay in Moanda, because there was secretarial and nursing work available at an Anglo-American manganese mine. All their white employees lived in a town which was closed off from the township of Moanda. We stayed overnight in the luxurious guest suites and the company directors wined and dined us. However, both Lesley and I felt that this was not the right place to settle, so we set off on foot to Koulamoutou. Two days later, after much walking, a few lifts and a monkey hunt, we reached Koulamoutou, but discovered that we didn't like our German friend (I always was a hopeless judge of character). So we didn't stay. Instead we took the advice of a Frenchman whose family included a baby gorilla. The Frenchman recommended Port Gentil as a pleasant place to find work.

On our way to Port Gentil we stopped at Lambarene because from there on there was no roads and we would have to continue by river or air. Lambarene was particularly interesting because it was where Schweitzer had founded his hospital. Schweitzer was a remarkable man, a cross between a saint and a crank. He had such reverence for life that he didn't permit flies to be killed and he even used to feed titbits to the ants which lived under the floorboards. He refused to allow the hospital to be modernised; there was no running water, not even in the operating theatre. Now that he was dead things had changed, but not much. A place was still set and served at every meal for the dead man, and his rooms were kept as a shrine and a museum.

Lesley didn't want to inquire about working there, so we walked on to the river to look for boats to Port Gentil. We watched scores of logs which had been felled in the forest being strung together with rope and made into a raft which would be floated downstream to the sawmill at Port Gentil. It looked a very wet way to travel and there was no guarantee that the raft would arrive intact. We walked to the airstrip to see if any planes were going there; we found an army pilot who said there was a military flight leaving at 7 a.m. the next morning and we could fly with it for no charge. The following morning, having spent the night at the Catholic mission, we returned to the airfield. There was a large crowd of soldiers, their wives, children, luggage, chickens and goats, and we all clambered aboard an old army bomber. The bomber roared into the sky. After half an hour wisps of smoke began appearing through cracks in the floor and I noticed with dismay that smoke was also pouring out of the ventilators. The air had gone very cold and moisture started dripping from the ceiling. No one else seemed perturbed and we landed safely. The only trouble was that either I had misheard what the pilot had said, or else somehow we had boarded the wrong plane – because we weren't in Port Gentil, we were in northern Gabon.

We intensified our search for somewhere to settle. Having now been travelling for seven months, we were exhausted, but it was our exhaustion which kept driving us forward – we were determined to find the right place to stop. It was a search which led us from the north slowly down to the furthest southern point. We never found the right place because as soon as we started exploring Gabon we forgot what it was we were looking for.

Both Lesley and I enjoyed walking; we grew accustomed to the sweltering heat, the constant sweatiness of our bodies. Lesley carried a postcard of some snow-covered mountains which she would look at deeply – she said it made her feel cooler. There were frequent rainstorms which poured down so torrentially that within seconds we were soaked to the skin. It was rarely worth sheltering because the rain passed over quickly and we would be dried out by the sun in ten minutes, and soaked in sweat in less time than that. In addition to deep mud, the roads were also sometimes blocked by fallen trees, and avalanches of red mud where the banks had collapsed. The forest steamed visibly, the mist lingering among the trees whose trunks were decorated in lacelike patterns of intertwining vines. Over the top of the forest lay a thick smothering blanket of creeper – the only patches of sunlight were where dead skeletal white trees stood in stagnant pools of black water.

In villages we bartered pencils and paper for bananas and smoked porcupine; we chewed strips of porcupine as we walked and stopped to swim in every river we passed.

We came to a pygmy village with huts made of pieces of bark. An old man invited us to drink some palm wine. Another pygmy man pointed at us and made paddling gestures in the air and I realised that somehow he also knew that we were the girls who had paddled down the Congo. I was amazed at how far the news had spread. Admittedly we were easily recognised because few (if any) white people stopped at their villages, certainly never on foot, and certainly never young female whites. The pygmies all started chattering; their speech had a musical quality which was almost a chant or song. The tallest among them was no more than four and a half feet tall, but they were perfectly pro-portioned. The one who had pointed us out came over, indicated that we were to finish our palm wine, leave our rucksacks in the care of the villagers, and follow him. He led us first on a forest path and then through the trees on game trails for a couple of miles. Something was going on – I could hear music – and we hurried faster. Ahead of us was a clearing. The pygmy motioned us to be quiet and to sit in the dark shady undergrowth just behind the edge of the clearing where we would not be noticed. He squatted down beside us.

In the glade were several groups of pygmies. The first to catch my eye were some clusters of girls, their faces dramatically painted with strange patterns of indigo blue and white. Some had lines dividing their faces in equal halves from their forehead down the nose to the point of their chin, one half was painted blue and the opposite half was dotted with large white spots, or painted white and dotted with blue spots. Other girls' faces were divided by double blue lines into quarters, which were striped with oblique lines or painted plain white, and all the girls had flowers and cowrie shells threaded into their hair. They were watching the men performing a sort of play depicting a hunt to the music of a drum and some horns. There were six actors who were the hunters and four pygmies who I thought represented wild animals. Each held long pieces of wood which could have been meant to symbolise elephant tusks, or horns. One of them had corkscrew-like pieces of curly vine that had grown wrapping itself round and round the branch of a tree; another one had forked sticks. All four wandered among the saplings on the far side of the glade, stopping to sniff the air and stamp the ground. The hunter-actors crept stealthily in a line around the perimeter of the clearing and swayed in time to the rhythm. They carried bows and had short quivers made of reddish bark and filled with arrows which were slung over their shoulders. The bows were only about a foot long and were arched into a fat D-shape. I longed to take a closer look at their arrows. Both Lesley and I were careful not to move a muscle, not even to wipe off the sweat which ran down our faces despite our being in the shade.

The music of the horns had slowed to a low falling and rising cry; the hunt continued. The small patch of sky above the glade was an ominous pearly grey and it looked as if rain was imminent.

The girls began to dance. Their bodies rocked backwards and forwards; they whirled their hips in a swift circular thrusting movement; their arms were outstretched sideways and trembling. As they danced they sang a high-key warbling song which rejoiced in ecstasy, blending into one with their vigour and the lavish mightiness of the forest. They were oblivious to the swarm of flies which had just arrived in the clearing. The flies were a type that the French called *'ferroux'*, and they bit savagely. It was sheer torture not being able to slap them dead or whisk them off our arms and legs. Our little man indicated that we should leave. We slipped silently away. As he led us back through the forest I tried to ask why the people had been celebrating. If I understood him correctly, his answer was that the forest had been angry with the tribe, so they were dancing to make it happy again. How delightfully simple.

Among the other forest tribes we found various unusual tribal markings, including a rather beautiful style of arrowheads etched in the centre of their foreheads reaching down between their eyebrows. Some arrows pointed down, others up, and the more elaborate arrows had many barbs. Another interesting feature that I noticed was the sharp-filed teeth of some men. Even this custom varied – in one region I saw a man with every tooth filed into double points. Sharpened teeth usually implies cannibalism. The eating of human flesh was common among many tribes, and some even ate the sick and the dead. In parts of the equatorial rain forest there was no wild game or meat – it had all been eaten by their ancestors – and tsetse fly prevented the keeping of domestic animals. People required protein in their diet; without it they couldn't survive. The only available protein was human meat. The Fang tribe of northern Gabon had always been known for cannibalism. It was done through necessity, and was performed in accord with deep-seated superstitions and tribal traditions. I reckoned that in theory this custom was rather like the Christian church who took communion and symbolically ate bits of Christ's body and drank his blood. Whenever we realised we were among cannibals Lesley and I would exchange glances and remember Heko saying: 'Don't worry, we don't eat white people.' We never had any cause for alarm.

One morning in a village I watched some children playing a game. They fetched bowls and tins to use as drums, and three young boys began drumming. They were only about eight years old, but they already knew how to pound out rhythm and to change the beat from one rhythm to another. The other children were dancing and singing; they wriggled their hips and stomped around exactly as they had seen their parents do. The music became more powerful and the dance more frenzied. Suddenly with one accord they all pounced on one little boy. They pretended to tear him apart, eat him, and then they all ran round chuckling and rubbing their tummies. It was slightly disconcerting to watch, but it was only a game.

Gabon was by far the most primitive country I visited. A different custom was that of a tribe we came across in southern Gabon: when one of their women gave birth to a male child, the father would go out into the forest, find someone of a neighbouring tribe, discover his name and then kill him. Certain parts of the body were eaten in a ceremony of baptism and that was how the child received its name. When cannibalism was declared illegal the chief protested and pointed out that without this ceremony the future generations of male children would not be entitled to have names. Tradition was not something which could be altered or replaced and cannibalism could not be stamped out by a mere law. It was their way of life, it was part of the forest, and it was not going to change.

The eating of human flesh was often a privilege reserved for men only; the women had an equally primitive habit and it was one in which they excelled. Female natures were not gentle and soft; they didn't lead a gentle, soft life. Their ways were hard and cruel, they were often vicious and spiteful to each other, and their revenge was through poisons. Some of the types of poison were cunning and fairly harmless, like the ones to which they apparently addicted their unsuspecting husbands, administering a dose each day in his food. It guaranteed that the husband would never leave them, and if he did then within three or four days he would come back with a craving for home cooking. Woe betide the person who aroused a woman's wrath. One of their favourite poisons was made from the finely chopped whiskers of wildcats, and when the person ate or drank these hairs they would catch in their stomach lining causing ulcers and a great deal of pain.

We were still travelling despite the exceptionally heavy rainy season which had turned the roads into seas of mud. My brain felt as though it was about to burst. It was full up, there was no more room in my head to store any more information. My senses felt saturated and could no longer listen, see, or feel. I wanted to curl up in a ball and pretend I was hibernating. I needed to stop, to settle, and to digest everything.

We found a pleasant African village, we were lent a spare hut, and we moved in. Our home was a small three-roomed hut made of planks of wood, shaded by mango trees, with a flowering yellow bush growing outside the front door. Chickens scratched around outside in the sand and came in the door whenever we left it open. We made tables and stools from other rough planks and tree stumps, and we decorated the walls with curly vines and potted creepers. We lived there for a couple of weeks, passing the time lazily by sleeping and eating. We bought food from the local market, such as fish, rice, dried beans, and even fresh bread. We cracked open coconuts for their milk and bought jugs of palm wine for 20 CFA (5p). We joined the village girls for their hairdressing sessions when they braided our hair in their styles and we tried to put their hair into buns, but their hair was so springy, coarse and short that we had to give each girl six buns.

The villagers accepted us as part of the village and no one thought it odd that we were white. At first the young men were a bit tedious and kept propositioning us. Their propositions were sly and they would ask in silly ways like, 'Are you kind?' I had to say 'No' quickly before Lesley said 'Yes' thinking that someone needed her help.

Our best friend in the village was a tall good-looking young man called No-No. He was a deep-thinking, slow-talking and unaffected person. He wasn't frivolous like the other young men, who regarded fun in terms of nightlife and glamour, and beauty in terms of hotels, industrialisation and development. No-No loved being in the forest; he was a born hunter. He and his brother took us hunting forest pigs, fishing, and boating on the mangrove swamps in an old dugout. No-No always brought something special with him, like a jar of sugar-cane wine, or some roasted anteaters which he de-scaled for us and served on plates of banana leaves. He knew instinctively the things which would interest us; he showed us how to make dressings for wounds from crushed herbs which developed penicillin-like moulds, and when a jigger flea burrowed in and laid its eggs under one of my toenails (which itched like mad), No-No made me wait until the eggs were ripe and then he took me to see his cousin's tame monkey. He gave the monkey a sliver of bamboo and I gave the monkey my foot. It examined my foot carefully, checked between each of my toes, and noticed the swelling of the jigger eggs under one nail. It chattered, picked up the bamboo sliver, used it very gently to cut my skin and lift out the sack of eggs. No-No said if we tried to do that we would have broken the sack and made a terrible mess. We gave the monkey a pile of mangoes as a present.

I had another health problem which was more serious. It had started a couple of months before as mild bronchitis, but had grown increasingly worse. Often I felt as though there wasn't any oxygen in the air and I was suffocating; I coughed all day long, and when I couldn't get enough air to cough I

would collapse which sometimes frightened me. The local tobacco I smoked aggravated my chest, but nothing would have
induced me to give up smoking. Nights were very bad; my lungs
felt like they were full of liquid. I choked if I lay flat, so I slept sitting upright. Lesley had been doing everything she could to help
me, laying me upsidedown and thrashing my back to bring up
the gunge, and it was thanks to her that I had lasted this long.
However, now I needed medicine. No-No made an appointment
for me to visit the witchdoctor.

On the appointed day No-No collected us early in the morning.
He was carrying two chickens which was the fee for the cure, and
we set out to walk to the witchdoctor's hut situated on the coast
five miles away. No-No said he had asked for two treatments, one
to cure my bronchitis, and the other was to be a spell to make me
give up smoking. The witchdoctor had agreed to both and had
gone off into the forest to gather the necessary plants.

We arrived at a group of three huts which were made of dry
palm leaves. One was an open-sided sun shelter and beneath it
five very old men sat crosslegged. No-No told us that the one in
the centre was the witchdoctor, who was a hundred years old,
and the other four were wise men and sages. One of them indicated that we should sit on the straw mat facing them. The
witchdoctor looked older than a hundred – his black skin had
fallen into folds of wrinkles which nearly covered his eyes, his
head was bald except for a few white popples of hair, and his
arms and legs were so skinny that his joints looked grotesque. He
was sitting in the lotus position; his bearing was tranquil and ser-
ene. He greeted us quietly in his native tongue and acknowledged
the chickens which No-No had put in front of me on the sand. To
the side of the chickens was a wide calabash full of clear liquid,
probably water. I wondered what was going to happen.

A young boy came up, took away the chickens, and gave the
witchdoctor an instrument which looked like a home-made sitar.
The old man began to play. He strummed the chords as though
he were in a dream; the soft music blended with the far-off roar

of the waves down the beach. Three young boys appeared wearing short cloth wrappers, with cross marks painted on their chests. They danced in a flowing movement around the shelter where we all sat. The five men opposite us seemed to be in a trance and I began to feel more and more relaxed. The boys were now dancing in slow, long, bounding steps, and when they halted each of the wise men took a twig from a pile behind them and put them in the calabash of water. They looked like ordinary brown twigs, but immediately they touched the water it began to bubble. The witchdoctor started to chant a strange melodious song and the water fizzed until it was seething. One of the wise men dipped an old enamel mug into the liquid and handed it to me. I drank it down slowly; it tasted bubbly and slightly bitter. When I had finished I gave back the mug, which he refilled and returned to me. I wondered if they expected me to drink the whole calabash, but after the second cupful he put it aside. Then the witchdoctor put down the sitar and picked up two old but clean washed beer bottles. He inserted the twigs inside them, filled them up with fizzy liquid, and looked at me with penetrating, sharp eyes. He spoke to me and No-No translated what he was saying. He told me that the cure had now begun to work. I must drink both the bottles of liquid the following day then replenish them with water. Every day I must drink both bottles, until the time when the twigs no longer fizzed, and that would indicate that I was well again.

Then he commenced the magic which was to make me give up smoking. He asked No-No and Lesley to go away for a while; I was to stay but must close my eyes because this part was something I was not allowed to see. They left and I shut my eyes obediently. I waited.

The five men started to chant in sonorous unison; there was movement around me; I heard crackles, thuds, snaps, an insistent hollow pounding noise, and the chanting grew louder. I smelt an odd pungent smell — oh how I longed to open my eyes. I raised my chin slightly so that I would be able to see through my eyelashes without appearing to open my eyes. I couldn't see well, but someone was circling me sprinkling something on the ground, the others were sitting hammering their fists against their chests. The pungent smell was so strong that I felt dizzy; I wondered what on earth I was doing here and reflected that I didn't even want to give up smoking. The noise ceased, the wise men stood up, they came over to me and each one said something which sounded like a blessing. Then they left. I didn't know how to ask the witchdoctor if I was allowed to open my eyes yet! I wished No-No and Lesley could come back. I shut my eyes and waited. A stick tapped me on the knee and I opened my eyes. It felt more as though I had awoken from a sleep. No-No and Lesley were walking towards the shelter chatting and smiling. The witchdoctor went over to speak to No-No and I scrambled giddily to my feet.

'Well, have you had your two chickens' worth?' asked Lesley. I felt lousy. No-No joined us and said the witchdoctor wanted to know if I had felt a pain in my chest. I answered yes because I thought that was what he wanted me to say, and because I had indigestion from drinking so much fizzy liquid. We said goodbye to the old witchdoctor, shook hands, picked up my beer bottles, and wandered back to our village.

Over the next days I discovered that I hadn't given up smoking, though I had cut down considerably. Each day I religiously drank both bottles of medicine, and each time I refilled them the twigs still fizzed, but my cough was definitely on the mend. Lesley and I left the village soon after that; I was almost better and we were impatient to get moving again. The sad thing about moving on was always saying goodbye, especially to No-No, but we soon forgot the sadness in our delight at the new things which opened up ahead of us.

We found some Greek engineers building a road, and a small aeroplane whose pilot offered us seats. I enjoyed the air turbulence of the flight, but most of all I liked the different perspective

163

we had of the forest with its muddy meandering rivers and marshes. We landed in Mouila. Lesley and I had already been to the south-east and the south-west corners of Gabon, but Mouila was south-central and had a character all of its own.

We set out to explore the town which was situated on both banks of a river. We crossed the main square with its flagpole, rows of concrete offices, overgrown flowerbeds and flame trees in blossom. Most of the buildings were old French-style colonial houses with arches and pillared verandahs and we, in our long skirts, felt like a memory from the past. An American girl teacher invited us to lunch. She was the first white and also the first female teacher that the school had ever had. She told us about the local belief that a mermaid lived in the river. Many people claimed to have seen her, everyone knew that she was very powerful, and for assured good fishing the mermaid demanded an occasional human sacrifice. A few years ago construction had begun on a bridge to span the river and connect up both sides of the town, but no one had asked the permission of the mermaid. The bridge collapsed. None of the locals believed that it was a fault in the design which caused the collapse and two young children were sacrificed to appease the mermaid's wrath. She accepted these sacrifices, and when the engineers tried again to build the bridge it was successful. The mermaid was not just a figment of the imagination. She was in fact a manatee – an aquatic mammal which is probably the basis of all mermaid myths. A manatee is about six feet long with a fish tail and a snub face which resembled a large seal.

Evening came, we went to mass at the Catholic mission church whose seats were made of rough cross sections of tree trunk, and we stayed the night at the house of the four Catholic sisters (who all looked identical to us). They were fabulous people, they sparkled with the joy of life, and Soeur Gabriel who was in charge of the cooking deserved the highest praise. They didn't rely on imported foods; they grew vegetables and bought local produce from the town, transforming everything with superb French cuisine – which was a lovely change from the repetitious rather bland African diet. The sisters had found a way to stop the village children raiding their mango trees. They hung some tin cans full of 'magic spells' from the branches. All the talk of the evening was about the forthcoming celebrations which were to be held in Mouila in five days' time.

On the day of the celebration Mouila bore little resemblance to the sleepy sedate town we had first explored. As we walked into the main square we were bombarded with noise, colour, and confusion. The first thing I saw was a red and white painted African somersaulting high against the blue sky above the crowd. At the top of his arc he flipped his legs over his head and vanished upright back into the midst of elephant masks, raffia wigs, tall feathers, plumed head-dresses, worn by men painted in different colours and dressed in grass skirts, monkey-skin kilts, or the pelts of civet and wildcats. I didn't know what to look at, everywhere I turned I was dazzled by stupendous sights. I was jostled by a real elephant. It was only a baby, less than three feet tall, and there were four men hanging onto its tail trying to make it stand still, but even at that size the elephant was strong enough to tow them along in his wake like waterskiers.

A medley of music filled the air. Rhythms were pounded out by drummers who were oblivious to everything except the powerful hammering of their hands producing the resonant thunder of their drums, the interweaving cadence of the beats evoking wild feelings of abandonment, festivity, and stirring everyone to dance.

I looked up and saw a group of men who were dancing on stilts ten feet tall and wearing heavy round wooden masks. The dance of the stilt-men was an exciting and skilful exercise; they moved with the music, they jiggled and hopped, pirouetted and twirled, while down below them were men dancing upsidedown using their hands as feet and wearing many-layered costumes of grass which reached to the ground. These men symbolised spirits; their role was to protect the stilt-dancers and they performed this by a ritual of leaps and somersaults. One particular spirit could jump so high that when he somersaulted he was on a level with the painted masks of the stilt-men. He whirled and cavorted among the other spirits, bounding clean over the top of them in a display of jack-knife and swallow movements, and seeming to float suspended in the air balanced on the rumbustious crescendo of rhythm.

15
A Nightmare at Sea

A chance meeting with a Frenchman called Maurice took us to Libreville. He offered to fly us there in his aeroplane. Actually, Maurice was only going to stop for lunch in Libreville and would then be flying off for a week. So, he suggested that Lesley and I could stay in his hotel room until he returned. The hotel was the most exclusive in the capital; it was a tall, ultra-modern tower right on the seafront. Maurice showed us to our room, on the tenth floor of the hotel, with a fabulous view of sea, golden sandy beaches and palm trees. We assured him that we would be very happy there.

When he left, Lesley and I walked downtown looking for the post office. It had been about three months sine we had been able to post letters home; it was difficult to find post offices in the forest. Libreville had a big, modern post office, and while we were there we checked with *post restante*, although we didn't expect anything because we hadn't known or told anyone where we were going. Much to our surprise there was a card for us. It was from Chimu. Its message was even more surprising: 'Am in Hong Kong. I just read about your Congo adventure – in the *South China Morning Post.*'

We left the post office and strolled along the seafront. A taxi screeched to a halt, a man jumped out, came running up and hugged me. It was my brother-in-law. I can't begin to describe the shock and happiness I felt. He had arrived by plane that morning from Lagos, where he'd had business, and had come to Gabon to search for us. My parents had become disturbed when they heard nothing from me for so long; they weren't alarmed, but they had taken the opportunity of giving my brother-in-law photographs of me and Lesley, and asking him to go to Gabon and look around for any sign of us. So he had decided to start his search from Libreville, had put our photographs in his pocket, and wondered how on earth to set about finding us. By coincidence, he was also staying at the same hotel as us. We spent three glorious days together and when he finally left I cried for hours. My family were very important to me, but I had been away so long that I had almost begun to think that they were just a figment of my imagination.

Our first task in Libreville was to find some employment and other lodgings so that we wouldn't be homeless when Maurice returned at the end of the week. It was a disheartening search. We could find no work which interested us and the city had a terrible shortage of housing, quite apart from the rents which ranged from £500–£1500 per month for a flat. We soon discovered that all the prices in Libreville were equally astounding and were told that it was the second most expensive city in the world (second to Caracas in Venezuela). The high prices in Gabon were caused by the shortages and by the fantastic wealth generated from the off-shore oilfields, plus inland mines of gold, uranium, manganese and iron ore. There were no local fruit, vegetables or meat because Gabon was infertile and couldn't grow anything but forest. There were no public buses in the city; everyone was rich enough to have one or two cars and most of the French expatriot schoolchildren went to and from school by taxi.

In spite of all these negative factors I liked Libreville; it had a magnetic quality that made me want to stay. The Gabonese and the French seemed to mutually loathe each other, but we didn't look French, so both sides were friendly towards us.

Libreville seemed to belong to the French and they ran banks, shops, service industries, worked as shop assistants, barmaids and even prostitutes. In most black African countries all semi-skilled work was reserved for the Africans and unless you had special qualifications you couldn't get a work permit. This was the first time we had seen white people doing non-technical jobs. Of course, it didn't mean that Lesley and I would find jobs, because the jobs were for the French and we were English. We were outsiders.

We were asked to appear on Gabonese television (in colour) and afterwards we gave interviews on radio and to newspaper men. Instant stardom followed. Four-hour lunches of lobster and crab with diplomats and chic French people led into champagne cocktail parties, dinners of frogs' legs and palm hearts, night-clubs and midnight feasts of prawns down on the beach. Our accommodation problem was solved by three people all offering us temporary empty lodgings, and since we didn't know which to accept we said yes to them all and moved from one to the next playing a game like musical chairs which we named musical flats.

We acquired a selection of friends. They were an odd assortment, like Mad Meurde, a fighter pilot trainer who was so paranoid about being poisoned by his *boyess* (female servant) that if he saw her touch his food or glass of drink he would throw it away immediately. He warned us never to take a taxi after dark because we would be driven into the African district, killed and eaten. He also warned us of the dangers of travelling in Gabon and said that when a black person saw whites in cars they would hurl rocks through the windscreen. Our other paranoid French friends had obsessions about not drinking any water that originated in Gabon, so they bought imported bottled water from France and even used it to make ice cubes. When the shops ran out of bottled water, they were forced to clean their teeth with whisky.

Our four best Gabonese friends all looked rather similar and were called Mavungo, Maganga, Mapangou and Makouma. We never sorted out which was which. Three of them held very important jobs, and one was a policeman whom we met in a bizarre encounter. One day one of Lesley's admirers had presented her with a chunk of fresh steak, so we decided to barbecue it for lunch down on the beach. It was going to be a huge meal for just Lesley and me, so we walked for miles along the beach to build up a good appetite. We reached a deserted bay of golden sand, and the morning passed in a haze of surf. We barbecued the steak on a fire of driftwood, and after eating we stretched out naked in the sun to sleep.

When a shadow moved across me I woke up, opened my eyes, and there above me stood an enormously tall policeman.

'Passports,' he demanded.

I shuddered and said, 'Please turn away while we put our clothes on.' We wrapped up in towels, passport examination was very thorough (luckily they were in order) but the policeman then arrested us for being nude. I explained that we were only tourists, we had seen many topless African women in the bush, so how could we be expected to know that it was illegal not to wear clothes. I kept him talking for quite a long time, reasoning with him, because I knew we must, at all costs, make him forget about arresting us. If we were to be taken to the gendarmerie then we would be in heavy trouble. Every single policeman would play power games with us, and since the crime was being nude the price of our freedom would doubtless be to sleep with every officer who fancied it.

The tall policeman began to look less stern and finally he relented. He cautioned us, 'You must never again be naked on the beach. However, I know a beach further away where no one will find you. I will drive you there.'

I wanted to burst out laughing at the absurdity of it all. He drove us to another bay and while Lesley went swimming (in her bathing costume) I sat and wrote my diary. A shadow fell across the page and I looked up. There stood an enormously tall naked policeman. I thought it best for me to act as though I saw naked black policemen every day of the week and I chatted with him as I continued my writing. After a while he went away, came back fully dressed, and asked what time we would like him to return with the car to drive us home. And that was the beginning of a long friendship.

Christmas was in two weeks' time, we had completely forgotten about it, and we started trying to think of somewhere nice to go and celebrate. Christmas had always been a very important family occasion for me; this was the first time I had spent Christmas away from my parents and it made me feel rather sad. Our first idea was to go back to Père Alphonse in the Congo, but the long rains were falling and the roads were closed. We thought of Mayumba instead, a coastal village where we had met a fascinating old-time Frenchman. Then we decided to change our minds again and stay in Libreville. Still undecided, we began to wish we could leave Gabon; we'd had enough of it. Its magnetic quality was still strong, but I felt as though I was in a vacuum. I'd become restless and fidgety, little things annoyed me, and I didn't know what was wrong or what to do about it. It was time to leave.

We had been travelling now for ten months without a proper rest; we were physically exhausted. We longed to speak English again, to be able to fully express ourselves in a conversation and ease the mental strain of talking in a foreign language all the time. We poured over the map to look for an English-speaking country; it was surprising to see that 50 per cent of Africa was Francophone, and our choice was only southern or east Africa. We had been told that work permits were very difficult to obtain in east Africa, whereas in South Africa they were easy. We had to find work soon because our money was nearly finished. That created a secondary problem; most countries would not allow anyone through their borders who could not show sufficient funds to support their stay, plus onward air tickets. We did have open-dated vouchers for air travel anywhere, but not much money.

We went to the airport to see if there were any private planes going outside Gabon. We were offered a lift to France, but much more interesting was the mention of a sanction-busting meat flight to Rhodesia. While we were at the airport, President Mobutu of Zaire arrived. There was much drumming, dancing, parading and saluting, and we met the Zaire press secretary who invited us out to dinner and said that he could arrange visas for us to Zaire. The visas were issued and it looked as though our problems were solved. We would go to Zaire and hitch-hike south. The only snag was getting to Zaire; it wasn't permitted to enter it via Congo, it wasn't wise to enter via Angola which was in the throes of heavy war, and the only way in was to fly to Kinshasa. That was fine, then we heard about the Compulsory Expenditure Law, whereby every visitor was obliged to spend a minimum of £20 a day, for each and every day of their sojourn. Well, even if we could have afforded that, it wouldn't have been possible to spend such an amount in the forest.

'That doesn't matter,' the Embassy replied. 'The official at the point of departure will calculate how much money you should have spent, and you just have to pay him what is due.' Crunch.

Next we tracked down the men who ran the sanction-busting meat flights to Rhodesia. It was a difficult bit of tracking, but very rewarding because they said they were always happy to help people who couldn't afford scheduled airlines, and that we could fly with them at the end of that week, or any week. What a relief. At last we could relax.

We went to take the meat flight a week later but, unfortunately, on the interim flight the company had helped three other tourists – who had gone straight to the South African newspapers and sold their story of flying with the sanction-busters. So, naturally, the company had decided never to help another traveller.

Libreville had trapped us again. With a sickening, sinking feeling I heard the metallic clang of a door swinging shut, and the click as it locked us in.

We went to the scheduled airlines office, but there were no
flights to anywhere except Europe until after Christmas. So then
we went to the harbour; we were determined to board the first
southbound boat. Easier said than done. Even if a boat was
going south they couldn't admit it, because international politics
forbade ships to stop at South African ports. According to the
shipping lines, every ship was going north. The harbour con-
troller confirmed that the ships' papers said they were north-
bound, but added that many ships also had a second set of
papers, carefully forged to show that they came from somewhere
else and were, in fact, on route to South Africa. Once out at sea,
they would switch papers and head south. We walked back pensively along the beach to town, looking at each option again, rack-
ing our brains for a way out. Every moment of every day was
spent trying to make a getaway, but we were thwarted at every
attempt.

During the days we dashed from the harbour to the airport.
Every possibility was a dead end. We mishandled a couple of
chances, like the presidential flight to Burundi, and our stupidity
only made our frustration worse. Every piece of information we
received conflicted with what someone else had said. Every office
we visited was either closed, or else the person we wanted to see
was out, and after waiting for an hour they would say something
like that he was out because he was on holiday for two weeks.
Yes, someone was handling his business but they didn't know
who, so they went to find out but didn't come back, and by the
time you had found out, then that person had gone home for
lunch, and the offices all closed in the afternoons. It made me feel
frantic.

On one of our afternoon visits to the port, we saw a couple of
new arrivals anchored just outside the harbour, and the tugboat
driver agreed to take us out to them so that we could ask where
they were going.

The first ship was going to France. We chugged over to the
second which was a dilapidated cargo boat. One of the African

deckhands told us they were going to Pointe-Noire on the Congo coast, and that, from there, we would easily find a connection to Capetown. So we climbed aboard to speak to the captain. He was a tall, lanky Frenchman, rough looking, and he obviously hadn't shaved that morning, but his manner was pleasant and courteous. He introduced himself as Jacques, opened some beers and we sat down to talk. He said that he knew of a boat which was going from Pointe-Noire to Capetown in about three days' time, and that he himself was sailing for Pointe-Noire in two hours, so we'd better be quick if we wanted a ride. We were thrilled; at last here was a real chance to get away from Libreville. We thanked him, and he smiled awkwardly. He said that he had never before had the pleasure of carrying two young ladies and he hoped we wouldn't find the company too uncouth.

I stood at the ship's rails watching Libreville fade away. I said a quiet goodbye and prayed that I would never return there. Then I moved round to the prow of the ship to feel the wind in my hair, to blow the past out of my mind, and open it up to the future. The ship's engineer came to join me; he was a young Belgian lad, probably only twenty, with a baby face that was not yet weathered or scarred with the tough life of a sailor.

He asked me if I knew that it was Christmas Day. I felt a stab of regret that I hadn't known and that for the first time in my life I hadn't hung up my Christmas stocking, given or received any presents, or cards, or sung any carols. I tried to dismiss my gloom by telling myself that the captain and engineer never celebrated Christmas on their boat and then I decided that this year would be different for them.

I found Lesley; we searched around for basic materials, went to the main cabin, and leapt into action. Lesley began cutting up newspapers to make a sort of Christmas tree which we decorated with blobs of colour and tinfoil stars; strips of tinfoil also served for paperchains and flowers; we pinned them up; and, finally, painted as many Christmas cards as we had time for before the captain and engineer came in. They laughed with surprise, said it looked wonderful, and the captain brought out two bottles of champagne. They also had a treat for us – Christmas dinner. It was a magnificent feast of caviar, lobsters, shark steaks, followed by another fish course, then a meat dish, then roast muscovy duck, salads, and a huge selection of cheeses. Thank god neither of us felt seasick. The captain talked to us about his experiences in twenty years' tramp steaming round the African coast, and we sang carols, in French and English.

Our journey on that ship was a pleasant one. Lesley passed the time happily fishing off the stern, while I was up on the bridge, learning to navigate and manoeuvre the ship. After one day, Jacques, the captain, handed me the charts and put me in charge.

On arrival in Pointe-Noire, the captain radioed to *L'Augure* (the boat which was going to Capetown) and explained that Lesley and I would like to go with them. *L'Augure's* captain replied that he would be glad to have female passengers and it was all settled. We were so pleased that everything had gone according to plan and we thanked Jacques for such an enjoyable voyage. He said he was happy to have been able to help us and although he didn't know this other captain very well he was sure that we would be well looked after. Jacques refused to accept any money for our fares from Libreville – he told us that he hadn't enjoyed a trip so much for years. We were to change boats after dark when we wouldn't be spotted. Our baggage was put in one of the lifeboats, and late in the evening we said goodbye, climbed into the lifeboat with two crewmen and were lowered into the water.

The men rowed us over to *L'Augure*. There was a lot of movement going on under cover of darkness; the port was being used as a supply point for the Angolan war and every ship was busily engaged in secret activity. Jacques had pointed out Russian ships discharging Cuban troops, a freighter unloading armoured cars and tanks, and cranes that were shifting crates of guns and ammunition. We passed silently round the stern of a Chinese registered ship which was carrying army lorries parked bumper to bumper on the deck, and the lifeboat nudged up against the side of *L'Augure*. Rope ladders were let down, Lesley and I climbed aboard, and the lifeboat disappeared into the night.

We were taken to meet *L'Augure*'s captain who was sitting in the main cabin with his engineer and some of their African crew. The captain and engineer were both French and, since they were in the middle of having an argument with the crew, Lesley and I sat down on a corner seat. The captain was a thickset, swarthy man, and his heavy jowled face showed the ravages of many fights and too much alcohol. He sent the crew away, reached for an open whisky bottle, sloshed some into his glass and two clean glasses, and called us over to his table. I hesitated. I didn't want to meet him; I didn't like the way he looked at me, and I loathed the taste of neat whisky. At that moment, a commotion broke out on deck, the captain swore, slammed his fists on the table and went out to see what was happening. The engineer stayed behind. He was a skinny, old man. We said hello and took the opportunity of explaining that we were very tired and would like to be shown to our cabin.

From our cabin porthole, we could see the black silhouettes of unlit ships, but where Jacques' ship had been was now an empty space. It was too late for us to change our minds.

Three days later, we were still anchored in the harbour at Pointe-Noire. The only thing which had altered was our predicament. Lesley and I had been separated; I was kept locked up in a cabin most of the time and was only allowed out under surveillance onto the decks.

The day after we had come aboard *L'Augure*, the captain had said he was sorry but we couldn't stay in the cabin where we'd spent the night and he gave us separate cabins instead. That didn't matter at all, but the thing which did upset me was the way he followed me around like a dog behind a bitch on heat. In the morning, Lesley and I had explored the boat, comparing it with the last one. The captain accompanied us on our tour, putting his large hairy hands on my arms or shoulders whenever I stopped, pinching me, pawing at me, and standing underneath the bottom of every steep iron stairway so that he could watch us going up.

That night, I locked my cabin door and reckoned I was safe. The handle turned, someone hammered on the door, the captain's voice shouted that I was to open the door at once. I climbed into the bunk fully dressed and lay down to go to sleep. The captain kicked the door down. I reacted with anger and indignation, and he said gruffly that he only wanted to talk to me. But he didn't talk; he came over to the bunk and tried to pull down the covers which I held gripped firmly up to my neck. I yelled at him to get out of my cabin. He left. I got up, closed and barricaded the door with a table, and went back to bed. Five minutes later, the captain forced the door open again, my barricade crumpled like matchsticks, I sat up in the bunk and demanded to know why he couldn't act like a normal human being and leave me alone to sleep. He just looked at me with a greedy gaze that travelled up and down the outline of my body. I tried to reason with him, still he said nothing, he just stared. He must have finally seen my point of view because he nodded, then walked out. I turned over and went to sleep. I was woken by two large hands which were groping through the covers. I lost my temper and he went away again. Throughout the night I repulsed his advances with a mixture of reason and anger, and by the next day I felt worn out.

At breakfast, I asked the captain how much money he would like for our fares to Capetown. He replied that he had plenty of money and that we must pay in kind, by my favours. He gestured to his cabin and said he was ready for payment straight away. I objected and reminded him that he had understood my views last night.

'So now I will make you understand mine,' he said, and from that time on I was made a prisoner in another cabin with one small round porthole which faced out to sea, a bunk, and a very

stout door which was locked on the outside. I didn't mind being
locked up, but I wished the boat would get moving. The captain
was a constant visitor to my cabin and he harassed me until I
thought I was going insane. I tried every tactic I could think of to
make him leave me alone. My tone had to be one degree more
powerful than his and I had to make sure that I outwitted him.
My displays of outrage were quite successful but their effect was
not long term. Indeed, nothing had a lasting effect on the captain. His stage of silence and sulking was over, but now all his
conversation consisted of what he wanted to do to me. Sometimes, I could reason with him, sometimes not. I often explained
that he didn't appeal to me; I tried feigning illness, and he gave
me some aspirin; when he forced me down on the bunk, I faked
such a terrible coughing fit that he brought me a glass of water. I
don't know why he didn't just simply rape me and have done
with it. Something was holding him back.

I was impatient for the boat to get to Capetown and asked why
weren't we moving. The captain replied that *L'Augure* was not
going to Capetown, it was on its return trip from there and now
it was heading north up to Gabon. Then he threatened that if I
made any attempt to escape from the boat, he would inform the
Congolese authorities that he had found two stowaways and had
evidence that they were spies. If we were to successfully escape
from the boat we could be sure that every soldier and policeman
in the Congo would be after our blood.

I wondered to myself what evidence he would think of to
give against us, but I knew how much the police would love to lay
hands on two white girls accused of spying. Guilt or innocence
has nothing to do with it. If caught, we would certainly be tortured for secret information, kept in appalling prison conditions
without trial for months or years, and have little chance of being
rescued because there was no British Embassy in the Congo.

Apart from this continual persecution, I was well looked after
and took my meals with Lesley and the two Frenchmen. Lesley
was being guarded by the crew and she seemed to spend all day

fishing off the stern. Occasionally we met on deck and had time to catch up on each other's news. Her nights were eventful too, because, although she had managed to barricade her cabin door, she was awoken several times each night by crewmen wriggling in through the portholes. She was very distressed about the way I was being treated and was furious when I told her that the boat was heading north back to Gabon, and what the captain had threatened, if we tried to escape. We had no choice but to bide our time.

Our fourth day on board *L'Augure* was New Year's Eve, which was also the Congolese Independence Day, but this year nobody intended to dance. There was a curfew in Pointe-Noire and anyone seen in the streets after dark was likely to be shot. It didn't seem possible that it was the same merry little holiday town which we had visited three months before. *L'Augure* had swung round on her anchor; I could now see a couple of other ships and a dock beyond with a railway yard. I leant against the porthole and whiled away the hours just looking and thinking. The Cuban military allies were a sinister sight.

Just before midnight the captain fetched me from my cabin and we joined the others on the deck behind the bridge. At midnight exactly, all the ships began to flash their lights, dozens of distress flares were lit and rocketed up like fireworks; fog sirens wailed, horns whooped and claxons howled. It was a celebration I knew I would never forget. The captain had poured a tumbler of whisky for each of us and everyone wished each other a happy New Year. The captain stood behind me breathing heavily down my neck. Wherever I moved, he followed.

When the echoes of the sirens had died away and all the ships had returned to darkness, the captain escorted me down to his cabin for a private party of our own. I refused his advances, so he beat me up and left me lying in a heap on the outer cabin floor. He went away, locked the door, and shortly afterwards the boat's engines started up. I felt the floor begin to move and I realised we were on our way back to Libreville. I desperately wanted to cry.

The captain was on duty on the bridge for the rest of the night, but he found many opportunities to slip downstairs and clumsily attempt to lie on top of me as I lay on the floor curled tightly into a ball. He failed to make me lie flat, so he kicked me instead.

New Year's Day was marked by the fact that, since we were now at sea, I was officially removed from my prison cabin and installed in the captain's cabin. It meant that I had more freedom during the day to walk on deck, chat with Lesley, and try to think of a way to end this nightmare. Lack of sleep and worry had made me very lightheaded, and my body looked rather bruised and battered, but my mind was surprisingly clear. I felt nothing at all, no pain, no feelings, no emotions.

My relationship with the captain was becoming a battle of wits; every tactic I adopted he parried very deftly and with a panache that I almost admired. My more feeble excuses were treated with the contempt they deserved and my more ingenious moves produced equally crafty counter-offensives. The preservation of my virtue was not the thing that mattered – I was fighting for a principle that no one had the right to bully me.

One morning I stole a kilo of raw garlic from the kitchen. I immediately ate ten large cloves – they really stung my mouth – but they had the desired result. I stank from every pore of my skin and my breath was so foul that everyone stayed well clear of me. Even the captain wrinkled his nose and hurried away. How pleased I was! I sat in the sun writing my diary undisturbed. Then the captain returned and solemnly emptied a whole bottle of eau-de-cologne over me. He sat down close beside me, put his grease-stained arm around my shoulders and started kissing my ear, very wetly and very loudly. My appearance was enough to turn off the most ardent of lovers; I had rubbed cooking oil into my hair to make it lank and greasy, and had washed my face in diluted vermilion red ink to make my complexion florid. The captain thought I had sunburn and suggested we moved into the shade.

I was beginning to understand something of his character. He was not a complicated man; he was coarse, vulgar and violent because his life had moulded him in this way. He had no conception of the finer side of life because he had only known the constant voyaging at sea with no other company besides one dreary old engineer and a crew who despised him; no other sights but the rough and ruthless ocean interspersed with occasional rowdy drunken stopovers in the same old ports with the same baggy whores.

One afternoon I was fishing off the stern of the boat. The African crew's quarters opened onto that area and I thought that having other people around would make the captain leave me alone. I was wrong. He stood behind me and kept trying to hug me , so I kept pretending I'd caught a fish and would go leaping heavily backwards onto his toes. The crew were baffled; Lesley had said they'd been asking her what on earth was going on between the captain and myself, and when she told them, they asked her to relay their sympathy. The crew were a rough bunch, but they weren't nasty or vicious. Lesley had become friends with many of them; they respected her and she was left in peace at nights. If there had been anything they could do to help me, they would have done so. The engineer wouldn't have lifted a finger to help me, so I never asked him, and besides there was nothing anyone could do. It was my problem and mine alone.

Lesley had a brilliant idea: she discovered the locker containing the boat's medical kit which she searched for drugs or sleeping pills. Unfortunately, it consisted mostly of bandages and healing creams, but she found a few tranquillisers, enough for one good dose. We dissolved them in a teaspoon of water and in the evening I distracted the captain's attention while she poured it into his whisky. Dinner was like all meals, rather subdued, though the cook had been brightening up our life by asking us to tell him our favourite dishes and cooking them specially for us.

At bedtime I settled down in a chair with a book and to my immense relief the captain fell asleep. This was the first night that the captain had left me alone for long enough to sleep. In the past, even when I had fallen asleep, it was never in a bed; I slept upright in a chair and dozed lightly because I was always awoken by groping hands. The captain stirred and shouted for me to join him. I called back that I would come when I had finished the chapter. The night before this I had also sat up in a chair reading, and been harassed so many times that I had locked myself in the loo where I spent the rest of the night. The captain had tried to batter down the door, but the lock had held firm. In the morning he had unscrewed and removed the lock.

The days passed in battle and exhaustion. Sometimes I felt I was going crazy and I wondered when it would end. The captain still followed me everywhere. Whenever I stopped he began to squeeze, stroke and pinch me. His teeth were stained brown with nicotine, his chin was always stubby and his breath smelt. He often tried to kiss me and I responded with clenched teeth and wheezing, rattling noises from my nose.

Inevitably, I received the final ultimatum. Either I went to bed with the captain, or we would be handed over to the police in Libreville with the evidence to prove that we were spies. There was no British Embassy in Gabon either and I doubted that our influential friends would be friends if we were in trouble. But we weren't yet in Libreville. In fact, according to the engineer, we were moving exceptionally slowly and Libreville was still three days ahead.

I said a quick, silent apology to Lesley, in case his threat was put into force, and I called the captain's bluff. I explained, as clearly as I could, that nothing was going to make me change my mind. I was, by now, filled with a cold, hard rage, my mental powers felt sharp and crystal clear and I knew I was holding control over at least half the situation. But strain and tiredness were fast tearing me apart.

I reached a kind of breaking point. Suddenly something happened inside my mind; it was as though I had been lifted out of my body and was watching the play from afar. The four of us assembled for lunch in the lounge cabin. The captain flopped

Above: Lesley in *La Pirogue*, one of the few surviving photographs from the Congo.
Below: Myself with Basotho girls, Lesotho, Southern Africa.

Above: Desert landscape in South West Africa.
Below: Fish River Canyon, South West Africa.

With Xoza at the beginning of our journey, eastern Transvaal.

Above: Toni on Toroka in northern Kenya.
Below: A Kalenjen family in the Cherangani Hills.

Typical African girl painted white for initiation ceremony.

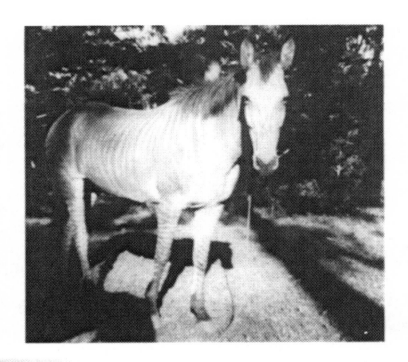

Above: The zebroid.
Below: The Turkwell river, Kenya.

Galeb woman and child, Ethiopia.

Above: The camel at Lake Rudolph.
Below: Along the shores of Lake Rudolph.

down heavily into a chair and leaned back, hooking his arms behind the chair. The rope with which he had tried to whip me the previous night was still lying on the floor. Without any idea in mind, I took the rope and tied the captain's hands at his back. Lesley helped me. The engineer didn't understand what was going on and he got up with a puzzled expression.

'Sit down,' snarled Lesley. He sat down. We tied him up as well. There was a bottle of tomato sauce on the table, so we splattered some on the captain's head to look like blood. Neither of us were following a plan; we were making it up as we went along.

'Get up,' I ordered the captain. 'Walk up the stairs to the bridge.'

He started to protest, so we gagged him with his handkerchief, pulling it tightly through his mouth and knotting it behind his head. His chin waggled up and down as he tried to shout, but the only noise was a throaty grunting. I opened the door to see if there was anyone around; the corridor and stairway were empty and I noticed an iron bar lying outside the kitchen door, so I picked it up. Lesley hustled the captain up the stairs. As he turned to walk onto the bridge, the ship rolled and he tripped over the raised doorsill. He went crashing headlong and lay sprawled across the bridge floor. The big wooden steering wheel was in the hands of one of the African crew and there were three others lounging beside the radar equipment. They were all friends of Lesley. When they saw the captain gagged and bound, blood everywhere and me wielding an iron bar, their eyes bulged and their jaws dropped open. I faced the crewman at the wheel and commanded, 'Turn the boat. Set a course for Capetown.'

He goggled. No one moved. It was a classic moment, and it was now that we needed chance to intervene for us.

'I said turn the boat. Are you coming with us, or do you want to go for a swim?' I put on my best gangster drawl and snapped out all the pirate clichés I had heard in old films.

The crewman smiled, 'Angel, we're with you,' and he began to turn the boat. It turned steadily and I screamed inwardly –

183

chance, it's all up to you. Is it going to be real or not? Chance
ignored us, and a voice at the back of my mind told me what we
could be letting ourselves in for. The sentence for piracy was ten
years' imprisonment. We would have to sink the ship on the
South African coast, but what would we do with the captain and
engineer? If they escaped, the crew would face charges of
mutiny. No, piracy was not for me.

I glanced at Lesley and shook my head. She shook her head
also. The crew nodded and grinned and nodded again more en-
thusiastically. That did it, we all burst out laughing.

'Okay, you can set the boat back on course for Libreville and
please untie the captain.'

The captain chose to agree that the whole thing had been a
joke and he laughed as heartily as the rest of us. Life returned to
normal, though he began to treat me with an air that bordered
on politneness. I spent the evening sitting out on the point of the
boat's prow, suspended above the waves, watching some dol-
phins, shoals of flying fish, a big turtle and the silver sliver of the
new moon.

I attempted to sleep the night in Lesley's cabin, but I was removed and disciplined. So I dozed in a chair with a book. The
captain was on the bridge; he came down to check me every hour,
groping, pawing and whining at me. As a last resort I changed
tactics again, reverting to one which had not been successful
before because the captain hadn't really caught on, but now I felt
that he was more ready for it. I flooded him with respect and civ-
ility, doing everything possible to evoke his sense of gallantry
and awaken the spirit of the gentleman.

For the first time in the voyage he appeared for breakfast in a
clean shirt, he shaved twice in one day, and he began to try to
please me. To counter my respectful treatment of him, he pretended to fall romantically and dashingly in love. He now walked
behind me quoting poetry and crooning love songs, while I
munched cloves of garlic as though they were peanuts. He still
persisted in trying to kiss me and I developed a bigger and better

range of blowing, squelching noises from my mouth and nose. But it didn't stop him loving me and he asked me to marry him.

We arrived back in Libreville harbour and I was again locked in the cabin so that I couldn't escape. The next stop was to be at Abidjan on the Ivory Coast of west Africa. I couldn't take any more of this torture. Pain and exhaustion had driven me to the end of my tether. Lesley had comforted me that we would surely find a chance to escape; she had packed our bags and put them in the kitchen. But no chance came our way; my door was never unlocked and the porthole was sealed closed. Through the porthole, I saw the pilot's tugboat arrive; he moored alongside *L'Augure*, and boarded the ship to steer it out of the harbour. Soon we were moving and, eventually, the engineer unlocked the cabin door. The pilot handed *L'Augure* back into the captain's hands and he was just climbing back into his tug. Lesley was waiting outside my door; we grabbed our bags from the kitchen, ran across the deck heading for the gap in the rails where the tug boat had been tied and was now casting off. As the boats moved apart, we threw our rucksacks forward and made a flying leap, landing squarely on the open deck behind the pilot. The pilot glanced over his shoulder, but his expression didn't alter and he didn't ask why or what we were doing. He didn't say a word, he just dropped us at a wooden jetty and went on to the next ship.

Lesley and I hitch-hiked into Libreville. I didn't believe it was true. I kept looking behind me, but the captain wasn't there. We were standing in the airline office, I felt weak and shaky, I could hear Lesley asking for two tickets on the first flight anywhere. The hostess replied there was a plane to Johannesberg which was scheduled for the coming night. We reserved seats and bought the tickets with our air-travel vouchers. As we walked out of the office we started to voice our fears.

'Do you think the captain will let us go?'

'He can easily radio back to Libreville with a tip-off, and they would certainly check the airport.'

'He's bound to be wild with anger.'

'He's foiled every other plan we had.'

'No, I don't think he's finished with us yet.'

We walked for miles along the northern beaches to a deserted bay where we felt safe. We slept and swam and surfed and slept some more. We dreaded going to the airport, something was certain to go wrong. If we weren't arrested, then perhaps the plane wouldn't turn up, or else it would be full.

At sunset, we walked to the airport; takeoff was not until 4.30 a.m., which left us nine more hours to wait. I was very scared as we sat in the public lounge, every moment I expected to feel the heavy hand of the law on my shoulder and to hear, 'Come with us, we want to question you.' I jumped nervously every time someone walked behind me. The chairs were hard and uncomfortable. I fidgeted and wanted to go pacing up and down. A Gabonese man came over.

'Excuse me.' I leapt a mile. He continued, 'Are you waiting for the 4.30 flight?'

'Yes,' we said cautiously.

'Come with me. I can show you a comfortable and quiet place to rest.' He led us to a manager's office which was closed up for the night. There were long sofas and air conditioners. Our new friend, Samuel, brought us coffee and croissants from the bar and promised to make sure we woke up in time for the plane. We slept until our flight was called.

I went through passport control in a cold sweat of terror. The suspense was worse with every minute, nothing had gone wrong yet. The plane had landed, then we boarded it, there were seats for us; we sat down. The plane was not remotely similar to the single-engined noddy planes we were used to; there were no chickens and goats, and there was only one person in each seat. I fell asleep, slept all the way to Johannesburg, until the plane circled for landing when I pressed my nose to the window and saw thousands of English-style suburban houses; nearly every one had a swimming pool in its little garden, and the man in the seat behind us said that the swimming pool population was second only to Beverley Hills.

I bit my nails and waited for trouble as we approached the passport barrier, but there was no problem. They didn't even ask us to show onward tickets and holiday money. I was stunned that nobody queried us, nobody stopped us, and that the captain had let me go free. We cleared customs and came out the other side.

Into another world.

16
Rhodesia

I had often heard Johannesburg described as a concrete jungle and there is no more apt description. The buildings are closely packed, towering skyscrapers with black-tinted glass. To me it seemed as dense and awe-inspiring as the equatorial rain forest, except that here the undergrowth was a tangle of shoppers and people hurrying along the pavements.

We went into a department store which was full of familiar items. Everyone was speaking English, but there was one startling anachronism: everyone seemed to be carrying a gun. The woman ahead of us had a small pistol in her handbag which I noticed when she opened her bag to pay for her purchases, and as men raised their arms to take goods down from the shelves I saw the shoulder holsters inside their jackets. We bought some bread, cheese and paté for lunch and ate it in one of the leafy green city squares, sitting on a bench marked 'Whites Only'.

We both felt overwhelmed. Lesley's eyes were wide and glassy and I, still with swelling bruises, kept glancing over my shoulder to make sure that the captain was not there. I had no feelings or reactions towards anything that I saw. I felt numb and I suppose I was in a state of shock. I think we both felt the need to settle down.

We did not know anyone or anything about this part of Africa, so once again we let chance decide where we would go. I marked some matches: Johannesburg, Durban, Capetown, Botswana,

Zambia, and Salisbury and Bulawayo in Rhodesia. Lesley picked. It was the match marked Salisbury.

We left immediately. It took us two days to hitch-hike to Salisbury and it was tarmac roads the whole way. It was odd to be in a chilly climate; the air was sparkling clear and as crisp as the apples we bought at a roadside farm stall. There were fruit orchards, prize bulls, dairy cattle in fields of green grass. It all looked so normal, so English – I felt as though I were waking up from a very long dream. Lesley and I hadn't taken into consideration that there was a war going on in Rhodesia, but it didn't seem dangerous; the people we had met said it was just a spot of terrorist trouble and would soon be under control.

We found a hotel and, in the morning, we bought a newspaper to look for jobs. There wasn't much and the only thing which interested me was a big advertisement that said, 'Manager wanted for Dog Kennels'. I thought it might be fun to work with dogs, so I made an appointment for an interview.

Hunter's Moon was fifteen miles from town. It was a seventy-acre property located among pine trees in the rolling hills to the north-east of Salisbury. I liked the kennels and the owner seemed to think I was a very capable person because he offered me the job, starting right away. I accepted. There were about 100 dogs and I had a staff of two white girls and ten Africans. My new home was a whitewashed cottage, with a houseboy/cook, a television, telephone and a bed with starched, white sheets. I settled in. Everything was so strange, yet so natural; it was like recovering from amnesia, seeing and hearing familiar things, having to learn again everything that had been forgotten or lost somewhere in the recesses of my mind.

There was no nursing work available for Lesley in Salisbury, but many of the hospitals in the rural areas were short-staffed. We had realised that we must not expect to find work so close that we could live together and, besides, nurses usually lived in hospital accommodation, so it was no shock when Lesley enlisted for a hospital in Bindura, sixty miles north of Salisbury. It would only take an hour to hitch-hike there and we could visit each other easily.

Weeks passed. I no longer looked over my shoulder to see if the captain was there, though often at nights I had nightmares and woke up screaming. My cottage slowly became home for me. I painted huge murals on the walls, of trees with fins like rocket-ships and of green mountains with crater lakes. I started a collection of caterpillars, some with long, black, silky hair growing thickly from nose to tail, others with bodies coloured orange and turquoise; some were the size of my index finger. I wondered what kind of butterflies they would become and I fed them on a variety of leaves from my garden, which had over-grown flower-beds, a rockery and a thick lawn.

My life in the bush outside Salisbury could have been uneventful because I had a lot of spare time, but I filled it by learning to train dogs in obedience, teaching French to the children of a neighbouring farmer and taking a course in reading dynamics.

1 February 1976 was my birthday, I was now twenty-five years old, and Lesley came to spend the day with me. She had just received a letter from a man whom she had met a long time before, when she was in South America. The man had been making a world tour because he had cancer and was left with only one year to live. He had set his affairs in order, sold his estate, made his will and set out to enjoy the time remaining to him. During that year, he and Lesley had continued to write to each other. That year had ended in December; it was now two months past his deadline and he had written to tell Lesley that the doctors had announced him completely cured, there was no further trace of cancer in his body, and he asked her to marry him. Lesley said that she had decided to accept and she had booked herself on the next flight of the week. I remembered how once I would have been distressed by the parting of our ways, but now I felt only pleasure in seeing Lesley's happiness. I was glad she was going to do what she wanted most. She was almost thirty; she had travelled enough and it was time for her to settle

permanently. That evening, when we celebrated my birthday, was the last time I saw her, but I knew that our parting was not final and that I could never find a better friend.

I left Hunter's Moon after about three months – suddenly I yearned to leave civilised life and go back to the bush for a while. I chose the eastern region of Rhodesia because it was mountainous and wild.

It was strange to go without Lesley, but it felt lovely to be out on the open road again. There wasn't much traffic as sanctions had created very severe petrol rationing, though every car that did come along stopped to offer me a lift. People were warm and friendly and by evening I had arrived in Melsetter. I didn't want to stay there, I wanted to get to the Chimanimani mountains, where there was a base camp for climbers. I found a lift with an instructor of the Outward Bound school; he looked at me and said, 'But surely you're not going to climb like that?' and his gaze moved from the sandals on my feet, my long skirt, two jerseys, ending with my rather empty rucksack.

'Yes I am,' I replied.

He shrugged and added that the Outward Bound school had now been closed because of the terrorists and that the range I was intending to climb was all along the border with Mozambique. I wasn't really listening, I was watching the blue, jagged silhouettes of high mountains looming closer with every mile. When he dropped me at the base camp he thrust a map into my hand, saying that I'd better be careful and I mustn't get lost.

The base camp was run by an African who told me that no one had been there for ages. I spread out the map and he showed me the route up the mountains to the climbers' hut at the top and, when I discovered that I'd been in such a hurry that I had forgotten to pack any food, he lent me a saucepan, plus a bag of maize meal and sugar. The other thing I had forgotten was my sleeping bag, so I made a bed of a pile of dry leaves.

At dawn I set off up the narrow path into the mountains which rose vertically in magnificent, grey, craggy cliffs and ravines. Within an hour I had lost the path. I didn't realise I had lost it until I found myself trying to scale a sheer cliff. I could have made it, but it was obviously not the correct route, so I retraced my steps looking for the path, but got even more confused and started following imaginary paths round perilous rocky corners and up steep-sided ravines. I sighed with annoyance. There seemed no point in going back again, since I had the map I might as well just keep climbing, and work out where I was later on.

It was a glorious day, the sun was hot, cactus and orange flowering aloes grew from crevices in pitted and knobbly rock covered with patterns of grey lichen. There were tumbling streams of icy clear water, and when I reached the first plateau I saw thorny trees hung shaggy with beards of pale green feathery trailing moss which swayed gently in the summer's breeze. Ahead of me the mountains rose again, shimmering in the heat-haze. By mid-afternoon I was nearly at the top of that range. I had put my sandals away in my rucksack, hooked my long skirt between my legs and tucked it into the waistband, enabling me to climb faster. It was tough going, sometimes the rock was perpendicular, but it was so craggy that there were plenty of hand and foot-holds. Much of the way I followed a sharp ravine full of slippery rocks and, eventually, my path was blocked by a waterfall where I took a long, icy bath before reaching the edge of a precipice overlooking a view of perhaps eighty miles of pine forest, scrub and farmsteads. After I had rested I stood up, flexed my shoulder muscles which were a bit sore from carrying the rucksack, and continued my scramble up the mountain. All around me was a sea of rugged, grey peaks against a cloudless, blue sky. Between the mountains stretched flat plains of short, wiry, green grass strewn with yellow everlasting flowers. Out of the flatness jutted some groups of tall, thin pillars of rock, like statues weathered out of recognition – desolate. A movement caught my eye; it was a herd of small antelope which had seen me and were bounding away in effortless, long, springing leaps. I ran too, all the way across the plain and across a second plain, then I stopped and listened. I could hear a waterfall somewhere to my left, so I followed the noise and came to where a stream poured over the rocks into a wide pool.

There was a large cave beside the pool. I slid out of my rucksack and dumped it on the sandy cave floor, went outside and gathered armfuls of dry grass to make a bed, then collected firewood from some spindly trees downstream, and settled down for the evening. Maize meal and sugar tasted like porridge and was very filling. I had built the fire just inside the mouth of the cave because I knew the night was going to be cold, and I kept it burning warmly. Then it crossed my mind that this was terrorist country, so I killed the flames, but ensured that the embers smouldered hot and red. A second thought came to me: I was alone. A chill ran down my spine. I had never been alone before, I had certainly never been alone, lost in wild mountains at night, and I was still scared of the dark. I wondered if I ought to panic. I had two options: either I could huddle in fear in my cave and sink into the depths of terror, or I could disregard my nervousness and sleep soundly in my cosy, grass bed. At that moment, the full moon rose slowly above the jagged skyline. I curled up in my bed and watched the moonshadows. I had become part of the night, it had become part of me. I slept with a deep and untroubled sleep.

In the morning, I dived into the icy pool, then sat down to eat a panful of porridge, and looked at my map to work out my position. It was a fairly detailed map, but I couldn't tell what any of the details were. There seemed to be an awful lot of streams, so I calculated my position from the number I had crossed the previous day. That tallied with the sunrise in the east and I concluded that Mozambique was either to my left or straight ahead, and Rhodesia must be somewhere behind me. So I set off to the right.

Three days later I was still completely lost. I had realised that all those lines which I had thought were rivers were in fact contour lines and, inevitably, found myself in the mountains on the

Mozambique side of the border. The view was breath-taking, and I was sure that I could even see the Indian ocean. At this height in the Congo I would not have been able to see such a distance; it was the lack of humidity and the clarity of the air which made the difference. Here I had noticed how every shape had a sharply defined outline, and even though the days were hot the air had a quality of crisp freshness. I turned round and headed west back towards Rhodesia.

Those three days were an unforgettable time of happiness for me. I found no paths, I saw nobody. The only sounds I heard were the songs of the skylarks and the barking of some baboons. I climbed peaks, wandered across meadows of flowers and along enchanting valleys where the streams widened out into successions of sparkling clear rock pools. As the afternoon shadows lengthened, I found other caves to build my nest in, and at dawn I would watch the mist rising from the mountains, steaming up from fissures in the rock and evaporating in the early heat of the sun. My porridge lasted well and was not even finished when, late on the third day, I walked over a spur of a mountain and saw, with great surprise, that down below me on the grassy plain was the climbers' hut. When I reached the door, I was greeted by the African attendant, who was just leaving to go down to the base camp. He said that the area had been closed to climbers (because of terrorists) since the day I set off. He went down, but I stayed overnight and I reasoned that terrorists wouldn't come over the top of this rugged range, since it would be much simpler for them to go round the ends of it.

I didn't watch the attendant leaving and, in the morning, I didn't know which path led down. I set off, arriving safely at the base camp by midday.

I spent a month touring the eastern highland regions of Rhodesia. Travel was very difficult and local people constantly warned me of the danger of terrorists. I did my best to be sensible. I didn't deliberately tour the troubled areas, but it seemed there was trouble wherever I went. If I heard reports of shootings then I would go somewhere else, but I was not prepared to give up my travels in Rhodesia because of something that might or might not happen to me. I didn't sleep out alone any more; when I found myself stuck at sunset in isolated places, I often managed to find an army observation post where the soldiers offered me their protection.

In the Inyanga district I went to look at the ruins of an ancient, walled city built by an unknown civilisation in about AD 1300. There were twenty-five square miles of ruined terracing with water channels and furrows that comprised a highly sophisticated irrigation system. Scattered in the hills were ancient stone forts of approximately the same date; what remained now were the stone ramparts of the central compounds, other stone walls of complexes which had enclosed some huts with curious deep pits underneath them, and around every fort were the broken-down outer walls. The area now belonged to Rhodesian National Parks Trust, and when I met the head ranger, Bill Thomas, he suggested that I might also like to spend a couple of days with his rangers, learning a bit of bushcraft, visiting more gorges and waterfalls.

Everyone I met was kind and helpful. The farmers who gave me lifts when I was hitch-hiking always asked me to stay or stop for a meal. Their hospitality was unbelievable and they made me feel completely at home. On one occasion, when I stopped for a cup of tea at a farm in the hills above Silver Streams, I stayed for four days. There was an old, grey pony there which I rode on long, leisurely outings through the wattle plantations, until someone reported seeing forty-eight terrorists crossing the farm. The risk was a way of life which everyone accepted. The menfolk alternated their time fighting for six weeks, returning to civilian life for four weeks, then back to the army for six, while their wives volunteered to take over the police duties, ran the radio network and also managed the farms. No one (except me) went anywhere without a gun, and the curfew banned all vehicles from the roads after 5 p.m. Every evening at the farm the men sat by the log fire talking about weapons, recent attacks and the progress of the war. Because Silver Streams was so remote, the army sent us two soldiers to guard the homestead, but most of the other outlying farms just relied on their radio alert systems and security fencing.

Many of the farms where I stayed had horses which the farmers let me borrow. It occurred to me how nice it would be to travel again with a horse of my own, but for now I confined myself to just riding around sheep farms, trout farms, coffee farms and the misty Vumba mountains. Finally, at the end of the first week of May I returned to Salisbury.

Salisbury did not have the atmosphere of the capital of a war-torn country. There was no curfew, no danger, no need to listen for disturbances at night. Even so, I could not ignore the frequent announcements on television about the intensifying struggle against terrorists. I didn't wish to get involved with politics, but I felt a tremendous sympathy for both the black and white Rhodesians who were fighting side by side against guerilla communist forces trained by the Cubans and armed with the latest Russian equipment.

In addition, I feared that Rhodesia could easily plunge into a very bloody civil war. The dissension stemmed from tribal conflict. The majority of the black Rhodesians were Shona-speaking tribes, gentle and mild by nature, while the minority group were Matabele, an old offshoot of the Zulu people whose ways were proud, fierce and domineering. It seemed to me that the Matabele would never accept the ruling of the Shona people.

I continued my travels. There was no part of Rhodesia that I couldn't reach in one day's journey from Salisbury. When I got a lift, the drivers would invariably drive like hell while I kept their rifle or shotgun on my knees and watched for signs of trouble.

One day I was waiting at the crossroads in the bush outside Fort Victoria. The late afternoon sun had slightly blurred the air, making outlines less distinct; it was not a good time to be sitting beside the deserted road. I was aiming to go to Zimbabwe ruins, but when a car finally came along the driver was going west to Shabani. He stopped to suggest I might like a lift, so I climbed in. I didn't want to go to Shabani and when we passed a turning to an eland research station I asked to be dropped there.

I walked for several miles through the bush, found an old timber house, and knocked on the door. It was answered by a warm, welcoming, grey-haired game warden, who invited me to stay, and I spent the following day helping and looking round the research station. It wasn't quite as one would have imagined: it was just a vast area of the bush where eland and wild game abounded. There were a group of ramshackle sheds full of parts of broken Landrovers and eland horns which were about two feet long and twisted upwards in spirals. Another barn held tons of home-made leather harness and wooden yokes for oxen. There were three African game scouts skinning a kudu (another type of large antelope) that had been found nearly dead in a poacher's trap, some tame eland wandered around and a rather wild horse plunged about in a corall. The game warden, John Posselt, believed that eland could be domesticated like cattle, and since eland are browsers and cattle are grazers, he reckoned that they could be herded together on farms, which would double the meat value per acre. Eland meat tastes much the same as beef and the animals are sturdy beasts, larger than cattle. So, to work out his theory, tame some eland and study their ways, he had built himself this timber house in the wilds of a game reserve and, as yet, no one had told him to move. John was a quiet, modest, likeable man, who wanted nothing from life but to be left in peace to observe the game and live off the bush. However, he needed to go into town for the rest of the week to attend to some business – and he asked me to stay and look after things in his absence.

He left me with four small dogs and a shotgun. There was no security fencing, radio system or alarm bells, because the house was well protected by wild animals like the hippo that I could hear noisily pulling up grass outside the window.

While I waited for my supper of roast kudu to finish browning, I looked along the bookshelf and picked out a book called *How to Survive in the Bush*. I noticed the record player and a collection of music which included many of my most favourite, from Pink Floyd to Tchaikovsky. I curled up by the log fire with supper, music and book — it was one of the nicest evenings I had spent for ages.

Over the next few days the African game scouts gave me lessons on how to skin animals and cure the hides, and in tracking. They taught me to recognise the different spoor of animals, to read from the prints the size and weight of each animal, to calculate the time of their presence from the depth of the imprint in relation to the dampness of the ground, to follow game by detecting broken twigs and upturned stones, and they began to teach me to identify the edible varieties of plants, berries and roots. I was a good pupil. I needed to learn about survival in the bush, I still remembered the hunger Lesley and I had suffered when we crossed Nigeria on horse-back, and I was determined not to make the same mistakes twice.

One morning I walked down to the lake where I found a canoe. The paddle was inside it, so I climbed in and went to explore the lake. I paddled warily up through the crocodile breeding grounds. The sky was heavy and overcast, the water reflected its gloom, and a log with two eyes sank silently underwater as I passed. I headed the canoe up a creek between tall, feathery, silver reeds, skeletal white, dead trees on whose branches perched three hooded black and white fish eagles. Some Egyptian geese flapped and scuttered out of my way and the water rippled. The creek became a narrow, rocky stream where I played in the rapids until a storm started to blow and gusted so hard that it pushed me back onto the lake. I raced across the lake with the storm winds, got a fright when a hippo surfaced close to the canoe, and I paddled even faster to the shore.

The sensation of paddling stirred a chord in my mind and released a flood of memories. But I didn't yearn to be back on the Congo, I was totally happy. Although sometimes I missed Lesley, it seemed natural to be alone. I felt completely free.

The game warden had said I could ride the horse which had been broken-in on the day I arrived. She was a pretty little brown mare, and I asked one of the game scouts to saddle her for me. I spent the next three days on horseback. I packed huge picnics into my rucksack, which I wore strapped tightly to my back while I rode, and though the mare was nervous she never misbehaved. We cantered for miles across flat plains of tall, dry grass with *kopjes*, rocky hills made of piles of rounded, granite boulders. Eland scattered at our approach, but some of the more inquisitive ones bounded up to us. I saw zebra, kudu, impala, troupes of monkeys, and on the rocks of the *kopjes* I saw scores of hyrax, small brown animals the size and shape of guinea pigs which are apparently the closest relation to the elephant. I noticed a strange formation of stones which, on closer examination, turned out to be the ruins of an ancient fort with terracing. In some other hills I found a fortified cave, the remains of a human skeleton, and some bushman paintings. Many of the *kopjes* had traces of the bushman art, faded primitive red and brown pictures of buck and antelope painted on the sides of vertical rocks.

On the second day, while I searched for bushman paintings on a *kopje*, I jumped down onto the rocks of a sunny hollow – and met a leopard. He had been lazing in the sun there. He leapt up startled when I landed within a few yards of him; we both froze and stared at each other. I waited for him to run away. He was probably waiting for me to run, too, and he began to flick his long tail from side to side. The rock wall behind him was richly covered in primitive paintings of two-headed beasts and I was sad that I couldn't stay to look at them. I turned slowly and stomped off angrily (I knew better than to run away from a leopard which would give chase just for sport). Once out of his sight, I ran and kept running and leaping down the hill until I reached the bottom. Puffing and panting, I looked around for the horse and realised with dismay that I couldn't remember where I had tied her.

By the end of that week, I had made up my mind to travel on horseback around southern Africa and, when I returned to Salisbury, I set about looking for a companion. I didn't know where to start looking. I was staying with an eccentric but kindhearted man who kept thirteen dogs. I lay in the garden with Rufus, the red setter, and pondered where I would find a girl companion. I was adamant that it must be a girl because I had so enjoyed travelling with Lesley and I felt that male company would be more of a hindrance than a help.

It was a hot day. Rufus was wagging his tail, which acted like a fan and kept me cool. I had a sudden idea that I should speak to Rhodesian television and ask them if I could be interviewed and also take the opportunity to say I was looking for a companion. I telephoned them, met one of their producers that afternoon, and was interviewed on television within a few days.

Bundles of letters arrived after the interview. Ten of them were from girls who sounded potentially companionworthy, the majority of others were from girls who were still at school, including one aged twelve whose parents told her she could come with me, and the rest were from people who were interested in what I'd done, families who invited me to stay at their homes, or to parties, barbecues, to go hunting, shooting and fishing.

In between jaunts, hunts and picnics, I hitch-hiked all around Rhodesia, visiting ancient ruins and areas renowned for bushman paintings. The Matopos hills near Bulawayo were one of my favourite places. I walked for miles over sheets of sloping granite and, when I stopped to rest in the shade of overhanging rocks, I tilted my head upwards and saw beautiful friezes of bushman art on the ceiling. Cecil Rhodes was buried in the Matopos hills; he too had loved the area. He had come here whenever he had problems and he would stride among the hills thinking deeply about his beloved country. His wish was that he could create the foundations of a multi-racial country which black and white would share in harmony. I stopped going to the Matopos after terrorists shot and killed a couple of tourists there.

My very favourite haunt was Zimbabwe, a ruined city which had been built by an unknown civilisation and for an unknown purpose. The date of construction could have been any time from several thousand to several hundred years ago. Zimbabwe was a mysterious place, with a powerful atmosphere. A chain of ruined stone forts led to the Great Enclosure, a magnificent walled citadel with monumental phallic towers. Above these ruins, on top of the highest neighbouring hill, was a complex acropolis. The stonework of its fortified walls and gateways was a masterpiece of craftsmanship, displaying pointed obelisks and herringbone patterns of coloured stones.

I spent many days exploring the labyrinth of narrow passages which led between vertical rockfaces, past ruined guard rooms and sentry points. On the summit of the hill was a natural rock formation of colossal, flat boulders, balanced on one another, creating the effect of a supreme temple. Its commanding view of the surrounding territory gave the temple an almost tangible feeling of power and, despite the heat of the days, I saw that my arms were covered in goose-pimples.

During one of my visits, I met a sprightly old English archaeologist and we discovered some caves with tunnels leading under the hill. Roof-falls and rock barriers made it impossible for the archaeologist to accompany me, so I crawled alone down the tunnels, using a candle to light my way. After a spooky but uneventful hour I returned to daylight. An African was with the archaeologist and, catching sight of me, he began to scatter handfuls of red leaves on the ground. He said that the tunnel now belonged to the ancestral spirits and my presence would have disturbed them, but that his gesture with the leaves should calm them and send them back to rest in peace.

In general, Zimbabwe was deserted and I saw no one at all. One day, as I returned from there, I was walking along a path in the bush, when a jackal sprang up from a thick clump of grass beside me. It leapt straight at me, its lips snarled back and its teeth clicking with anger. It was so unexpected, so sudden, and I had no time to think as I struck out with my hands to ward it off. Its teeth latched onto my right wrist. I couldn't shake the animal free; one of its canine teeth was hooked deep into my wrist. The flesh tore open and the jackal fell to the ground. As it hit the ground, it leapt straight up at me again; again my fists shot out to protect myself and again my right hand got entangled in its teeth. It was a full-grown black-backed jackal. It shook its head from side to side violently, snarling continuously, tightening its grip on my hand. I smashed my left fist down on its neck, then I grabbed for its throat. Quick as a flash, it dropped my right hand and bit my left. I staggered backwards, it jumped at me again. I don't know for how long we fought, but every time I knocked it to the ground it seemed to just bounce right back up again. My mind was numb and my hands were even number. I was aware of nothing but the jackal's yellow snapping teeth and gurgling snarl. When it hit the ground awkwardly and rolled over, I aimed a kick at its head; it sank its teeth into my foot. I stamped downwards and kicked with my other foot. Then, suddenly, the jackal turned, slunk off into the bush, and was gone.

I stood still wondering if it had been real. The blood dripping from my hands told me it had been real and my brain told me to stop standing there motionless and go and find a doctor. So I started walking back towards the road, but I couldn't walk properly; I seemed to be limping very badly and leaving a trail of blood from one foot. I eventually reached the road, waved a red dripping hand at the first car that came along, and they drove me to a doctor. I didn't talk much, I just kept seeing the jackal bouncing back up me time and time again. Jackals are nocturnal, timid, and they rarely attack people. Either it had been a female with young pups nearby and she felt threatened by my presence, or else it had rabies. I didn't remember anything about the jackal that would give me a clue, but it made no difference. Even the slightest chance of its having been rabid was enough to warrant a course of anti-rabies injections. The doctor cleaned away all the blood, stitched my wrist and bandaged both my hands and also my foot. There were thirteen tooth holes in me.

It was a frustrating but fascinating experience, trying to live without the use of my hands. For the first week I was very helpless, I felt as though I was wearing boxing gloves, my fingers were useless and I couldn't even move my wrists. It made me realise how much people relied on their hands and without them I had to invent alternative ways of getting things done. The simplest of actions, like opening a door, required major strategy. But I was determined that two useless hands and one lame foot were not going to interfere with my life.

Entertainment in Salisbury revolved around the sporting clubs, and there was a club for everything – the polo club, the race-horse club, the trotting race club, the jumping society, the sailing club, waterskiing club, canoeing club, gliding club, etc. As soon as the anti-rabies course of injections was over, I went crocodile hunting with some professional hunter friends, and among the things I learnt was that crocodile meat actually did taste like lobster – so much so that there was a factory in Rhodesia for canning the meat which was labelled 'Mock Crayfish'.

Within two days of returning to Salisbury, I caught myself pacing up and down my bedroom floor. That meant only one thing – it was time to travel again. I had not been successful in finding a girl companion. I wondered if I would ever have the courage to set out on my own on horseback. Perhaps not. So far, all that I had done was to start off in a nice, secure Landrover, and all the rest had just happened to me. However, I longed to ride horseback around southern Africa and, although my plans were terribly vague, I had already applied for permits for horses to cross the borders of South Africa, Swaziland, Lesotho and

Transkei.
Many of my Salisbury friends asked me what I was searching for. To their minds one couldn't travel without a purpose and a goal. My aimlessness bothered them and they wanted to know why I travelled. It was a question for which I had no answer. I travelled in much the same way that other people stayed still – it was the way of life that suited me. As for purpose and goals in life, I didn't have any. Purpose sounded too single-minded for me, too restricted by fixed ideas; I preferred to be flexible. Also, I rejected the concept of goals and ambitions; they implied success or failure. I wasn't interested in measuring myself against others or in competing with them.

The war was escalating. Military call-up was now for eight weeks in the army, two weeks civilian life, though many didn't take the two week break; they preferred to stay and fight. The position was not good – cars and farms were being attacked every day; terrorists were coming in from Botswana as well as from Zambia and Mozambique – but morale was high and the threats of Mozambique's President Machel had been demoted by the newspapers to page four, side column, small print.

A couple of close encounters with terrorists made me realise that the time had come for me to leave Rhodesia and I decided to go on my own. I didn't tell this to my parents; I avoided mentioning it, and merely said that I was now going to South Africa.

I was not at all confident about riding alone; in truth, I was terrified by the thought. However, if I could manage it alone, it would prove to me that there would be nowhere on this earth that I wasn't free to travel when and how I pleased.

17
A South African
Slaughter-House

I sat at the top of the acropolis watching the sun go down over the ruined city of Zimbabwe. It was my last farewell to Rhodesia, whose country and people I had loved deeply, and where I would unhesitatingly have made my home if I were ready to settle. In the last rays of the sun, the ruins glowed with the memory of their golden past. I felt that a phase in my life had ended. Now the future lay before me again, wide open. Then I remembered the 5 p.m. curfew, so I raced back, driving by moonlight as I knew it was unsafe to turn on the headlights. I returned the car I had borrowed to its owner, who was also en route to Johannesburg. In the morning, we joined the convoy to the border. It was a two hundred mile run. There was no trouble, and, once inside South Africa, there were no more soldiers, no machine guns and no petrol rationing. There was a lot of traffic; the roads were tarmac, but inferior to those of Rhodesia, and the atmosphere had changed. Faces didn't sparkle and laugh like the Rhodesians, all the people I now saw look drab and dismal. My driver was a friendly but rather dour Afrikaner (descendant of the Dutch settlers). He spoke English with a thick accent, explaining that his normal language was Afrikaans, pointing out how all the notices were written in Afrikaans, English and the Bantu tongue, and telling me that South Africa was ruled and governed by the Afrikaners. It seemed that the two white groups did not mix socially, or intermarry. They had separate churches, there were separate schools for their children, and the TV programmes alternated every evening between Afrikaans and English.

In Johannesburg, I stayed with an English girl who was a friend of my family. Jane was married and couldn't come with me, but she entered into my plans with great enthusiasm and we immediately started searching for a horse. With masses of money, it would have been easy to buy a horse but, although I was far from penniless, it was essential that I kept a large reserve in case of an emergency. I had to find a horse that would be inexpensive. It didn't matter if it was cheap because it was in bad condition, there was no hurry; I could wait while it fattened up on a farm. Farms were the obvious places to look for horses, but it was not easy to meet farmers in Johannesburg and, when Jane and I went out into the countryside, none of the people we asked had any wish to sell their horses. I telephoned some horse dealers, but that was a waste of time because their prices were too high. One of them suggested I should contact the municipal abattoir, so I rang them and asked what day they auctioned horses for slaughter.

I had no idea what an abattoir was like and when I went along I found an enormous yard with long rows of square enclosures made of thick iron bars. All except the first row were empty and I passed many pens of forlorn-looking cattle before I reached the horses. The horses stood listlessly, some were alone, others were bunched six to a pen. They were pitiful creatures, their heads drooped low, their emaciated bodies so thin that every bone showed through their scarred and haggard coats. I felt glad to know that they would be slaughtered by the end of the day. There were not very many people around, no other white women, though there were quite a few Afrikaans butchers, some farmers who had come to see their animals sold, dealers hunting for possible bargains, and the rest of the crowd was made up of African rag-and-bone men looking for beasts to pull their carts.

Metal gates clanged open and four fleshless, miserable ponies clattered over the cobbles into the auction ring. Everyone leaned against, or sat on, the rails and I found a space at the front between a group of butchers and farmers. The auctioneer was a large Afrikaner, who raised his arms, poked his fingers in his ears and began to count rapidly in a loud voice. I couldn't understand a word he said, but I watched his eyes darting among the crowd as the men nodded their bids or indicated them with almost imperceptible movements of the hands. The auctioneer slowed down, then yelled sharply, and the ponies were ushered out. I asked the man beside me what price they had fetched and he said 70 rand (£50) each. I was stunned and said I'd expected prices to be much lower. He replied that in Johannesburg meat was expensive, the Afrikaners liked horse meat, and the leftovers were made into dog food. Then we chatted about why I needed a horse. The next one was already in the sale ring – it was not nearly so wretched-looking and it had four black feet. The only thing I knew about horses was that black feet were good because white feet were softer and tended to go lame. I couldn't understand what prices the auctioneer was calling, but I signalled a bid anyway. My friend beside me tugged my arm sharply and pointed out that the horse had a broken leg. I thanked him, sighed helplessly and asked if he would suggest what horse to bid for. After about forty horses had been sold, each one more battered than the last, I started to despair. There were only two more lots to come. I clenched my fists and willed a suitable horse to be among them. Next was an old mare with her foal, the auctioneer recommenced his indistinguishable gabble until his yell signified that they were sold, then the last pen was opened and a thin, rakish bay gelding plunged into the ring. He was not special, not beautiful, but he looked strong.

'What's wrong with this one?' I asked my neighbour.

'Dunno,' He turned to the man behind us. 'Oi Bez, whose is this horse?'

None of them knew who it belonged to, no one had seen it arrive, and no one was here to watch it being sold. All they could tell me was that it had no broken legs. The bidding began and the horse hung his head dejectedly. I caught the auctioneer's eye and nodded, he could count me in. Every time he looked at me I nodded again, the bidding rocketed upwards until there was only myself and a rag-and-bone merchant. My friend beside me had slipped away. The auctioneer looked from me to my opponent; I was still bidding though I didn't know what price had been reached. I noticed my friend standing behind my opponent, he tapped him on the shoulder and said something to him. The man smiled, looked at the auctioneer and shook his head. The auctioneer yelled, the horse was mine.

The crowd began to disperse and I stood there stunned. I was too dazed to think, I had no idea how much I paid for the horse, I just stood and stared at my horse which stood and stared at the ground. When someone asked me to remove my horse, I realised that I didn't have a halter, nor anywhere to put him, nor a truck to take him away in.

The men around me burst out laughing. The one who had been so helpful offered to lend me a halter, another said the horse could graze at his farm, and the man called Bez volunteered to drive us in his small cattle truck to wherever we wanted to go.

I wanted to go to the eastern Transvaal. I had decided that it would not be fun to start out riding from Johannesburg, the surrounding countryside was flat, monotonous farmland. I didn't want to ride in order to get to somewhere else. The ideal place to start my ride was in the beautiful, mountainous region 250 miles north-east of Johannesburg. I asked Bez how much he would charge to go there and out of sheer kind-heartedness he offered to drive us for just the cost of the petrol.

'How soon can we go?'

'Tomorrow,' he replied.

The abattoir agreed to keep the horse overnight and feed him. Bez checked his teeth and said he was only about eight years old. He reckoned I'd bought a bargain, and we all wondered if he was rideable. His ribs were showing through his copper-coloured coat, but his condition was not so desperate that he couldn't start travelling immediately, provided that he had frequent rests and masses to eat en route. It was lunchtime, I already felt exhausted by the day, especially when I thought of how much I still had to do before I was ready to leave the next morning.

I zoomed off to the city centre where I bought a piece of carpet and some underfelt to use as a saddle, some rope, a compass, a Michelin map of southern Africa, and a camera. Then I rushed home to Jane's house, cut the straps of mine and Lesley's old green rucksacks and stitched them together to form saddlebags, packed my meagre belongings and finished in time to sit down to a champagne dinner. Jane asked me what route I planned to follow, so we spread out the map and I drew a straight line from the top of the eastern Transvaal through Swaziland to Empangeni on the Zululand coast (since the only other person I knew in South Africa was an old school friend who lived there). I judged that if we went in a straight line, I stood less chance of getting lost, and from Empangeni I would turn right and follow the coast to Capetown. The whole journey would take many months, it was a distance of about 1500 miles as the crow flies, but I doubted I'd stick to any planned route.

All I needed now was a name for my horse. There were so many names I liked that I decided to call him a different name each week of the journey. The first week he would be called Xoza, which was more normally spelt Xhosa and was the name of a tribe of Zulus who had run away from Zululand during the horrors of King Shaka's reign. They had founded the country which was now called Transkei. The X of Xhosa (or Xoza) was pronounced with a click sound between the tongue and upper palate, and the pronunciation of the whole word was like the spelling 'causer' or 'coursa'.

In the morning, Jane woke me up bright and early, and we drove across the sleeping city to the slaughter yard. Bez was already there with his truck and Xoza looked at us with curiosity. The truck was open-sided but had a framework of iron bars to prevent the horse jumping out. He allowed me to lead him up the loading ramp and into the back of the truck where I tied the halter so his nose was resting on the cab roof. The rush-hour in Johannesburg was now in full swing, but Xoza stood quietly as we wove through the traffic and for the next seven hours until we arrived at our destination, a randomly chosen timber farmhouse somewhere between Tzaneen and Lydenburg. The farmer and his wife were Afrikaners. When Bez asked if I could stay the night with my horse they replied sweetly, 'Our house is your home, please be welcome.' They showed me a paddock where I put the horse, then Bez left because it was already dusk. The farmhouse had no electricity, light was provided by parafffin lamps and the telephone had a crank handle.

The farmer sent one of his African labourers to help me with Xoza in the morning. The horse was easy to catch because I had put a long neckrope on him. Then I made another rope into a halter with an equally long leading rein, and the African held him while I fitted the underfelt and carpet on his back. The twin rucksack-saddlebags weren't heavy and they rested comfortably either side of the carpet. The horse didn't flinch, he seemed gentle-natured and quite used to people. He never laid his ears back and didn't mind when I tightened a cinch rope over his back and under his stomach to hold the saddlebags firmly in place. I had decided not to try and ride him on the first day – just leading him would give him time to get used to the sight and smell of me, and I would also be able to see how he reacted to things. When I asked the farmer which direction was to Blyde River Canyon, he told me to follow the main road. I explained that I meant by path through the bush, but he replied that it was impossible, there were no paths through the bush and, besides, there were some mountains in the way. His wife gave me a massive bag of home-made biscuits and cakes; I thanked them both and set out.

The road was tarmac – I hated every inch of it. The verges were full of litter and broken glass from drivers who would chuck their empty beer bottles out of the windows as they went along.

Xoza's hooves made a dull, clopping noise on the tarmac as he wasn't shod. The farmer had said I wouldn't find a blacksmith anywhere in the eastern Transvaal and I knew that the hard road would wear my horse's hooves down to the quick.

Within an hour, I was in a passionate rage. If I was going to have to tour South Africa on tarmac roads then I might as well be in a car. We turned down a track which led towards the mountains. Xoza pricked up his ears and arched his neck. It was suddenly a good day, the sun shone, green grass rippled in the warm breeze, and when the track ended we made our own way through the mountains. From the peaks we gazed across choppy seas of mountains, and I selected ways that looked feasible. At a steep gulley we stopped. I glanced at the horse wondering if it was too treacherous for him and saw that he was watching me, clearly worried that I might not be able to scramble down. I started down, Xoza came slithering past and waited at the bottom for me to catch up. There were many places in those rocky hills which I thought were too rough for a horse, but Xoza was astonishingly surefooted and I slipped or stumbled more often than he did. When we came to a stream, I unloaded him for a rest. I held onto the end of his rope and lay down in the water to cool off. The horse took a long drink from a deep pool, then waded further in, lay down in the water too, and rolled vigorously.

Late afternoon we came to a dirt road with various farm lanes leading off it. I picked a lane which was marked with the name of a farm in the hope that the farmer would sell me some sort of food for the horse and would let me sleep in a barn. The lane led through a tunnel of trees and emerged into sloping, landscaped gardens with a colourful profusion of flowers and peacocks strutting across the lawns. A farmer came up to greet me warmly and invited me to stay. During our conversation, I mentioned that the horse needed a blacksmith; he said he had once been a qualified farrier and would be happy to shoe my horse for me. My luggage was put in a large wood-panelled bedroom with an old, wooden four-poster bed and, while I bathed and changed, the farmer shod Xoza. He did it really nicely and he said that, though the horse had never worn shoes before, he had behaved well. All their fields were full of crops, so Xoza spent the night in the garden, munching a small haystack of lucerne (very tasty to horses) which had been heaped on the lawn for him. His drinking bowl was the ornamental stone birdbath.

Before I left the next day the farmer taught me how to make hobbles out of a leather rimpey made from kudu hide. It was a simple method of fastening Xoza's front legs nine inches apart so that he could shuffle around to graze but not run away. He said my horse was going to be a real beauty; he thought Xoza was almost pure Arab, with probably a bit of Basotho (mountain ponies of Lesotho renowned for their strength and hardiness). When we had loaded the baggage onto Xoza, I looped the leading string of his halter to form reins. It was time to try riding him. The farmer gave me a leg-up onto his back. I sat comfortably between the saddlebags with my legs hanging just in front of them. The horse leapt up and down a few times when the farmer let go of his head, but both I and the luggage stayed in place, and despite having only a rope halter, I found him very easy to bring under control.

Riding him was lovely. At first he tiptoed along in his new shoes, rather like a man wearing high heels for a joke, and when he got used to them he walked with long, swinging strides, his head held high and his tail floating out in the wind. Bez had told me that it was very tiring for a horse to walk all day, and much less of a strain if we often changed paces. I had worried that my weight, together with my luggage, would be too heavy for Xoza to carry at fast speeds. He was less than fifteen hands high (five feet tall at his withers), but Bez had pointed out that I weighed only 110 lbs, my luggage was 30 lbs, and 140 lbs was nothing to a horse. So I put Xoza through his paces and was delighted to discover that he could triple, which was a sort of flat trot, so smoothly that I didn't bounce at all, I just stuck my feet out forwards, leant slightly back and balanced very restfully. His canter was like sitting in a rocking chair and all the time he carried his head high and his ears so pricked up with pleasure that they nearly met in the middle.

We reached Blyde River Canyon, the second deepest canyon in the world. It was spectacular with craggy mis-shapen bald rocks and a river meandering between strangly eroded cylindrical peaks. The canyon sides were vertical cliffs, the cliff-tops were smooth short grass and we galloped for many miles, close to the edge. Through a steep valley we descended into the canyon, where we both swam in the icy sparkling river. While Xoza grazed on some lush grass, I went off rock climbing, exploring caves, playing under waterfalls and marvelling at some deep symmetrical round potholes carved by the river in smooth black rock. I led Xoza along the canyon floor, the sun blazed down, the cliffs soared up majestically on both sides, and I saw nobody else. In the evening, when we were up again on top of the cliffs, we camped in the shelter of some pine trees. Xoza was feasting on grass and I was wishing that I had remembered to buy some provisions, when I saw some people. They also saw me and started walking over. They were young men, dressed in army uniform, and completely stunned to find a girl and a horse camping out in the wilds. They came from a military training camp nearby and, while three of us sat chatting, the other two went running back to the camp to fetch a thermos of coffee. They returned with the coffee, a picnic of meat pies, jam buns and fruit, plus presents for me of an army ration pack for four days, an army water bottle which was far superior to my tatty, leaking flask from Nigeria, and also a camouflage jacket so that I could be more invisible. The jacket had eight pockets and became one of the most useful things I ever owned.

Over the next three days we galloped south along the edge of the cliffs in the wind. The canyon grew wider until the opposite side disappeared and we found ourselves on top of an escarpment, the lowveld stretched far below to the east. One day at noon we rested beside a viewpoint called God's Window which

213

looked out over a breath-taking panorama, and that night we camped on the cliffs overlooking a gigantic single sharp pinnacle of rock. Our camping spot was a leafy hollow where a stream trickled down over the cliffs. I was woken several times during the night by heavy footsteps, and even heavier breathing, blasts of warm air, and the gentle muzzle of Xoza brushing my face to make sure I had not gone away. At dawn, a thick mist blew up from the lowveld, it came over the escarpment and obliterated everything, including Xoza. I had to leap out of my cosy sleeping bag and go to search for him. He was hobbled, but he'd wandered off. I found him standing right on the cliff edge. He was a ghostly silhouette, and behind him the sun was rising as a translucent white orb through the swirling grey mist.

It was winter; that meant there was no rain, and the days were warm and sunny. I seldom saw people and the only signs of habitation were the farms far below, sprawled across the lowveld.

Towards the end of our first week, both Xoza and I were tired. Admittedly, we had travelled quite fast, but we had rested for more time than we moved and we broke our journey at least four times a day to unload the weight off his back and let him graze. Despite the frequent stops, I found that I never had a moment's spare time; I was days behind with my diary (it wasn't possible to write as I rode), and when we camped there were a million other things to do, like bathing in streams, collecting firewood, making tea, cooking food, remaking the carpet saddle, adjusting the straps of the saddlebags, greasing Xoza's ears, fetlocks and tail to kill the ticks, and oiling his hooves with gungy old motor oil to prevent dryness or cracking. Every single thing that had to be done had to be done by me and I realised what a difference it made without Lesley to share the burden of the work, but apart from that I didn't mind being alone. I was never frightened, I never had time to be. The moment my chores were finished I fell asleep. Sometimes I woke up at night with nightmares that the horse had gone, but he was always close by and, very often, he would shuffle over to check up on me.

We went through Graskop, bought a bag of crushed mealies for the horse, some supplies for me, and we camped for a couple of quiet days in a glade in the pine forest. From there we made our way down the escarpment and into a region of mountainous overgrown pine plantations, criss-crossed with cool grassy tracks. All I saw were endless green forested hills, and when the paths ceased to exist we pushed our way through the undergrowth. Some of the plantations were overgrown, others were carpeted with bouncy beds of accumulated years of pine needles. Often I walked and led Xoza, to ease my aching muscles, and I discovered that, if ever I showed any hesitation at the top of a slope or in crossing a stream, Xoza would not follow me. It didn't matter if I had only stopped to scratch my head, he was instantly suspicious and, even if it were just a small ditch, nothing would persuade him to cross it. If I didn't hesitate, then there was no problem, except when I should have hesitated and we found ourselves sliding rapidly down long, steep mountainsides on moving beds of pine needles. At streams I learnt to act a pantomime, testing crossing places, shaking my head, finding an easier place, smiling hugely and saying confidently, 'If you can't cross here then you're an idiot,' and when he faltered because, in fact, it was a raging, rocky stream, I had to look at him with surprise and exclaim, 'Don't tell me you're chicken! Come on at once.' He learnt to follow wherever I led, and never to doubt my wisdom.

Some of our routes were so steep and slippery that I put my shoulder hard against his chest to slow our descent, and others were so marshy that I had to chop down branches, make a path and take his hooves in my hands to place them on sure footings. There were, of course, many near-disasters, but the only major setback was when I mislaid the compass. The result was that we spent three days hopelessly lost. In the evening of the third day I was arrested as a poacher. It was nice to see people again, even if they *were* pointing guns at me. Besides, I was innocent, my aim with a catapult was not yet sufficiently accurate to kill any of the small forest antelope, quite apart from the fact that I had eaten so much food in the last six months that I was quite content to go without eating for a few days. When the foresters realised that they were aiming their rifles at a very defenceless white girl they all laughed heartily, decided they had made a mistake and invited me back to their house for the night. They lived at a site in the middle of their plantation, and since the log hauling was carried out by mules, Xoza also had company, and mule cubes.

After that I managed to find several forest sites and met some incredible people who lived in wooden houses on hilltops. I met millionaires and hermits; an Irishman building a yacht that looked like Noah's Ark; and a Scottish family just existing quietly and never going away, because there was nowhere else they would rather be. They had dogs but no mules, so we fed Xoza a meal of high-protein dog food.

Our first proper rest came after two weeks of travel, when we stopped at a forestry commission yard. Xoza went to stay with the carthorses; he was looked after by the herdboys and spent his days grazing somewhere up in the mountains. At night he came down to his stall in the carthorse shed; he was only half the size of the carthorses, but he ate so many bucketfuls of horse cubes I felt sure he'd soon equal them in weight. His ribs still showed, but his coat shone like red silk. I stayed with a young South African forester called Gavin. We spent the days wandering through the plantations and, while he did whatever it was that foresters were supposed to do, I gathered fircones, climbed trees, and we picnicked together on the flat rocks of gushing streams.

From the moment I met Gavin, we had a firm friendship. Gavin never treated me like a guest. We both did exactly what we felt like, regardless of social politeness and conventions, and we spent long evenings in deep talk. Foresters are a strangely interesting type of men, very withdrawn, lonely and introspective. The older ones have long lost the art of conversation; they are nervous and embarrassed in company because they have forgotten what is the accepted way to behave. So they never seek company, they withdraw completely into themselves and are trapped there. Gavin was only twenty-seven, he still had time to change his mind, give up his reclusive ways, and adapt to normal life. But he had no desire to do that, he was content to retire into himself and to let the passing years close the doors. Our discussions tended to be amusing because Gavin talked to himself as often as to me. I felt as though I was in a crowded room with a debating society. He said it was an easy and companionable habit, and I wondered how long it would be before I too started talking to myself.

We also spent a lot of time exploring the caves which we found in sunken basins of rock hidden behind walls of undergrowth. Taking torches, chalk and ropes we clambered down their mouths, followed narrow twisting faults and passages in the dolomite rock, sometimes wriggling along flat on our stomachs because the way was only two feet high. It was cold and so dark that when I turned my torch off I felt swamped by the blackness. Impenetrable blackness. Even on the darkest night my eyes were able to adjust so that I could see shapes and shadows, but here in the caves I could see nothing but solid black. The tunnel opened into a cavern and I shone my torch around it. The rock was made up of very thin, horizontal layers of soft stone alternated with ironhard bands, creating a multi-shelved effect. It was unearthly. I walked along carefully and, looking closely at the rock, I saw weird circular coral-like growths and crusty shapes. These had been produced by seawater polyps, at a time when this area of southern Africa was under the sea. It was believed that South Africa had contained an inland sea, whose shoreline had curved round, bounded by the high range near Johannesburg, the mountainous eastern Transvaal, Swaziland and Lesotho, and that dated these caverns at, at least, three million years old. It was a staggering thought and I realised that, if we were to dig around, we would surely find prehistoric fossils and dinosaur bones.

Many other passages led from the cavern and we spent the rest of the day exploring them all. One of them led over a landslide

and I squeezed through a gap into an ancient gold mine. I crawled along the shaft where wooden props collapsed in dust when I
touched them. The dust was nearly choking me but I went gingerly on
along the shaft. The atmosphere reeked of decay. I found an old
pickaxe, and a place where the gold reef had been laid bare and
picked clean. I was going to continue on, but I felt, or imagined I
felt, the ground tremble faintly under my feet. Panic gripped me,
the air seemed stifling hot, my torch was growing dim. I wanted
to run but forced myself to move slowly and gently, just the
touch of my skirt was enough to turn the pit props into powder. I
cursed myself for having wandered so far. I didn't dare shout to
Gavin in case the vibration of my voice brought the roof down. I
heaved a sigh of relief when I reached the landslide where I had
entered the mine-shaft and called to Gavin, but there was no answer. I started crawling back towards the main cavern, dragging
myself along on my elbows and toes. The main chamber was
empty, though I could hear Gavin's voice singing somewhere
deep down inside the mountain. I found him in the third cavern
and he asked me if I was ready to go home yet. It was raining, so
we ran home, lit the fire, bathed, changed into dry clothes and
opened a bottle of wine.

The next two days were spent re-designing Xoza's tack. When
we had set out, I had had very little idea of what was required,
but now I knew that the top of the saddlebags must be raised to
the level of his backbone, I must add a chest-strap to prevent
them sliding backwards as we went uphill, and a crupper to his
tail to stop them sliding onto his neck. Then, in addition to the
all-round cinch, there must also be a girth attaching the bottom
of the two saddlebags to stop them flapping as he cantered. The
saddlebags themselves needed large pockets sewn on front and
back to hold things which I would want to reach for, such as my
waterbottle, camera, handkerchief (because I was still allergic to
horses), diary, biro, tobacco, etc. The pockets couldn't just be
deep bags, it was essential that I should be able to put my hand
on the item I wanted without having to rummage around for it.

Xoza and I were ready to go. Gavin hugged me farewell and wished me luck. I felt rather miserable and, having enjoyed security and company, I was alarmed at the prospect of setting out alone. When I thought about the future, I was scared. A voice in my mind told me that I was doing what I had chosen to do. I realised that I had never been happier, that the life I had chosen was one which I loved wholeheartedly, that the security which I still craved was not something which could be given to me, it had to come from within myself. What I made of my life was my responsibility, though chance had much to do with it. Now I seemed to be steering upwards, riding high, riding free, scooping up life's ecstasy and terror in handfuls, throwing it in the air and catching it again.

18
Prospecting for Gold

The line I had drawn down my map chanced to cross several small, rustic towns which had been created in the time of the gold rush of the 1880s. Much of the appearance of the towns was unchanged. I felt I had arrived in the past. In Pilgrims Rest, White River and Barberton all the old buildings had hitching rails and there were horse-troughs outside the hotels. The streets were lined with a jumble of funny little tin-roofed shacks built by the miners. After Barberton we detoured into the mountains to visit a ghost town, Eureka City.

Eureka City was a deserted corrugated-iron and wood town, with doors that hung off their hinges and squeaked in the gusts of wind. The buildings had fallen into ruin; empty, nothing left, no one, not a footprint on the dirt roads, not a sign of life. Desolation swept over me. I pulled my faded brown sunhat lower to shelter my eyes from the dusty glare, looked back at Xoza's hoof-prints down the main street, and rode out of town. We camped the night in the Valley of Death, which had once been littered with the bodies of thousands of men dying of fever.

In the days of the gold rush men had found heavy gold nuggets on the ground and fat reefs of gold underground. In the mountains I had seen many old mine workings, just simple shafts, dug by axe and shovel, and often only large enough for one person to crawl along, working like a mole and pushing the rocks back out for his family or colleagues to crack for gold. I had been told that the gold reefs were created three million years ago by the inland sea. Rivers from the mountains had carried down great quantities of alluvial gold which had sunk to the bottom as soon as the river reached the sea, and the tides had swept it into fissures in the rock along the sea's shoreline, so that the slopes of the curved belt of mountains from Johannesburg to Swaziland were the area which was later discovered to contain some of the richest gold deposits in the world. I rode along the ancient coastline, through hills clad in pine forest becoming hills carpeted with wild flowers. In clumps of large red and orange daisies there were stone cairns which marked out the claims of present-day gold prospectors, but no one was digging. The gold that remained was not commercially worth the effort of mining it. We wandered along near a stream which meandered over smooth rocks in a series of pools and waterfalls which we paddled in, swam in, drank from and rested beside. I lay back in the sun and watched a tawny eagle soaring and circling high overhead. When I was hungry, I chewed biltong (strips of dried meat), or cooked plants which were like artichokes, and found other roots that when pounded to powder could be made into porridge. One of my best meals was a feast of flying ants – they tasted like mushrooms fried in butter.

The stream went west, we continued south through the bush without paths. Tall, tangled, dead grass grew as high as Xoza. We pushed our way through, disturbed some waterbuck, and trod in the paths that they made for us. In the evenings I checked Xoza and myself for ticks. I usually pulled many off him, and less off myself. Some were just crawling around, but others had already buried their heads under my skin. They didn't hurt, even when I pulled them out, but they were unpleasant little insects and impossible to kill unless you cracked them between fingernails or burnt them to death. Their nastiest aspect was that some carried tick-bite fever. The other troublesome insects had been the flies, which left me alone but bothered Xoza. I picked a young twig off a pine tree and attached it like a browband on his halter.

The pine needles were six inches long and hung down over his eyes; their movement as he walked kept the flies away.

We entered into a barren rocky range of mountains and much of the time the ground was so rough that I was on foot leading Xoza. We scrambled higher into the mountains; it was hot, dry, and the grey-brown views between the jagged peaks shimmered in the heat-haze. I noticed a mauve blur in a far-off valley. It was a group of jacaranda trees in blossom beside a small stream. Under the trees was a lean-to shack made of bits of wood and cardboard, with an awning of torn canvas patched by squares of yellow and green. In the shade of the awning sat two figures. They didn't notice me. They were chattering loudly in Afrikaans and the old woman was intent on her work of trimming the old man's grey beard with a long knife. They looked like gypsies. Their faces were wrinkled and weathered deep brown; the woman was wearing a dazzling pink crochet beret, but her orange skirt and purple patterned blouse were sadly tattered and faded. They saw me and exclaimed with surprise. The old man came over and we shook hands. He was even older and more wizened than I'd thought on first impression; he smiled a broad semi-toothless smile and bid his lady to put on the kettle for tea. Then he helped me unload Xoza and I hobbled the horse and left him to graze. I stayed for three days with these Afrikaners, who were a delightful couple. She spoke no English, but he talked enough for both of them. He took me on long walks in the hills, searching for rocks with seams of gold, and he spent many hours teaching me to pan alluvial gold in the streams. Once I had got the knack of swilling the sand and water in the pan so that the sand circled at a faster speed than the grains of gold, then the two would separate out. Each panning was a long business. It took up to an hour before all the gold was extracted and it certainly wasn't a way to get rich quick because it took thirty pannings to fill a teaspoon of gold. The small egg-size nugget which the prospector showed me had taken him three months to accumulate; he estimated that he had sifted 1000 tons of sand and it was worth about £600. I liked the glitter of gold in the sunlight, and when he melted the nugget in a ladle in the furnace the colour became so densely gold that it turned green. All around their campsite were piles of rocks flecked and veined with gold.

The old man had a tremendous knowledge of geology. He told me that these mountains were the oldest range on the earth's crust and that in Swaziland I would see the very oldest rock existing in the world. He was a fascinating man, a prospector all his life, like his father had been. He first struck lucky with gold when he was sixteen, and he said that since then he had been married five times. His fortunes had rocketed up and down. When he was wealthy, he was a reckless gambler, so his riches never lasted long, and when they were finished he returned to search for more. Now he was old he searched in a leisurely way, the gold was only an excuse to live in the wilds, where he had found peace of mind. The prospector and his current lady love lived on unleavened bread, berries, small game and fish from the stream. The stream also gave them running water, the sun gave heat, the trees gave shade and firewood, and when the sky turned stormy there was no more beautiful sight than the mauve jacaranda flowers glowing luminously against the dark and turbulent clouds. My stay was during the time of the full moon; I slept out in my hammock between the trees, watching the night sky, listening to the sound of the bullfrogs by the stream, Xoza sighing happily in his sleep and the far distant echo of pounding drums in an African village.

Before I left, the old man showed me how to recognise some of the semi-precious stones I might find in the mountains, and so I set out as a prospector. Except for my youthfulness, I hardly looked different from these old people: my skin was tanned deep brown, my sunhat was battered and worn, my clothes were my bizarre Chinese silk jacket and a faded long skirt. I put my baggage on my horse and set out leading him up the rough, rocky trail.

My days as a prospector were fun and rewarding. Xoza and I

went along the top of the mountain range between the rocky wilderness and the cool green pine forests. I found a small amount of gold, some opals, and some verdite which is a vivid green rock. It feels similar to jade, and because this is the only part of the world where verdite can be discovered it is valuable for its rarity as well as its beauty. I found rocks containing asbestos fibre and stones of every colour from pink, red, purple, blue and turquoise. Every day that I lifted the packs onto Xoza they were heavier with stones, so I sorted my collection and the ones that I wasn't going to keep became ammunition for my catapult.

The mountain range continued southwards into Swaziland, and since the South African tourist board had twice assured me that I needed no permits or documents for the horse to cross the frontier I was rather surprised when I discovered at the customs post that the horse could not cross the border without an export permit to leave South Africa, an import permit to Swaziland and a vet's certificate, (and the same again to cross from Swaziland back to South Africa). Well, more than surprised, I was wild with anger at S A T O's inefficiency. It would take me a month to obtain the necessary papers by post, the rainy season had just begun and I was not prepared to sit and wait for a month at the frontier. I rode on and looked for an unofficial way across the border.

The trouble with that idea was that I met a high, barbed-wire fence which appeared to surround Swaziland. Despite my anger, I laughed at the thought that, if Scotland could have Hadrian's Wall and Russia could have the Iron Curtain, then there was no reason why Swaziland shouldn't have a wire fence. In addition to the fence, the mountains had become a formidable barrier of sheer cliffs and vertical ravines. I spent all day looking for a way through and my temper was not improved by finding that the South African side of the border was African settlement land. The Africans were friendly, but their goats had eaten every blade of grass in the region. I kept going, determined not to stop until I reached somewhere Xoza could graze. Then, in the twilight, way ahead, I saw the glow of green grass. Xoza quickened his steps and we turned down a farm lane. The farm was run by an English farmer and his wife. I was not the only visitor. There was also the farmer's sister, brother-in-law, granny and grandpa, and a couple whose car had broken down nearby. There was plenty of room for more; it was a huge old rambling farmhouse with no electricity, lots of tilley lamps, and a fireplace in every bedroom. The large dining-room table was piled high with roasted meats and fresh vegetables. After supper, the nine of us formed a council of war to work out how to get Xoza and myself into Swaziland. Grandpa was the most determined, egged on by granny, who tried to outdo him with absurd ideas, and brother-in-law who thumped the table with his fist to emphasise his contributions, while the man from the broken-down car pointed out the snags in each plan and the fact that the border was sure to be patrolled by guards. Everyone said that, even though it might be illegal, I must go to Swaziland; it was a beautiful country and I would love it. It was the farmer who thought of the smugglers' route, and the council put their heads together to devise the final plan. We put it into operation early in the morning.

My luggage was put in the farmer's car, while I rode Xoza to the valley through which the smugglers' route ran. The stream in the valley was only three feet deep and we waded up its bed to the barbed-wire fence. At the fence, I met my accomplices, all except the break-down couple who were beside the farmer's car on the road, pretending they had broken down again, and keeping watch for any trouble. They agreed to hoot the horn to warn us of approaching persons. The farmer and brother-in-law jacked up the fence with forked poles until the wires were high enough for Xoza to walk underneath, while the sister climbed an anthill to look out for border patrols. The rest of us went through, and granny and grandpa wiped out the traces of Xoza's hoofprints as the farmer and I took him to the smugglers' hiding place which was a deserted mine tunnel. We hid him inside, with a bundle of lucerne to keep him quiet, and then raced back the same way we had come. Back at the car I said goodbye to my allies and the farmer drove me to the main road border post, crossing officially into Swaziland. A few miles farther on we drove off down a rutted dirt track which eventually led us to the mine. Xoza was fine. The farmer took me down another shaft to show me a deep dark underground lake in a cave. We swam, the water was icy cold, and every splash echoed far into the tunnels. We dried off in the sun, loaded the baggage onto Xoza, the farmer handed me a shoulder of roast beef to chew as I rode, and then he was gone.

I rode into Mbabane, the capital of Swaziland, and right along the main road through the city centre. The atmosphere was light and cheerful. I tethered Xoza in the market-place, bought some woven grass baskets, filled them with presents for my family (and my rock collection), went to the post office and sent them off to England. We continued on and out the other side of the city until we came to a farm, where we stopped. The owner of the farm was an African/Asian, married to a Swazi girl. They were charming, and when I asked if I could put Xoza in one of their fields they said that he could have free run of the farm. I was welcome to stay for as long as I liked. It was rather an unusual farm, the perimeter fence was in good repair but all the other fences had fallen down and the cattle, sheep and goats went where they liked. No animal was ever sent to market, they just lived peacefully at the farm until they died of old age (though some got put in the deep freeze). Xoza loved the farm. He joined the dairy cows at milking time to go into the shed and eat cattle food, and he joined the chickens at noon to eat corn. He hadn't seemed tired, but we had been travelling now for six weeks and I felt sure that a week of rest would be good for him. He badly needed a blacksmith, but the farmer shook his head and said there was no such thing in Swaziland, all the local horses were unshod. I looked again at Xoza's hooves, the shoes were wearing thin and one had started to tear loose, so I borrowed a hammer and pliers and tightened it up again. Horse shoes were only meant to last for about a month. I wondered how much longer it would be before we found a blacksmith.

The day I arrived in Mbabane, I met an Italian called Armando, who was very lonely and ardent. We spent a great deal of time together and while I painted a huge mural of golden hills on one wall of his apartment he would cook the most sensational dishes of lasagne or pizza. He never ceased to astound me with the incredible things he said and did in all seriousness. The sad thing was that he was so serious he didn't see himself as funny. He made romantic speeches to me, but got hiccups in the middle; he'd walk along talking earnestly, and trip over; if he thought I was looking at him he'd strike casual poses, invariably against trees that were rotten and collapsed under him. He was so offended when I laughed, poor thing.

I enjoyed being with him, there was never a dull moment. It was impossible to tell what he would do next, but it was certain that whatever it was it wouldn't turn out as he'd imagined. At the end of my week in Mbabane, he asked me to stay permanently. To all his lengthy, impassioned speeches I replied with blunt honesty. I would not even contemplate the thought of stopping travelling with Xoza, it was unthinkable. The whole of my future lay ahead of me, and the idea of giving it up now was out of the question.

From Mbabane Xoza and I headed south at great speed as I was in a hurry to see what lay ahead. There were grassy mountains, evergreen valleys with streams tumbling down to rockpools then vanishing completely underground, and there was a hailstorm which caught us out in the open. We sheltered under a flimsy fern tree which was smashed to smithereens by hailstones the size of golfballs. We couldn't run to anywhere else and the hailstones nearly knocked me senseless. I stood there being bombed, with a river of water running off the front of my hat, a cold dribble down the back of my neck, and I laughed and laughed. When the hail ended it lay on the ground like snow. Many trees had been knocked over and the whole landscape was a mass of torrential rivers.

The season was changing, dry to wet, winter to spring. The change of season meant far more to me than the passing of time. Time was a meaningless word; hours that were lived intensely seemed equal to days of lesser experience; hours could also drag long and slow, being tediously dull, but afterwards it was as though they had never been, and other hours could pass in a flash if I was not aware of them. It felt good to have lost the habit of trying to make or save time.

Leaving Swaziland was a painful and hair-raising business. We were scratched to ribbons in thorn thickets and I came to blows with some sharp rocks in a river. In order to get back to the border post to have my passport stamped out, I spent hours crawling on my stomach through a game reserve. We went west to nurse our minor wounds in the Indian ocean. The ocean was warm and coloured aquamarine. There were white waves to surf on, the beach was desolate empty miles of golden sand, backed by immense dunes so steep that I played for hours jumping down them in leaps and bounds, pretending I could fly. The night skies were studded with a million stars and I slept buried in the warm sand beside the campfire which smouldered all night. The wind howled, the waves thundered, and the bleakness of the coastline was overwhelming. We didn't stay long because the only drinking water I could find was a rather saline spring behind the dunes, and Xoza said the spear-grass also tasted salty. Sandstorms raged all night and day, so we took off and galloped with the wind along raised dykes across the vast inland marshes. We galloped virtually the whole way to Empangeni.

Empangeni was important because it was where the line on my map ended, and because Dee lived there. Dee had been my best friend at school and it had been nine years since we last met. It was lovely to see her again. Dee's house stood facing some acres of wasteland. It was a small, overgrown cottage hidden behind a high hedge, and Dee was exactly the same nutty, exuberant person I had known at school, except that now she was married with two babies.

Unfortunately, during my stay I was attacked by a large dog. I had decided not to have rabies jabs. There were rabid animals in the bush around, and that week some pet cats had died of rabies, but I felt confident that the great dane which savaged me was not rabid. I'd had enough of pain, and the thought of another series of large injections in my stomach was too much. I was prepared to take the risk that the dog was healthy. The dog's owner was not. He took it to be put to sleep and its head was sent up to the vet labs at Pretoria for tests. If it were proved that the dog was rabid then I would start the anti-rabies jabs immediately.

I was growing restless. The results of the dog's autopsy still had not arrived after four days and inquiries produced the answer that the vet labs had mislaid the dog's head. There was no point in waiting longer. I drew another straight line on my map. It went from Empangeni to the centre of Lesotho, a barren plateau 10 000 feet above sea level. I said a tearful farewell to Dee and set off riding Xoza westwards across Zululand.

'

19
Tick-Bite Fever

Xoza was fresh. He cantered gaily along the tracks through the sugar plantations, and when we took short cuts in the narrow rows between the sugar-cane plants he was in seventh heaven, nose deep in the most delicious leaves he had ever tasted. It was a beautiful, hot day with a cool breeze. As I rode I re-read the letters from my family which Dee had gathered and kept for me. It was the first news I had received from them since I left Salisbury; I had wondered how they would react to hearing that I was riding alone and now I knew. Their letters told me that they had complete faith in me and that I was doing the right thing. It was difficult to fold the letters because my left hand was still sore where the dog's teeth had pierced right through the index finger at the nail. It was neatly stitched up with time-dissolving thread, so that I wouldn't need to have the stitches removed. That was fortunate, as after the sugar-cane plantations I was in the Zulu homelands, a region without white people, cars or tarmac roads.

There were dirt roads, but we didn't need to follow them. The open, undulating hills were traversed by grassy paths leading between groups of beehive-shaped huts. Each kraal (group of huts) was built around a central cattlefold and encircled by an outer fence of sticks. Each cluster was the home of one family and every wife had her own hut. Many of the people waved to me in a friendly way, others nearly fell over with laughter, and many ran off screaming at the sight of a white girl on a horse. The people were striking to look at: some women had greased their faces and bodies with red ochre, and their hair was rolled into a mass of short, straight braids, decorated with beads. Other women had greased their hair into an elaborate framework; they wore a score of necklaces, red-dyed cloth skirts, and round their ankles was a ton of ironmongery which clanked and jangled as they walked. Most of the men wore heavy earrings of metal loops, and their faces looked fierce. I went to visit one of the Zulu chiefs and was made very welcome. We all sat on three-legged stools. No one could speak any English; in fact, they were astonished that I knew no Zulu, they thought that everyone in the world spoke Zulu. They taught me their greeting, '*Sakubona*,' and how to say I was lost, where was the path, '*Duka, ipi ndlela?*' It was a pleasant language with many click sounds in the words. The chief called one of the women to wash my feet as a token of goodwill, and other women served us with sour clotted milk (made with the addition of blood and urine), which was refreshing.

On the second day I stopped late afternoon at a trading store to buy a bag of mealie meal. Among the dark shelves laden with tin bowls, beads and traditional red Zulu cloth blankets, I noticed a selection of hats. My sunhat was worn out, it had been given to me by the Chinese political prisoners in the Congo, so I picked out a floppy-brimmed beige cotton hat, and while I paid for it I started chatting to the big, amiable Zulu storekeeper. I didn't like hobbling Xoza all the time, so I asked the storekeeper (who spoke some English) if the horse could stay the night, and I would sleep in one of the nearby kraals. He replied that it was fine for the horse to stay and that he had a spare room but much to his sorrow it was illegal for me to stay. It was against the law for a white person to sleep in a black man's house, or to sleep anywhere in a native trust land. He would have liked to help me but he was afraid that it would bring serious trouble from the police in Eshowe, a white provincial town twenty miles away. He telephoned the Eshowe police station, who said they would come and collect me. While I waited for them, I sat outside on the stoop of the trading store, drinking a mug of fresh corn beer, watching the crowd of Zulus peeping at Xoza through the fence. I went over and poured some mealie meal onto an empty sack for him; he snorted down his nostrils with pleasure and clouds of mealie meal rose in the air, the crowd squealed with excitement and all tried to hide behind one another. The police arrived and drove me off to Eshowe. They informed me that not only was I not allowed to stay overnight in the native reserve, but also it was illegal to be there during the day unless I had a special permit which had to be issued by the magistrate.

Early morning found me standing in the magistrate's office being told that no way would they issue a permit to a lone white girl on horseback. The magistrate showed me an enlarged map of Zululand. Eshowe was a small white enclave on a road which cut across the middle of the trust land, and he pointed out the wide deep Tugela River thirty miles west which we would have to swim. He said that this district was the most violent part of South Africa, the Zulus of the trust land were well known for their savage killings and violence. Even black policemen refused to go on patrol there. This didn't worry me — I believed that the farther I could go from civilisation, the safer I would be. Townships or main road villages were far more likely to be trouble sources than the bush. After an hour of argument, the magistrate finally gave me a permit.

My main worry was Xoza's feet. There hadn't been a blacksmith in Empangeni. Xoza's hooves had grown long and the shoes were wafer thin. A lesser worry was my new sunhat which seemed to be absorbing the sun's heat. I supposed that this was due to the beige colour of the hat and to the design of the brim which was somehow reflecting the sunlight in front of my eyes and dazzling me. My head hurt, my eyes hurt, my brains felt as though they were frying and, when I thought about it, I realised that I ached all over. The pains in my back, arms and legs were, I suspected, due to the long hours I spent on horseback, which had never affected me before, but stiffness had been accumulating for months. It was a relief when our westerly route descended from the beautifully undulating, but treeless, hills down into thick, indigenous forest. However, despite its shadiness, I found the heat oppressive – yet I was also cold and I huddled for warmth in my camouflage jacket. I became very listless and when we rested at noon I stared into space. I wasn't lazy, I did all my chores, even remembering to rub cream into a growing sore on my leg, but I did everything in a mechanical way, and when I tried to catch up on my diary I discovered that I hadn't noticed anything for days. I had to keep my eyes shut because the daylight was too glaring, so I left it up to Xoza to pick our route. Sometimes I rode slumped over his neck, and I tied myself to his back so that I wouldn't fall off. Other times I felt fine, and I sang as I rode.

The Tugela River was as wide as the Thames in London, but luckily the current was not strong, and there was an old wooden dingy which ferried my saddlebags across. I led Xoza into the water and kept urging him forwards until we were out of our depth. He tried to turn round, but I wouldn't let him, he had to swim. I swam beside him, and when his head went under and his feet came up I hauled on his halter until his head reappeared on the surface. He had obviously never sum a river before, but he quickly grasped the idea and struck out powerfully towards the far shore. I couldn't swim nearly as fast as him, so I clung onto his mane and floated alongside, keeping my legs well clear of his hooves thrashing underwater. It was a long way. We emerged dripping up a sandy beach and onto the bank.

A track led from the river across the valley and up an escarpment which was a steep 3000 feet climb. The day was blazing hot with a scorching galeforce wind which spun dust-devils down along the Tugela valley. My head felt numb, but nothing hurt, and at noon I found a fresh water spring beside some wattle trees which vibrated with the singing of crickets. When the afternoon grew cool we slogged on up the steep track. Three of Xoza's shoes came off. At the top of the escarpment was a plug-like mountain peak, and beyond it was the small town of Kranskop where we spent the night. We stayed with a friendly English couple and I discovered that there was a blacksmith living at Ahrens only ten miles further on. When we arrived at the blacksmith's house, I found that he wasn't actually a proper blacksmith, he had taught himself to shoe horses because his wife's horses needed to be shod for show-jumping. He trimmed, filed and re-shod Xoza's feet in a way that could not have been surpassed by a top professional.

I was now not far from Greytown and the land ahead was all farmland. I began to sweat and toss in fever at nights and I soon realised that I was ill. My bones ached and one moment I felt as though I was burning up, then freezing cold. One morning, when I found a thermometer (in a bathroom), I took my temperature. It read 104°. I wondered what my temperature must have been when I rode all day in the scorching sun. In my stubbornness and determination to carry on travelling, we by-passed Greytown and continued west towards Mooi River. The fever had numbed my brain to the extent that I ceased to think at all. However, I remember well the evening I rode into the Braithwaite's farm. The farmer and his wife came out of the house as I arrived, and they took one look at me and cried, 'You're the girl with rabies.'

That shook me, and I gasped, 'No, it can't be.'

'There have been radio and newspaper bulletins about it; they've been trying to trace you for the past two weeks. You'd better come in and telephone the police immediately.'

Thoughts flashed through my mind: rabies was incurable and death was certain; the symptoms were depression, drooling, foaming and madness. No. Definitely no, I did not have rabies. I could not believe it. With a wry smile, I realised that I had already bet my life on it by refusing the anti-rabies vaccine in Empangeni. I felt calm as I picked up the telephone and dialled the police. The police said they would call me back. I still felt calm. My host had put Xoza in a stable, knee-deep in fresh hay and with a trough full of horse cubes. He was totally content. And so was I. There was no doubt in my mind, I knew I had not got

234

rabies. The Braithwaite's were super people and when, during dinner, the telephone rang Seymour answered it.

'Christina, it's for you. It's the police.'

I admit that my heart was pounding and I had to unclench my fists to hold the telephone receiver. The voice at the police station confirmed that they had been searching for me, they wanted to inform me that Pretoria vet labs had located the missing dog's head, carried out an autopsy and that the results had been negative. I did not have rabies.

In the morning, I continued towards Mooi River, via a mountain called 'the mountain that no one may point at'; if you pointed at it then disaster would befall. The farmer whose land adjoined it said of course I could ride over his farm, and he pointed in the direction I must follow across the fields. After several miles, we came to a small stream in a bed of tall reeds. It looked slightly boggy so I dismounted, tucked my skirt up high and left Xoza on the bank while I tested the stream's depth. It only came up to my knees. I led Xoza forwards into it. The tangled reed roots were a false bottom, they had supported my weight but they collapsed under Xoza, and he disappeared up to his withers in oozing, muddy bog. I pulled on his rope and he floundered desperately, but his legs must have been trapped by the reeds. There was no way he could free himself and every effort sank him deeper in the mire. He stopped still, and waited for me to rescue him. The water had closed over his back; every minute he sank slowly deeper in. I leapt into the bog beside him, I had to get the luggage off him so that he might have a chance of kicking his way out. The straps which secured the saddlebags were fastened under his stomach; I took a deep breath and plunged my heads and arms into the smelly mud, trying to reach the straps. I found them, but couldn't undo them. My knife, where was my knife? I groped frantically and found it in the front outer pocket. I flicked it open, took another breath and went down in the mud to cut the straps. The knife was razor sharp, the straps parted immediately and I hauled the sodden saddlebags onto the bank. Xoza's muscles strained in response to my yells of encouragement, but he could not move. The muddy water was now halfway up his neck, he was still sinking. There was no possibility of getting him out and there was nothing I could do to help him.

'You've got to do something,' I screamed at myself. 'You can't just watch him go under.' I scanned the fields and horizons for people but there was no one. My eyes rested for an instant on the heavy, brooding outline of the mountain that no one may point at. Then I turned – Xoza had sunk an inch deeper. I started to run back towards the farmhouse. It was noon; my head was burning with fever and whirling with fear. I ran, and kept running, for three miles back to the house. I hammered on the door. In tears and near to hysterics, I told the farmer what had happened. He said, 'I see, please come in, sit down and relax. Would you like a wash?'

'No,' I screamed, 'I don't want a wash, I want help. My horse is going to drown in five minutes.'

'Yes, quite so. How unfortunate, I'm awfully sorry that I can't help you, all my men are busy harvesting the maize crop. Perhaps one of my neighbours may have a spare lad.'

I burst into fresh torrents of tears. He was the sort of man who filled in forms in triplicate before taking any action. I threw a fit of hysterics so violent that he jumped up and said, 'Tell me what I can do to help you.'

I hustled him into his Landrover, stopped at a shed to gather an armful of sacks and some ropes and then we drove to where his farm manager and labourers were harvesting. He drove desperately slowly, and when we met the manager, the farmer inquired about work progress and added; 'Now, this young lady – er, what did you say your name was?' he asked me. I was still crying, my explanation was incoherent, but the manager seemed to understand. He ordered six men into the back of the Landrover and drove flat-out to the boggy valley. Xoza's head was just showing above the water, though it was plastered in mud and I guessed that he had been under and had fought his way back up.

The manager and his men stripped off their shirts and taking the ropes they plunged into the bog and deep down into the foul-smelling ooze to pass the ropes under Xoza's belly. I had also waded in, spreading some sacks in the mud in front of Xoza and trying to force other sacks down to where his feet might be, while the manager was tearing at the roots which were tangled round the horse's legs. The farmer stood well clear, he didn't want to get dirty. For a whole, grim, murky hour we wallowed in that bog, and finally, as the labourers heaved on the ropes, Xoza was able to flounder forwards and up onto the bank. He wasn't lame, limping or hurt in any way by the experience. I was in tears again.

The farmer drove back to his house with my luggage and the manager walked with Xoza and myself by another route. I wished I could express my thanks to him. Back at the house the farmer told me I stank too horribly to use his bath, so he gave me the garden hose to wash off the slime. Then he repented, offered me a bath and asked if I wished to stay for a day to recover my shattered nerves. All I wanted to do was to get on my horse and ride away. I knew I was in no fit state to do that, so I telephoned the Braithwaites and asked them to come and fetch me.

They drove over immediately, towing a horse trailer into which we loaded the bedraggled Xoza, and then we went home. There was something special about the Braithwaites; they treated me like an errant child in need of parental care and authority, and I adopted them as proxy parents. I couldn't have chosen nicer people. They quickly discovered that I was unwell and they marched me off to see their doctor. When I showed him the black-headed sore on my leg, he told me I had tick-bite fever. Further examination revealed that I also had bronchitis. He prescribed antibiotices and sent me home to bed. That night the fever burned as a raging fire, it burned until it could burn no more, my bed was soaked in sweat; by morning I was weak and exhausted, but the fever had gone. I slept peacefully for twenty-four hours, and then pronounced myself well enough to get up. I spent some happy, quiet days with the Braithwaites, and when I left they insisted on lending me a saddle and bridle.

When Xoza and I reached Mooi River, we turned up a track marked Sierra Ranch. The track was many miles long and when we arrived we found it was not a cattle ranch. It was a rootin', tootin' cowboy-style, luxury hotel, whose staff wore leather stetsons and tall, embossed boots. The hotel owner's wife was a lovely person, who invited me to stay as her guest for as long as I liked.

After a week's rest, I spread out the map again. I decided that I would ride west only as far as the foothills of the Drakensberg, then south across East Griqualand to the Transkei. It was now mid-December and I wondered where I would be for Christmas.

20
Lesotho

The soaring jagged range of the Drakensberg mountains loomed ahead of us. The next moment they were reaching out around us, and then we were high among them. We camped that night beside a waterfall, among trees which sprouted bunches of fern leaves from their tops. Dawn was early and by about 5 a.m. we were cantering on the grass along the ridge of a spur. Behind us lay the lowveld; to either side were parallel hill ridges like the prongs of a fork, all running west, gaining height and curving upwards into the massive wall of the Drakensberg. The mountain rose towering and near-vertical until it reached 10 000 feet, and above that was the high wilderness of Lesotho.

I wondered where my path led. Sometimes it was so faint that I could only detect it by spotting blades of grass that were broken or hanging over. The sun shone in a clear blue sky, the wind was cool. We saw no one all day, not a single trace of human life. No huts, no fences, no litter, not a sign that man existed in the world. There was peace. All was quiet, save for the gentle thud of Xoza's hooves and an occasional piercing whistle which was the warning call of a scattered herd of antelope.

The long spur of land met the wall of the Drakensberg. Its slope angled very steeply, so we made our way along its contour. That night we camped at an altitude of about 7000 feet, on a level hump in the shelter of a group of rocks. We were perched high in an amphitheatre, way above the tree line. There was nothing I couldn't see.

I hobbled Xoza, shared a bowl of chocolate porridge with him, and sat thinking about how much of my life I had spent on flat land and how different I felt when I was among mountains. I found power in them. I was filled with an overwhelming joy among the rocks which bulged stark and bare from the mountainside. Clouds flocked into the valleys below, jostling and spilling over, and some drifted mistily up towards me. There was one which reached my altitude. A full circular rainbow was reflected in the moisture and when the cloud moved behind me, the sun cast my shadow into the heart of the rainbow. It stayed until the sun sank behind the mountains.

The night was very cold. I huddled against the still-warm rock but at dawn I woke up freezing. I jumped around flapping my arms to revive my circulation. Xoza was also awake, grazing quite far away. I called to him to say it was time to leave. He looked up and started walking towards me. Not the shuffling hop of a hobbled horse; he strode with long swinging steps. I had tied the hobbles too loose and they had come off. I was amazed that he had not run away. I called again and he came trotting across the mountainside.

Mid-morning I saw two blanket-clad figures. They were on foot, herding a cow up the same path I had travelled the previous day. I had lost the path today but the only possible direction was forwards. I was now on foot – one small slip on the steep incline, and Xoza and I would have been lost. My feet were sore with the strain of every step angled against the gradient. I slowed down and when I looked behind I saw the cowmen were catching up fast. It occurred to me that they were probably cattle thieves, the Basotho (pronounced Basutu) – people renowned for persistent stock theft, especially at Christmas time.

They caught up with me during the afternoon, passing on a higher contour. We scrambled up to join them. I indicated that I was lost and they indicated that they were going up over the top of the Drakensberg into Lesotho. I nodded, pointed at them, me, and the jagged horizon above, and nodded again. They nodded back. I wondered how they would make the ascent up 3000 feet of steep cliff-topped mountain. Lesotho was like an immense fortress – it looked impregnable, but no doubt they knew a way.

A thick cold mist decended. If we hadn't kept up close we would surely have fallen to disaster. It was exhausting. We zigzagged interminably upwards, then along the foot of some cliffs and over a rocky path, and finally we emerged on the top of the plateau. The fog was even thicker and night was falling. The cowmen signalled me to continue behind them. I remounted Xoza and wrapped my blanket tightly around me.

We stopped after dark at an empty round stone hut. The men built a fire inside using a pile of dried cowdung. It was smoky but it didn't smell bad and it was warm. They were a villainous-looking pair, but they treated me with great respect and I felt quite safe with them. One of them unsheathed a long knife and they went outside the hut. I followed curiously. They walked round the cow, slapping her rump. They seemed to be arguing about which was the best place to cut a hunk of meat off her. I suspected that they were only going to do it because they wanted to provide food for me, so I interrupted and explained that I had enough food for the three of us in my baggage. Mealie meal and biltong weren't much of a substitute for prime steaks, but they sufficed. We all slept in the one hut. I curled up by the fire and slept deeply until the men roused me at dawn.

It was a ghostly morning. The landscape was an ever-changing scene of mountain peaks and horizons which loomed then vanished in the swirling fog. A couple of Basotho men went past on horseback like phantoms, swathed in blankets with wide-brimmed straw hats pulled low over their faces. At midday we reached a cave under an overhang of rock. The occupants hid in the dark recesses when they saw me, but my companions went and cuffed them on the heads and told them not to be afraid. The cave was partitioned and sheltered by low stone walls. The ceiling was blackened with smoke and as I looked round I saw that the cave sides were decorated with the ancient reddish paintings of bushmen who must have lived there in times gone by. I smiled in pleasure and tried to tell the inhabitants that I thought their home was beautiful.

We had steaming bowls of hot porridge for lunch and then the men went off to round up their horses. They returned with a wild-looking bunch of ten ponies, Basotho ponies, a breed which had developed on this plateau, renowned for their hardiness and surefootedness. Like Xoza, they could run trippling tirelessly over the hills. The men selected two, and then looked at me questioningly. I nodded and they selected a third. One of the children held Xoza's rope so that he couldn't follow us and we herded the other seven ponies ahead of us down a rocky path. It was strange to ride without Xoza but this new steed was fiery and fleet. We herded the ponies at a fast pace with wolf whistles and cries of 'Hai' to keep them on the winding track.

I had thought the hills deserted, but when I looked more closely I could make out the round shapes of stone huts which blended so well into the craggy background that they were almost invisible. We were riding through a sea of mountains, barren of trees or vegetation but for the coat of green stubbly grass and as we descended into the valley I saw patches where the Basotho scratched the infertile earth to plant their puny crops.

After about two hours we arrived at a trading store. Outside were groups of blanket-clad men and dozens of horses either parked or being loaded with sacks of meal; one pony was loaded with a large tin trunk and some battered suitcases. Despite the apparent poverty of the people, no one's blanket was threadbare and all the saddlery looked new and smart – bridles of embossed leather, long curbed bits, martingales, chest straps, cruppers. My tack seemed very shabby by comparison. I went into the store and bought some clip-on stars for Xoza's halter and some extra to give my hosts. They were busy roping sacks of grain onto the

242

backs of the seven ponies and then we herded them back up into the hills.

Bleak, windswept and barren, the roof of Africa seemed as if it had reached its maximum and could go no higher. The air was thin, the nights incredibly starry, the full moon shed light as bright as an overcast day. Sometimes I rode at night, which was spooky. I often thought about the dinosaurs which had roamed here, leaving their fossilised footprints in the rocks. By day we rested in sheltered valleys beside staggered pillar waterfalls, rockpools, among clumps of protea bushes with pink blooms, listening to the Basotho herdboys playing their flutes as they watched over their herds of woolly corkscrew-horned sheep. I saw no white people, no vehicles. It was not surprising in view of the roughness of the roads; even a Landrover would have had difficulty using them. My thoughts flashed back to when I had crossed the Sahara by Landrover, looking at the outside world through the windows, cut off from it all, and I reflected that Landrover expeditions and travel by horse have little in common.

As I rode I became part of the world. I lived in it, I didn't just pass through it. Everything that happened and existed around me had direct effects, moulding my day, my mood, and my whole being. Nothing was simply visual, it was all tangible. A mountain stream was not just a pretty sight – it was also water, the key to all living things. It came from deep inside the multi-million-year-old plateau. It was icy cold and made my skin tingle. It was refreshing and tasted sweet. Streams flowed, carrying the secrets of the forest and the songs of the hillsides. The rushing torrents expressed my longing for freedom. Their nature was ever-changing; as they meandered, so did I, and when they dawdled I lingered.

My life-style depended mainly on the weather which was responsible for the balance between rest and travel, for our speed when we galloped in the winds to outrun a storm, and for our direction when I saw black clouds gathering over a horizon. We played games of tag with the clouds. They would chase and we would run, dodge and sidestep out of their way. Then from a sunny hill I would watch the storm cloud break over a neighbouring dark hill, lightning forks flashing down to the earth and rain falling like a smudge of grey.

My moods and feelings didn't come from myself. They were reflections of the day, the landscape, and of everything around me. I loved being alone. I no longer had to be a person. I didn't need barriers against ridicule, or boundaries to contain what I was and wasn't. I was nothing. My existence merged into its surroundings. Many people I'd met said they hated being alone. They could only think of the loneliness. And yet I found my time and space almost crowded with thoughts and sights.

I was roused from my thoughts by Xoza who jerked his head up and stared at a group of Basotho people walking along the track. They were dressed in multi-coloured splendour – outrageous paper hats, rose-tinted sunglasses, painted bodies, and they carried an assortment of knobkerries and drums. When I asked them where they were going they did a pantomime to show that they had celebrated and were now going home. Rapid calculations told me that there were still about four more days to Christmas. It was time to find somewhere to be.

We headed south-east back to the rim of the plateau and there we encountered one of the most beautiful regions on this earth. Mountains soared steeply all around, their green slopes coloured with white and yellow flowers and white heather. Herds of antelope grazed on the grassy banks among weeping willows and clumps of white arum lilies which I had only ever seen before in vases on the altar of my home village church at Christmas-tide. I started singing carols as I rode along. White storks had chosen the more sheltered valleys as their summer nesting grounds, sharing them with flocks of large black birds with long, curled, orange beaks. The air was full of fluttering white butterflies and the streams were full of trout. I cut a willow branch, sharpened

244

one end and managed to spear a large trout.

It was impossible to get down the escarpment out of Lesotho. Wherever there was a track there would also be a boarder post and we couldn't officially leave Lesotho because we hadn't officially entered the country. We had to find some other way out. We followed along the perimeter of the plateau. Thousands of feet below us was the lowveld with the parallel arms of the Drakensberg sweeping up to buttress the cliff walls.

Within a short time we found a path which was a narrow shelf edged by cliffs that led through some very rocky tors. I dismounted and walked in front of Xoza. I kept slithering on the loose stones and whenever I slipped badly Xoza would stop dead so I could regain my balance by using him as an anchor. His neckrope was eight feet long and I held on tightly to it. I didn't even let go when he slipped and fell off the cliff. He was gone. With a numb sense of disbelief I looked at the empty space where my horse had been walking, at the skid marks going over the precipice, and then at the rope which I still held. I lay down on my stomach on the narrow path and leant over the cliff edge. Down below me was a steep valley. I scanned its rocky depths, but I couldn't see Xoza. But I still had his rope in my hand. I looked at the rope dangling straight down the cliff and there stood Xoza, about ten feet below me, apparently unhurt.

A fairly recent landslide nearby provided a series of rocks by which I could climb down. Xoza was waiting clamly for me to rescue him, so I explored each direction thoroughly in turn. But there was no way for him to go. The rocks were chest high. Some had flat surfaces, others tilted at varying angles. Where they were narrowly spaced he could perhaps walk on them and jump from one to the next, but in many places the gaps were too wide to jump. I traced alternative routes on the ground threading between the boulders, but every way was blocked by gaps that were too narrow for him to pass. It was like a game of roll the ball through the maze, except with this maze there was no way out.

There had to be a way. I explored every direction again, and a third time, but was forced to come to the same conclusion. There was no point in moving him. He was better off staying where he was. I sat down to think. The only way of extricating Xoza was by airlift. I would have to find a helicopter. Where I was going to find one in this wilderness I didn't know. I supposed there must be a mountain rescue team somewhere in Lesotho, or else perhaps I could find an army camp in South Africa. I wondered how many days Xoza would survive without food or water. There was no time to waste. I unloaded the luggage, hid it among the rocks, took out some sticks of biltong to chew, wrapped my blanket around me, said goodbye to Xoza, and set off over the landslide and back up onto the path.

Xoza whinnied. He thought I was abandoning him. He looked agitated, so I hurried on out of sight. The noise of some dislodged stones rattling and bounding down the valley made me halt, and I turned round. Xoza was trying to be a mountain goat. He was up on top of the boulders, very surely picking his way from one to the next, sniffing the rock and testing every foothold. I held my breath. I watched him slowly raising himself on his hindlegs to jump between uneven rocks, sliding because his iron shoes gave no grip on their surface. I could see no likelihood of him crossing the landslide unscathed and at any moment I expected him to fall. I could clearly imagine the charp cracking sound of his legs breaking. I found myself hopping from foot to foot in anguish with his every step. He sat back on his haunches and slid down a curved rock onto the ground. When he reached the place where I had climbed back up to the path he stopped. He couldn't continue at ground level and the rocks were too high for him to jump up onto them. I hurried down, hugged him, and went to collect the saddlebags. I carried them over to him and put them on top of each other as a step for him to climb up. Then I had a second idea. I tore my blanket into big squares which I tied round his hooves to help him grip the rocks. Now it was his turn again. He

246

made it onto the rocks, and he made it back up to the path.

As we set off again Xoza began to limp – well, he limped a few steps before I stopped. We looked at each other, then at the 4000 foot descent still ahead of us. Xoza sighed and walked soundly forwards.

Late on Christmas Eve in a small village nestling in the foothills of the Drakensberg, I met a man with unusual eyes. It was not entirely a chance meeting, although it was chance that had brought me to the village. I had already heard of him as being a philosopher, mystic or lunatic. He was a tall man, his brown hair was streaked with grey, his face was gaunt and pale. He was quite ordinary to look at, except for his eyes which didn't match.

'Hello,' I said, 'I've come to stay for Christmas.'

21
The Wild Coast

I couldn't think at all, my head reeled, my mind became more
and more fuzzy. I could only just manage day-to-day existence,
and the nights of fever. The black-scabbed swelling on my arm
told me that another infected tick had bitten me. Days were
marred by blinding headaches, sun too bright for my eyes, back-
ache, brain out of order, delirium. I wanted to be alone.

We halted frequently to rest under shady trees; I sat staring
into space, I didn't have the strength to remount Xoza without
the help of a tree-stump or rock, and when I looked at the path
I couldn't remember which way we had come from. The cool
winds became freezing gales that brought snow to this southern
part of the Drakensberg. Frozen fevered brains. I tied knots in
a piece of rope to mark each day that passed, but I forgot what
they were for, and untied them all.

In mid-January we reached Kokstad, a country town close to
the Transkei border. There I went to visit the doctor. He told
me I had tick-bite fever.

'There is no simple cure. There are twenty-four different
types of antibiotic pills. Try a course in each type until you find
one which works. And bear in mind that, when you take anti-
biotics, they also destroy the bacteria which provide you with
natural immunity from other diseases.'

That sounded to me like a poor deal, I would be better off
keeping the tick-bite fever rather than risking a host of other

illnesses. Another option was to lie in a darkened room for a few weeks until the fever had passed, so I unhitched Xoza from the surgery railings, rode into the town centre, and bought a pair of large dark glasses.

Next, Xoza had an appointment with the blacksmith. The only shoes in the smithy were a set that had been made sixty years ago for the carthorse which had pulled the milk waggon. The shoes were double-thick, heavy-duty, which, after they had been cut smaller and re-shaped in the furnace, fitted Xoza admirably.

The Transkei was reputed to be a wild and beautiful country, but all the white people I had met warned me not to go there. They pointed out that this rugged, remote country had been independent for only three months, it was unstable and Europeans had been attacked there. I didn't deliberately ignore their advice, I just found myself riding south across the border. It didn't look dangerous; the Pondo tribe were friendly and everyone called greetings to me. Women wearing beadwork skirts with hair rolled into string-like braids were tilling maize patches with short hoes; men dressed in red blankets were sitting talking vociferously in villages of decoratively painted mud huts; other men on horseback rode up to accompany me for a while; naked children stood like charioteers in rough wooden sleighs dragged by oxen which strained at their yokes. Sleighs were the common form of transport for local goods, and the network of sandy tracks was far more direct than the scanty road system I had been accustomed to. There were high mountain ranges, deep valleys, waterfalls, and tumbling green hills of smooth close-cropped grass. The clouds were low and occasionally I was swamped by mist which became denser until I could no longer see the path we were following. Wet cloud, obscure shapes, rocks and blurred colours loomed and vanished. Late in the day I heard voices through the mist; the voices led me to a trading store where I stayed the night.

Over the next few days I did find slight antagonism towards my white skin, but it was only gruff curiosity and it soon turned

Travels with Fortune

to smiles when they knew I was friendly. Most people mistook me for a man, and they called, 'Morning, sir,' so I lowered my voice a few tones to fit the part, but there was absolutely no reason to be afraid. The weather was so drizzly that I stayed every night in villages. I preferred to stay with people who could speak a bit of English, just in case there was a misunderstanding.

On the third night, I stopped in a small village, at the hut of the village shopkeeper, a superb old man of ninety-eight who knew many English words. His name was Sidney and, despite being a great-great-grandfather, he stood straight and was as bright as a sixty-year-old. His family invited me to stay. The younger generation were sent off to catch a chicken, while the middle-aged group brought a bed for me from a hut two miles away. During the evening the whole family and village came to visit; several of them had never seen a white woman before. African women were not permitted to eat with their men, but as a special treat they were to be allowed to watch how Sidney and I ate using a knife and fork. First, we were served with steaming hot thick porridge, then the chicken was brought into the hut, nicely cooked on a tray. African chickens are not the plump, tender birds you have in Europe, they are tough and stringy, and the only way to eat them is by holding the bones and gnawing the flesh off with your teeth. However, I picked up my knife and fork and the audience leaned forwards to see better. The fork was an interesting tangle of bent prongs, the knife was as blunt as an iron bar, and after a minute of sawing, I had made only a small dent in the chicken. Suddenly, a man burst into the hut; his expression was black and angry. Everyone shrank back fearfully. He was the chief of the village and he was livid because I had not asked his permission to stay there. I jumped up, shook his hand warmly and told him how pleased I was to meet him, how wonderful it was for a stranger to be offered hospitality, and how kind his villagers had been to me. To every question that the chief spat at me, I replied with smiles and chattiness, and soon he began to relax. He stayed to chat for two hours and when he left

250

he wished me a safe journey.

One afternoon, I saw a cluster of houses and I assumed we'd arrived at Lusikisiki. Wrong again. It obviously wasn't an ordinary place. There were outer entrance gates, the rows of houses looked more like barracks, and at the far end of the road was a larger house with a group of women standing chanting by the door. Men dressed in European fashion strolled up and down the road, staring at me in astonishment. I dismounted and asked one of them where I was.

'This is the Great Place of the Great One,' he replied with grand reverence.

'Who is the Great One?' I inquired.

'The Great One,' he paused dramatically, 'is the Honourable His Excellency the President of the Republic of Transkei, and Paramount Chief of the Pondos.'

At that moment a messenger came to inform me that I must report at once to the president's house to be received and welcomed. I glanced down at my mud-splattered skirt and even muddier bare feet, and asked if I could shower and change before being received.

'No, you may not keep the president waiting. You can go as you are.'

'Yes, but first I must unload and feed my horse.' This they accepted without argument. My baggage was put in a guest house, and Xoza was given a generous helping of maize from the royal mealie bins. I wanted to stop and wash my feet, but my escort said there was no time for things like that and hurried me over to the president's house.

I walked into a square room with a square carpet and a square of chairs set out along the walls. There were several men sitting down. I guessed that the president would be the largest one and I took a step towards him thinking that he would stand up and shake hands, but my escort dashed round in front of me and, walking like a scrunched-up hunchback, he flailed his arms in a circular, wheeling motion. That nearly flummoxed me. His whirling arms created a screen between the president and myself; the screen propelled me towards an armchair against the opposite wall. I stopped on my way to pick up a floor-rug and when I sat down I put the rug over my feet – I reckoned it was better to appear eccentric than grubby. The president spoke. I couldn't understand what he was saying because he spoke in his native tongue, but when he finished one of his counsellors translated it all for me. I had been very cordially received, welcomed and invited to stay at the Great Place for the weekend. The speeches were made at shouting pitch, and I had to yell my thanks to be heard above the raucous singing of the women outside the open door, while in a corner of the room a portable television was blaring full volume in Afrikaans.

The president offered me a drink. They were all drinking neat whisky, which I didn't fancy, and since there was nothing else available I asked for a glass of water. The man who went to fetch it and another man who was refilling the whisky glasses both walked as though they were doubled-up with stomach cramps and were careful never to turn their backs on the president. The water-bearer explained that they walked like that because it was considered impolite to stand up straight before the president.

After dinner I went out to say goodnight to Xoza who was wandering freely around the Great Place, and on the way back I bumped into the chief of police. Inevitably, he asked to examine my passport and visa – the white police in South Africa had never once checked my passport and I had forgotten about the passport-mania of the Africans. Unfortunately, I didn't have a visa for Transkei, my visa for South Africa had long ago expired, and my passport hadn't been officially stamped for months. The police chief paged through to the end and exclaimed, 'But you have no visa!'

'Oh dear,' I replied in consternation, then added brightly, 'but I'm sure the president will help me sort it out.'

The chief of police was a pleasant man, he didn't want to bother the president over such a trifling problem, and he issued me with a *carte blanche* visa to stay in the Transkei for as long as I liked.

From the Great Place, I headed straight for the sea. The weather had turned boiling hot. As we neared the coast, the sea breeze blew gently, Xoza sniffed the air and quickened his steps.

All the images and emotions inspired by the name 'Wild Coast' are appropriate. Though I'd thought that I would never see any-where more beautiful than the Drakensberg, the Wild Coast left me stunned. The mountains tumbled down into the ocean; some-times forest sprawled profusely to the beach's edge, forest so ancient that I saw trees which had petrified and turned to stone. The land was open, grassy, and on the slopes grew aloes in shapes like tall, branched candlesticks tipped by flames of orange flowers. Cliff-sided headlands fell sheer into rocky violent seas, there were caves, blowholes, isolated solitary spires of rock, eroded archways, and tunnels where the rising tides created thunderous booming sounds like cannonshots. Between the headlands were short, sandy bays, each one with a river estuary, so that to go along the coast we had to go up over the top of the headlands, then steeply down to the bays, and swim the rivers at their mouths. It was futile to go upriver, because nearly all had vast inland lagoons, while the mouths were narrow, and if we waited for low tide then often they were only waist deep. On the incoming tides they were an angry confusion of currents, and ac-cording to the South Africans they were infested with sharks. Usually we waited for low tide. By rocky headlands I gathered mussels, found oyster beds and caught so much crayfish that I never went hungry.

The coast was sparsely populated. The Xhosa tribe were not a sea-oriented people and they had retained the pastoral charac-teristics of their Zulu origin. The kraals were set back from the coast, though they herded their cattle wherever there was grass. They went far in search of new pastures, and since there were no roads along the coast the cattle also swam the river mouths.

Anyone going anywhere had to cross the rivers, and while I waited for low tide I occasionally met people who showed me the easiest or shallowest ways. A couple of rivers had rowboats, others had long sticks on either bank for the person crossing to use for feeling the sandbars and holding himself firm against the current. Some of the people I met were youngsters whose arms and faces were painted with white clay. It was customary here, as in many parts of Africa, for teenage children to be painted white and sent out into the bush to learn to fend for themselves. They roamed around for several months and the paint indicated to all who saw them that they were to be left alone, offered neither food nor shelter. Their period of isolation ended with circumcision or initiation and acceptance back into the tribe as adults. One of the girls spoke to me in a shrill, urgent voice and I guessed from her tone and gestures that she was warning me of danger. She told me that we would fall into quicksand if we continued straight on. I concentrated hard. She said that I must circle round, go up the hill, down to the left, across a river, and I would be fine from there on. It was surprising how well I could understand a foreign language when I concentrated. Everything was as she said, except that while wading the river I stepped off the sandbar and fell up to my neck in the water.

Not a day passed without swimming a river and one day we had to swim four. Each was quite a performance. To get the luggage across I put it in a large sheet of plastic, tied it into a bundle and floated it across behind us. I was always surprised that it didn't sink. While waiting for Xoza to dry off after the fourth river I saw a Xhosa man on the opposite side strip off and begin swimming the river. When he reached my shore, he came running at me, naked, with cries of lust, and his arms outstretched. It was fortunate that I was dressed and also that I'd just started trying to fold the huge sheet of plastic. As the man reached an arm's length from me, I thrust the plastic sheet into his hands and said, 'Please fold this up.' With the sheet between him and me, he had no choice but to take it and help me to fold it. Immediately that was finished I gave him some other things to fold, while I quickly saddled Xoza, then indicated that he should help me load the bags onto the horse's back. I tried to keep Xoza between us, but the man darted round and embraced me in a bearhug. He was repeating the same words over and over again and a trickle of saliva was drooling from his mouth. I tried to keep calm. He was physically far stronger than me and I sensed that if I attempted to wrestle with him he would get violent.

'Now look here,' I said firmly, then glanced over my shoulder at Xoza and changed my tone. 'Oh no, oh dear, the horse is free, quick, please pick up his rope before he runs away.'

The man looked at me, at the horse, at me again, he didn't know what to do. After a battle of minds, the man stepped back to pick up the rope. I was free. I made him help me tighten the cinch, then stand aside while I mounted and rode away.

Apart from that one strange man, the Xhosa people were wonderful to me. Everyone called me Nxosasana, as they had done throughout Zululand as well as Transkei. It wasn't a name, it was a term of respect.

January came to an end. I wasn't sure exactly when it ended and February began, so I spread my birthday out over several days. On the first morning I woke up laughing to a golden dawn that heralded a glorious day. Sledge paths led over the headlands, down rocky, forested, shady slopes to rivers, up hot hills, down to beaches where we galloped in the waves. An especially large river flowed out through a swampy valley, sandy swamp-land with flowering trees, mangrove root patterns, and red underwater moss. We wended across the swamps – knee-deep clear water, firm sand, blue herons and crested cranes stalking around, herds of antelope on the higher ground, glame lilies, the distant roar of the sea, and the splashing of Xoza's hooves. The swamp merged into the river, deep and terrifyingly swift. Xoza surprised me by his courage.

A big seal clambered ashore with us. It had been wounded on

the rocks, and though I tried to roll it down into the sea, it persisted in coming back. That was a pity, because after a while two Africans walked by, stopped, and it only took them ten minutes to cut the seal into piles of meat and blubber. If the men hadn't killed it, then the sharks would certainly have done. The men called me over and presented me with a chunk of meat which I roasted for supper. I didn't eat very much of it, because I put it aside to cool and my four-hoofed friend stole it. He was so used to sharing porridge or biscuits with me that he assumed he could eat whatever I ate.

Sunset crimson-streaked clouds as I sat watching savage waves thrashing rocks and spraying up against the cliffs. A gull was diving for fish, a hawk hung suspended over the hills, and a hyena's cackling sent chills down my spine. I hung my hammock extra high, remembering the ghastly stories I'd heard of hyena sneaking up and biting mouthfuls out of someone's head or snapping off a foot.

Earlier in the day, as I rested under a tree, my attention had been drawn by some specks like pepper dust on my arm. The odd thing was that the specks were moving, and when I stared closely at them I saw with horror that they were ticks, tiny pepper-ticks, and I was covered in them. There was little I could do about it, and anyway I still had the tick-bite fever that I'd caught in the new year. I wasn't delirious, although sometimes I was only semi-conscious, riding in a stupor. But Xoza seemed to pull me back to reality. He would stop on the crest of a headland, gaze around at the views over the rugged green hills and blue foaming ocean, prick his ears and dance along. Everything that I saw was touched by the outline of Xoza's pricked ears. It was as though I was looking at a painting filled with another's presence.

And so, at the edge of the kingdom of man, raising a small, defiant voice against the sea's roar, against the howling wind, I stood, and not alone. Xoza stood with me. Silent. Immense desolation and overpowering happiness. A single moment, leaving me bereft of all I knew.

22
Across the Kei

As we scrambled up a steep mountain, I realised that the higher I climbed, the more I could see. I saw the way that we'd come, the other ways we could have come, the problems we could have avoided or encountered. From the summit I saw the past and future spread out as the line along which we travelled. The future was wide open, every alternative route would in some way have different effects, every decision and change would alter my life. The fastest way would mean we swam the next river today instead of tomorrow, in which case we would be in line for an entirely new set of chance events.

A storm marched towards the coast, so we detoured inland to the forest and stayed overnight at the bungalow of Joseph Zibi, a Xhosa forester. By chance it was the eve of a very special occasion, the installation of a new chief, and the forester's place was a major gathering point for everyone who planned to attend. The air was full of festivity. I sat and listened to people chattering with clicking tongues. Joseph was the only one who knew any English, but he frequently lapsed into Xhosa and his sentences became a delightful muddle. Whenever I said anything, someone would jump up and shake my hand vigorously. I became rather confused. It was late, more people arrived, no one went home, no one went to bed, and finally I retired to my room. My bedroom was the central room of the bungalow, through which anyone going anywhere had to pass. It was like sleeping in a main road.

Joseph kept coming in, waking me up and saying, 'I assure you, Nxosasana, you will not be interfered with, please do not be afraid.' Every time I said thank you he thanked me back. Anyone currently passing through the room came over to see if I was awake, and so the night continued.

The following day we went en masse to the Great Place; it was a sea of mud, traffic jams of ox-sleds, dozens of horses, blanket-clad people with faces painted red or white, scores of bead coils round their necks, arms gauded with bracelets, legs laden with anklets, hubbub of voices talking, trilling, ululating, until some-one shouted for silence and the installation ceremony began. It took place in the cowfold. A leaning shelter had been constructed for the tribal elders and neighbouring chiefs, and as many as could squash themselves in besides, while everyone else crowded under bits of plastic. First came the speeches; the speakers dashed out into the rain, gabbled their speeches, but whenever one paused for breath an ox would moo mournfully from behind us. The chief asked me to make a speech, so I did. Standing in deep mud in tor-rential rain, I began:

'Sakubona. I am honoured to be here. As a subject of England and Her Royal Majesty Queen Elizabeth II, I bring greetings from my tribe. I wish they could see your beautiful country, I wish they could know how wonderful it is to be here; I am over-whelmed by your kindness and hospitality to a stranger . . .' It was a terribly prosy speech, but although few could understand English, I knew that they all could understand my praise.

All formality ceased after the ox started scratching itself against the leaning shelter which collapsed. The rest of the day was for eating, drinking and celebrating. Another ox had been roasted on a spit, there were flagons of maize beer, and soon everyone was dancing, oblivious of the rain. The party went on for three days; apparently it wasn't allowed to end until all the food and drink had been finished.

They were gregarious, sociable people, though dignified and very polite. They didn't fuss or crowd me, but they were happy to

258

teach me traditional beadwork, and before I left them each woman gave me one of her ankle bracelets of decorative beads and brass.

On a foggy day at the end of February, we left the Transkei. The terrain sloped slowly to the Great Kei River which marked the border with South Africa. The river was in flood, wide, deep and muddy. I rode upriver about a mile, so that if we were swept away in the current we should reach the opposite shore before being washed out to sea. There was a rowboat which ferried my luggage over, while I swam with Xoza and tried to keep near the boat because the men said they had seen a shark here the previous day. The current was not as strong as I had feared; we crossed safely, and so we re-entered South Africa.

It was probable that from there on the land would be farmed, fenced and full of white people, and I was pleasantly surprised to discover that it was not. The coast stretched ahead, bleak and windswept with jagged, red cliffs like blood-stained teeth. We camped beside a double river mouth and lazed there until the low tide mid-morning. The two rivers both looked as though they might be shallow enough to ford, but they were flowing very fast with floodwater, so I led Xoza to the first bank, tied one end of a long rope to him, held the other, and told him to stay there while I tested the river. As soon as I was in the main current the sandy river bed began to quiver under my feet. I sank rapidly downwards; it was quicksand. I hauled violently on the rope and Xoza backed away pulling me out of trouble. We walked a short way upriver and I tried again. This time, when I felt the sand begin to shift, I waded forwards to see if it were possible to cross the river before the sand sucked me down. Where the current was strongest, the sand gave way like a hollow vacuum. With every step I sank knee-deep in sand and the harder I pushed myself forwards the deeper I was swallowed. A bad patch sank me waist-deep with the river rushing over the top of my head. I yanked on the rope and Xoza again pulled me clear. After much trial and error, I found a crossing place where I didn't sink quite so badly and I reckoned that if Xoza were to gallop across he should be alright. He followed me in with blind faith in my judgement and when he started to sink I urged him forwards. He leapt and floundered, thrashing the water with his forefeet to free his hindlegs, and somehow he made it to the far bank.

The bank was a small island between the two rivers, and the second river was deeper but much easier to cross. We didn't wait around to dry off afterwards because the grey morning turned greyer, the clouds came down and mist engulfed us wetly, and within an hour it was raining heavily. Since the saddlebags were already soaked, there was no point in sheltering. I rode up and along the cliffs overlooking the sea, whipped by a strong wind which sent the waves below crashing in spray against the black rocks. The rain became so fierce that it was impossible to face into it, so we had to detour inland.

The day was hot and still. It was too hot for Xoza and me to be outside, so we took frequent dips in the sea. Then we puffed and panted up a cliff path which headed inland. The path joined a track which led to some stone gate posts marking the entrance to a private game reserve. We tiptoed through the gates unnoticed, hoping there were no lion or black rhino around. It was a lovely park, the track descended among red earth canyons and landslides down to the sea, there were herds of buck grazing beside the beaches, and at noon we rested on a hilltop between the sky, land and the sea. The breeze stirred. In the afternoon the breeze became a gale-force wind, head-on; we struggled along the beaches with sand blasting in our faces and eyes. I inhaled mouthfuls of sand, every step was a battle and we were soon exhausted.

That night I couldn't tell if I was burning with fever or if the heat was from my raw, sandblasted skin. The following day my eyes were blinded by the sunlight, my bones ached and a woolly fog blanketed my mind. I successfully ignored it all – we had arrived at East London. We stayed at the first farm we found, it was Glenmuir, with Chum, Fred and Pam. Fred drove me into the city and I collected my mail from *post restante*. It had been nearly three months since I had last heard from home. When we got back to Glenmuir, Chum said someone had telephoned to ask if Xoza and I had been past. It was a local call, from people called Wells. I was baffled. I knew no one in this area, and no one should have known about me. Before I could ring the number that they had left, the telephone rang again, and someone else asked if a girl on horseback had passed by. I asked him why I was wanted, he said he didn't know what it was about but that someone was looking for me. They had discovered where I stayed at Kei Mouth, then lost track of me, picked up the trail from a fisherman who had spotted us, guessed that I was aiming for East London, and threw a metaphorical net out over the area to catch me.

The mystery was solved when I telephoned the Wells. Robin Wells said he was a distant cousin of mine, with a farm near East London, and that my parents had received no letters from me since December, so they had traced Robin and asked him to inquire around for news of my whereabouts.

The Wells drove over in a small truck, collected Xoza and me, and took us to their farm. At the farm, Robin had built a stone fort; he considered this to be the Ciskei border, and as such it must have a fort. Outside the farmhouse stood three flagpoles (which had accompanied the Wells wherever they moved). At sunset the bugle was blown and we stood to attention while the flag was lowered. The notes of the bugle echoed over the hills and blended with the wind sighing in the trees. I was asked to choose the flag for the next day; I chose the skull and crossbones.

I stayed for a week with the Wells. Their farm was old and rustic. Robin's hobby was collecting and renovating horse and ox-drawn carts, carriages, gigs, waggons, and he had a fully equipped forge for remaking wheels and framework. He made

261

great wheels and it was a shame he didn't know how to make horseshoes. I filled my time by cleaning Xoza, and groomed him daily. He glowed with health and I remembered that, when I had bought him from the slaughter yard, the skin of his non-existent chest had lain in empty folds between his front legs. I found a blacksmith to re-shoe him, clipped and greased his ears against ticks, bathed him in cattle dip (as I had done at every farm since it was the only effective way of killing the ticks).

I bitterly resented what the ticks had done to me, the fever had taken hold of me again and I guessed it was either a relapse or a fresh bite. I was very sick and very tired. If Robin and Cynthia had known how ill I was, they wouldn't have let me go, but after a week, when I said I was better, I continued on my way. It was easy to know the way, I had only to follow the coast, I thought. But I remember nothing of the journey over the next hundred miles.

After Port Alfred I woke up again feeling free. Long, deserted beaches ran straight to faraway headlands; the beaches were backed by gigantic sand-dunes in parallel ridges which isolated the coast from the interior. It was bare and desolately wild; we galloped, keeping pace with the wind which blew strongly from behind us, pushing us along. The sand was whistling, roaring and billowing from the dunes like smoke from a bushfire. I saw shipwrecks, rocks, and a constantly changing variety of shells.

The sea grew colder every day that we moved south. Across the ocean lay Antarctica. Though the water was cold, the land was hot; it was summer in South Africa, the heat of the day did not begin to cool until late afternoon, and being so far south the daylight lasted late into the evening. I changed the pattern of our days, riding from dawn to mid-morning, then letting Xoza rest and graze for six hours until 5 p.m. and riding again during the cool, the sunset, the twilight and stopping as the stars came out at 8 or 9 p.m. I loved the evening rides; heading west we faced the sunsets. The waves surging up the sand were tipped with fire and as they receded they left crimson scallops of wet sand. Crabs came out to feed at the turning of the tide, flocks of gulls and sandpipers took to the sky as we came close.

High in the mountainous sand-dunes was a new lunar world, utterly beautiful; a strange, hazy fog encircled us from the storms, lightning flashed in the purple navy-blue bruised sky; ahead of us was a small patch of sunny blue, and the sunset through the hole was silver. I felt happy. Down on the beaches we galloped at the water's edge, the tide was coming in, when I looked back I saw the waves sweeping over Xoza's tracks, washing them away, leaving no trace that we had passed by.

At the point of one headland there was a stone cross; the original had been put there by Bartholomew Diaz. It marked the limit of his epic voyage in 1450, where he had turned back and set sail for home. It seemed strange for me to be coming from beyond his great journey. From here the coast I saw was the same as he had seen, unaltered.

The beach ended and tall cliffs of sand fell sheer into the rocky sea. We detoured inland into the dunes. It was a magnificent day, sand-dunes stretched to every horizon and occasionally, between their peaks, I caught a glimpse of the ocean. I was a bit concerned because the chances of finding fresh water and grazing for Xoza in this lunar world were one in a million, and it had been wonderful luck that the previous evening there had been a spring in a grove of trees right on the beach. At noon the dunes still stretched in choppy, barren endlessness and the sun burned down.

We climbed the highest peak and there in the desert below was a splash of green and the glint of water. Early evening our day finished where forest took over from the dunes. In the morning I needed a balaclava rather than a sunhat; despite the hot sun, the wind was icy, but when we got deep in the forest, the air warmed up and it was glorious. We followed an overgrown track among thick green scrubby trees crowded with roots, tangles of vines, and thorn bushes whose thorns were longer than my fingers. We cantered along tunnels of cold, dark shade and out into warm,

263

sunny patches. There were flowering creepers, orange flowers like lamps with yellow points of light at the tips, and across the track hairy spiders the size of golfballs had spun large webs.

We emerged into farmland – fat, English cattle grazing in lush pastures, whitewashed farmhouses nestled among the hills, and from my viewpoint I could see far beyond, to the sea, to the curve and a peninsula. An ugly, brown smog hung over the peninsula. As we slowly drew closer, I could make out the factory chimneys, skyscraper office blocks, outlines of a city. It was Port Elizabeth. We wandered along the coast towards it, enjoying the windswept desolation, and taking a last deep breath of fresh air before the city fumes filled our lungs. In the wind I heard the noise of cars on roads, aeroplanes, and a helicopter which disturbed the tranquillity by roaring along above the beach. It was probably looking for someone. I hid among the trees until it had passed. That evening we arrived at Swartkops, an old and charming riverside village just outside the city, and as I rode through the village streets a car stopped to ask if I needed a place to stay the night.

I stayed with the Swinnertons for two days; they were a young middle-aged couple, and it was a lovely transition back to the land of people. John was quiet and thoughtful and Betty overflowed with chat and vitality. Xoza was also enjoying good company, he was sharing a vast field with five other horses which were owned by horse-mad youngsters who each visited the field every day to ride, feed, groom and generally talk to their horses. It was obvious to me that this was the perfect home for a horse – to be among other friendly horses, people who loved them and daily riding and attention. A horse could not wish for a better life, so before I left I offered Xoza to Betty after my journey was over. The offer was not firm, but more of a thought for them to bear in mind over the next few months. From Swartkops I had to ride right across the big city of Port Elizabeth. Capetown was still five hundred miles ahead of me and anything could happen in the meantime.

23
Tsitsikama Country

On my first day in the Tsitsikama forest I found myself sitting by a path with my map and compass trying to work out where I could be. It was noon and very humid. Everyone had said it was impossible for me to go through the forest – it was a massive deep indigenous forest along the coast of the Garden Route, the oldest forest in South Africa. Naturally, I had decided to ride through and see for myself. Crossing the forest was proving difficult because the mountain ridges ran in straight arms at right-angles to the coast. Paths were almost non-existent. They were often only animal trails going nowhere, they went sharply up and down, and were totally overgrown. I had to unload Xoza in order to pass between closely packed trees, and when the path went where we could not possibly go, we turned back. Many of the mountainsides dropped almost vertically. To look down was terrifying and I couldn't think how the forest clung on. Tsitsikama meant 'water country', rivers raged in the ravines, waterfalls were everywhere, the water was coloured reddish-amber by ancient vegetable dye in the soil. It wasn't murky, it was sparkling and pure. The sun on the water reminded me of a glass of brandy held up to the firelight.

Over the next few days I learnt other reasons why the forest was impenetrable. It was astonishing how easily I could be thwarted. Just one fallen tree too high to jump, too low to duck, too dense or boggy to go round was an impassable barrier to us. I hated to go back the same way we'd come and be forced to follow the main road, so I pursued every single side-turning. After many frustrated attempts I found the old road which was quite pleasant. It took us via forestry sites and sawmills, where I met wonderfully kind people, but it was still too close to normality. I persevered with a near-fanatical determination to find ways into the remotest regions of the forest, fighting our way along paths which must once have been used, and in terms of going east to west I doubted we were moving very far. Our route zigzagged and looped in all directions, but at least we were now properly in the forest. When the trail was intersected by a well-worn footpath, I thought I must have been mistaken. Freshly broken twigs proved its recent use and I wasn't surprised to hear voices.

I rode into a clearing. There were some rough huts and a woodfire with spiralling smoke. The voices stopped, everyone froze. I smiled at the nearest group of people; it seemed like several minutes passed before they smiled back. The place appeared native, but the people weren't black, nothing looked quite right. As I sat with them and drank some tea I tried to figure it out. Unfortunately, no one spoke English, but it didn't sound like Afrikaans either. They didn't have the features of either black or white people, their faces were almost mongoloid. There were four men, six women, and one child. They all stared at me expectantly, so I spread out my map to ask them where we were. The map meant nothing to them, nor did any of the places I mentioned except that they repeated each word slowly after me and, when I offered them some boiled sweets, they didn't know what to do with them. I took a sweet and demonstrated, they copied me, only they didn't unwrap them first. Never mind!

More men came into the clearing, which produced much jabbering and more tea, then they showed me into a hut which I presumed was being offered to me. It was still early in the day, but I was happy to stay with these people. I left the next morning; I think they wanted me to stay longer, their gestures seemed to be saying that I should live there permanently. They were morose,

unattractive, uncommunicative folk. I hadn't understood who
they were or what they were doing there, the only thing I learnt
about them was that one of the men was so accurate with an axe
that he could split a match down the middle. It wasn't until much
later that, when I was telling this to a forester, he exclaimed that
I had met the woodcutters. He described them as a tribe descended from the Hottentots and early Dutch settlers, who lived
closed off by the forest. They interbred only within their small
number, and their genetic strain had grown so weak that now
they were nearly extinct.

Riding west towards Knysna I saw giant yellow-wood trees
festooned with grey-green beards of moss towering above the
dense primeval forest. Thick branches linked and tangled overhead, sunlight dappled our narrow, grassy path, Xoza cantered
effortlessly, and I allowed my mind to wander. Suddenly I saw
that the dark, shady patch three paces ahead was full of tusks –
long, pale tusks – belonging to monstrous cross-eyed elephants.

Emergency stop; I hauled on the reins, Xoza stopped dead,
spun round on a sixpence, and we galloped back down the path.
Elephants dislike horses, and since the Knysna elephants were
reputed to be among the largest in the world, I had no wish to
argue with them. The next morning we again met a herd of
elephants. They were browsing in a thicket, sending branches
crashing aside, and they made so much noise that they didn't
notice us creep past.

When we reached Knysna we had finished crossing Tsitsikama country. It gave me a great feeling to emerge between the
trees, to have found ways through the forests which everyone
had said was impossible. Very difficult, yes, but not impossible.
It was funny how people labelled things as impossible when
they'd never tried them and weren't qualified to judge. The majority of South Africans were afraid to walk in the grass because of snakes, afraid to swim in the sea because of sharks,
and afraid to wander the country because of black people. I had
been staggered by the massive amount of mis-information given

to me, like residents who said, 'I know this coast like the back of my hand,' but they didn't know how many rivers we'd have to cross, and they didn't mention the marshes; like seaside hoteliers who didn't know the tides, and who had never once swum in the sea since they'd lived there; like farmers who didn't know their land. Yet they all gave me advice. So many times I had been told it was impossible to ride where I wanted, but we had always found a way.

Impossible was also relative to the prevailing conditions and circumstances. A river that was impossible to swim during the rainy season could be crossed in drier months. A great deal was due to Xoza's courage and to the people who helped us. Without the aid of the men who rescued Xoza from the bog, Xoza would have been drowned; without the cattle rustlers I would never have ridden up into Lesotho; without the help of the Xhosa girls we would have fallen in quicksand; the list was endless of the people who helped and showed kindness, who made our journey possible.

A sandy track led inland, so we followed it. Late one afternoon we branched off down a farm lane. We were going fast, the drumming of Xoza's hooves merged with the chirring of crickets and the singing of birds which thronged in the trees. My little horse from the slaughter yard had covered 3000 miles in seven months, and the big tree at the end of the lane was our finishing post. Xoza was galloping, flying along. Cheering rang from the hedgerows, the evening threw streamers of sunlight between the clouds, and with a last valiant burst of speed we passed the post. Our journey together was over.

Part Three

East Africa

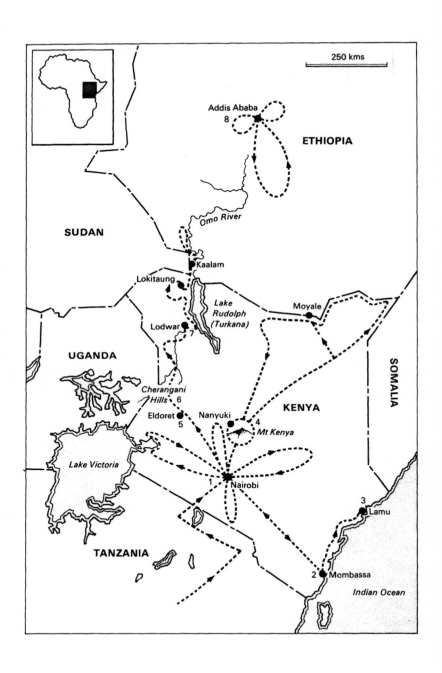

250 kms

Addis Ababa
8

ETHIOPIA

SUDAN

Omo River

Kaalam

Lokitaung

Lake
Rudolph
(Turkana)

Moyale

Lodwar

UGANDA

SOMALIA

Cherangani
Hills 6

KENYA

Eldoret 5

Nanyuki

4

Mt Kenya

Lake Victoria

1 Nairobi

3
Lamu

TANZANIA

2 Mombassa

Indian Ocean

24
Hunting for Horses

September 1977 drew to an end. My month in Kenya had already been two months long. I had arrived there in August and once again I was on my own. I had left Xoza in South Africa, at Swartkops near Port Elizabeth, in the care of the Swinnertons. He deserved the best home that a horse could have.

From Capetown I could have gone anywhere, but in fact I made my way north, through South-West Africa (Namibia), Botswana, Zambia, Malawi, and Tanzania, into Kenya. From there I intended to hitch-hike across the middle of the continent back to West Africa and up the western Sahara by camel. I had a sneaking suspicion that the journey would take two years. But now a letter from my parents told me that my brother was planning to get married in seven months' time. I wrote to congratulate him and to say I would be home in time for the wedding. Then I dug out my maps and wondered how on earth I could get there in such a short time.

Travel couldn't fight time. My journeys were not made for the sake of getting somewhere else. Destination was irrelevant. Pure travel is like dancing. It means moving in time with the land and the sky, being part of the music. That was why I decided not to re-cross Africa. I hadn't finished being in east Africa – here was the Rift Valley, the cradle of mankind.

I contemplated this as I sat on the verandah watching Chrissy trying to give a riding lesson to a group of three-year-old children mounted on Thelwell ponies. I was spending the weekend with Chrissy and her husband John in Karen, the outermost suburb of Nairobi, a very exclusive area of big houses all with many servants, where no garden was smaller than five acres and the horse population per capita was the largest in the world. We had met at a meet, the sort with foxhounds, cherry brandy, and English people in bowler hats, jodhpurs, gloves, and hunting jackets with carnations in their buttonholes. The hunt was following the scent of a drag and it led us at a gallop through the woods and out onto the rift escarpment of high rolling plains covered in tall dry grass that hissed and crackled as we thundered along. At the first check a group of Masai tribesmen with long braided hair, wearing nothing but pink faded blankets, gathered to stare in amazement, incongruous among the hunting horns and cries of 'tally-ho'.

I spent much of the weekend on horseback, riding out alone in the forest. The horse was a big, power-packed beast – it could have galloped a hundred miles – and in no time at all we were beyond the forest and out on the escarpment. I reined him in. The view of the Rift Valley and being on horseback combined into an idea. If I were to ride north from Nairobi up the Rift Valley, over the 10 000 feet Cherangani mountains and down into the deserts of the Northern Frontier District, then to Lake Turkana (Rudolph), I would reach Ethiopia. I could continue riding north across Ethiopia, down the Blue Nile into Sudan, and when we reached Khartoum the horses could go by boat to Cairo, while I sailed downriver through Egypt in a local reed craft. The whole idea tumbled out in a swift rush. I doubted it would happen like that, but it felt great to have a plan. Ideally I should not go alone – I needed to find a girl to come with me, two riding horses, and a packhorse. We would have to carry enough water and supplies to get us across the desert.

That same afternoon I located the first potential horse – a half-Somali mare, tough and sturdy, and also very wild. As soon as the saddle was girthed she went berserk, lunged backwards and flung herself to the ground. Then she collapsed and closed her eyes. I was afraid she had died, but the stable boy said she was only pretending. However, she refused to get up again and nothing we did would make her budge. Finally, we replaced the bridle with a halter and when we removed the saddle the horse rolled over, nibbled some grass, and stood up. By shaking a bucket of horse cubes in front of her nose we persuaded her to move, and after a few circuits of the garden I mounted her very cautiously. I was waiting every moment for her to plunge backwards and collapse. The stable boy rattled the bucket and she walked forwards. We judged the afternoon to have been a success.

In the evening I met an American girl called Toni who said she loved my idea of riding north. We immediately agreed to make the trip together. She was a primatologist and had spent the last five years in Kenya working for the national museum doing research into the behaviour of monkeys and baboons. She had now left her job and was planning to head back to America. She was pretty and looked younger than her thirty years. Her personality was strong, her opinions firmly decided and she was well informed. Although I knew that in many ways we were vastly different, I liked Toni and I thought we could get along exceptionally well together. The only problem was that she didn't know how to ride.

The next day I heard about another pony. This one was a full-blooded Somali pony and had earned himself the reputation of being a bucking bronco. He was running wild on a farm forty miles from Nairobi. Chrissy drove me there straight away. Apart from his wildness, the pony was perfect for our safari. He was small, but compact, sturdy and strong. His coat was fiery chestnut and crinkled in strange wavy lines which made him look striped. His mane stood up straight like a comb, his head was large and solid with a roman nose. He was in good condition and fat, despite the sparse dry season's lack of grazing. He had been born and raised in the Somali desert – he would know how to survive and look after himself.

It took me three days to lead him to Nairobi. Everything startled him. He kept stopping dead, snorting, stamping, walking one pace, then stopping again. By the time I reached Chrissy's house I was exhausted.

Over the next week I spent an hour a day riding the collapsible mare, which made little or no progress towards becoming a civilized horse, and several hours a day with my Somali bronco which I had named Zen. I started with him from the beginning breaking him in again. He objected to everything I tried to do. He disliked being groomed, tried to kick anyone who went near his hindquarters, and when I saddled him he bucked like a maniac before I'd even attempted to get on. In between times I went to see a third horse at a ranch a hundred miles north of Nairobi. It turned out to be a reject polo pony and though I rather distrusted thoroughbreds as not being tough and hardy like common horses, it was at least rideable. One disadvantage was that it was shod – we wouldn't find a blacksmith anywhere on this journey. Normally in Africa horses are not shod. Their feet grow as hard as the terrain in which they live, and the rockier the land the tougher their feet. Horses from a soft stable life have to wear shoes and if they go barefoot, they easily go lame. I returned to Nairobi to arrange transport for the horse, but after two days the owner rang me. He had changed his mind about giving me the pony for nothing and now wanted £150. I had to look elsewhere.

Nothing seemed to be working out right. One by one my lucky chances faded. I arrived to see one horse just after it had been shot dead, another was killed by a lion, others went lame or sick, and finally the collapsible mare had to be discounted because she fell ill.

It was then that I was offered the zebroid. A zebroid is a curious freak of nature, a cross between a horse and a zebra. It looks like a strange stripey mule. At that time there were only about ten of them in the whole of Africa, or in the world for that matter. I loved the idea of owning one and accepted without hesitation. The price was not high because the zebroid was wild, untrained and violent. Amber, the zebroid's owner, lived near Nanyuki at the foot of Mount Kenya and I set about finding a lorry to transport the animal from there to Nairobi.

Everything seemed to be moving so terribly fast I could hardly keep up. Toni was ill with mumps so I dashed madly around trying to get things organised, made lists which I lost on the way to town, and seemed to go more in circles than in a straight line. Friends offered advice on the proposed journey – warnings not to let the horses drink from pools of water, we would have to dig holes a few yards from the pools so that the crocodiles wouldn't attack; more dire warnings of hostile tribes near Lake Turkana whose customs included the castration of all strangers who crosssed their lands, other tribes who cut off women's breasts to make into tobacco pouches, and yet others who ran around naked with machine guns. When we entered Ethiopia we would be in bandit country, ambush and robbery could be expected, much of the country had never been mapped, three wars were raging there – one against the Eritreans, one against the Somalis, and civil war in Ethiopia itself between the imperialists and the Cuban-backed revolutionaries. None of this changed my plans. If we kept to the western side of Ethiopia and left via the Blue Nile we shouldn't have to cross either the Eritrean or Somali war zones.

I went to see if Toni was feeling better – she looked moronically swollen. She too had received warnings, ranging from lions to snakes and hunting spiders. We discussed each one in turn. Many were nonsense; for example, lions very seldom eat people. Only man-eaters will kill humans for food and man-eaters are rare. We decided to sleep in mosquito nets because we didn't think lions would attack them. However, a lion's favourite food is horse meat. We didn't have much idea how to overcome that threat.

Our main concern for the horses was to provide food for them as we crossed the Northern Frontier District. I bought three 150 lb sacks of horse cubes and hitch-hiked with two of them to the flying doctor service which agreed to drop them somewhere in the N F D and let us know where later on. The third sack I took to the office of a charter airline which occasionally flew supplies to Lodwar.

I enjoyed yet hated all the planning and preparation for the trip. It drove me mad with frustration. I just wanted to go, but I was rooted until everything was ready and everything was still not done. I had still not managed to move the zebroid to Nairobi, let alone make the tack and packs and tame the animals to carry them, and we still needed another horse.

No ranchers had any to spare, but they all mentioned some bands of wild horses which roamed freely over their ranches. I was welcome to take any that I could catch. When I discovered that each ranch was 50 000 to 100 000 miles square, I realised that it could be a long search to find the wild horses. Matters were further complicated by the short rainy season. Black cotton soil combined with heavy rain had produced a surface so slippery that not even a Landrover could cross it. I would have to go on foot. I hiked to an army base camp from which flights were made over the area. Perhaps the soldiers could locate the horses for me. They were tremendously helpful, the horses were pinpointed and I set off on foot to have a closer look. Eventually I arrived at a ranch house. It wasn't the one I'd set out for and, as no one spoke English, I couldn't discover where I was. Not that it really mattered because my Swahili was just adequate to understand that there was another band of wild horses not very far away.

With the help of some farm hands the horses were rounded up and we chased them into a corral. I picked out a lovely little mare, the finest of the bunch, strong, fat, young, and surprisingly docile. Perhaps she was too frightened to object but she offered no resistance to being haltered. We travelled back to Nairobi together in a potato lorry. The driver moved some of the potato sacks to make enough space for the horse to stand and I lay on top of the load level with the mare's head. She kept sniffing me and looking for my hand to stroke her. The truck dropped us at Karen polo club and I rode her through the forest the few miles from the club to the paddock in Toni's garden. It was wonderful to have caught and ridden a horse from the wild.

The following day I set off to collect the zebroid. The potato lorry man had agreed to make room for him. The zebroid had been rounded up and tied in a cattle-branding machine which was the only place strong enough to hold him. He had been starved for two days to weaken him, but he certainly didn't look weak. He was a magnificent beast, the height of a horse, but twice as thick and muscled. He was a monster-mule, startling in appearance — pale chestnut with his dark brown zebra stripes well defined.

Amber, the zebroid's owner, came up to speak to me. We had so far been on friendly terms but this time she was not pleasant. She said she had changed her mind, she now wanted £100 for the zebroid. Our previous agreement had only been verbal. If I wanted the zebroid I had no choice but to agree to the new price. I wanted the zebroid. She then tried to tell me I couldn't take him away until I had paid the full amount, but after some argument she agreed to let me move him.

The local vet had given the zebroid three times the recommended dosage of tranquilliser before we loaded him into the lorry, but it hadn't had any effect at all. When we tried to load him he kept bolting off. It took four hours to get him into the lorry and he nearly kicked it to pieces. He lashed out wildly if anyone even peeped in the back, so I travelled in the cab. We finally set off for Nairobi at 3 a.m. When we arrived at Karen polo club I managed to hobble him. He leapt plunging off the lorry but the hobbles held firm and by trying his neckrope to a stout tree, I managed to immobilise him for the time being.

The only way to control him was to lead him along in a group of horses, attaching him to one of them by a neck rope. I phoned Toni and asked her to bring a friend with some horses so that we could herd him along. As soon as the horses got near the zebroid they stopped. The zebroid brayed a loud hee-haw and the horses bolted away in terror. So next Toni and I enlisted the aid of four stable boys. We tied six long ropes round the zebroid's neck, then I released the hobbles. The zebroid charged off down the muddy track, towing all of us like a speedboat pulling waterskiers. We zoomed along, making furrows in the mud with our heels. Two of the stable boys fell over, the third let go, the fourth also fell over but held on to the rope and travelled for some distance on his stomach. Toni and I were still upright. The zebroid slowed down to thread between some trees and I quickly wrapped my rope round a tree. He had to stop. We waited for the boys to catch up, then, making ourselves into a solid wall, we walked along in front of the zebroid while he followed. The path grew more and more narrow until we were tightly bunched. The zebroid suddenly ran at us and those who didn't dive for cover were knocked flying. Toni landed in a stream, I was flat on my face in the mud, and the zebroid was gone.

We caught him; we re-caught him every time he escaped. Soon we were all unrecognisably dirty, but we had begun to get the upper hand. It was several hours before we emerged from the forest. The last half mile was on the road and, with one person ahead and one behind stopping all the traffic, we made it safely to Toni's garden paddock. Before letting the zebroid loose we attached a large label saying: 'If lost or found please telephone . . .'.

With a sigh of relief I asked Toni where the little mare was.

'She's dead,' Toni replied quietly. 'I put her in the stable last night and when I went to see her this morning she was lying dead on the floor.'

It was a terrible and tragic shock. We called the vet but he could find no cause or reason for her death. It was probably tick fever, or else a heart attack from fear. She had been so good and gentle; we were shattered with grief.

I returned to the slopes of Mount Kenya to search for yet another horse. Time was running out; if we didn't set off on safari within the next week then it would be too late for us to cross the desert on horseback. I assumed that somehow we'd be able to carry enough water to last the horses between the very rare waterholes, but I had no idea how much water a horse needed to drink a day. The heavy rainfall was a stroke of good fortune. It had been falling with unprecedented fury in the north. Waterholes would be plentiful and for the first time for many years the deserts would be grassy green. However, the rainy season was nearly over and we had to hurry to set out and across before all the water dried up.

Mount Kenya disappeared in black clouds and torrential rivers came flooding down the valleys. I turned and looked north, over endless ranges of hills dipping slowly towards the lowlands. Never had I seen such master-pieces of cloud and storms, sun and blue sky. In one stupendous view I could see five storms happening at the same time in different places.

I asked everyone I met if they knew of any horses for sale, and went on some wild goosechases. Within three days I found a good horse. He was a ranch horse, a fine looking dun. His one drawback was that he reared whenever anyone got on his back. The potato truck driver agreed to make space once more and arranged to collect him on 30 November. We had four days to finish our preparations.

While I had been away Toni had found a transport company which, in return for front page photographs of our departure, had agreed to transport the horses and zebroid to Nakuru, seventy miles north of Nairobi. This would mean that we could catch up with the rains. In any case, our animals were far too wild to ride along roads in the Nairobi district. We needed to be on dirt tracks where the chaos and disasters wouldn't be so dangerous.

We gave Zen some training sessions. I tried to teach him stop and go commands on a lunging rein. It was remarkably successful considering I'd never lunged a horse before and we only used a long rope tied to his halter. Then I saddled him and while someone held his head, I practised getting on and off his back. He didn't like it at all and immediately started bucking. However, on the second attempt he didn't buck, he was just too nervous to move.

We decided that it was time for him to meet the zebroid, so we moved him to the paddock. The zebroid adored Zen at first sight and Zen seemed to like him. With Zen there the zebroid grew tamer every day. He would take food from our hands and when we led Zen around he followed. He had the makings of an excellent packhorse.

I hurtled back up to Nanyuki to collect the dun but the potato truck was too full. The driver promised space on the next trip. Back in Nairobi I found that the transport offer to Nakuru had been rescinded, the camera we wanted had been sold, and every single arrangement had fallen through. We found another transport company and another camera. Time was critical. Toni went to Nanyuki to fetch the dun, there was space on the truck, but he escaped while they were trying to load him. Ten miles later he was recaptured and they tried again. He ran away so many times that he earned himself the name 'Toroka', the Swahili word for runaway. Finally they succeeded in loading him onto the truck.

The evening before our departure Zen and the zebroid ran away. We met them galloping down the main road. We chased them into a quiet road but it took hours to recapture them because they kept stampeding off round people's gardens. Then at dusk, as I led them back down a lane towards their paddock, a car came along. I waved at it to pass slowly, but the driver thought it would be more amusing to accelerate straight at us hooting and flashing his lights. The animals bolted in the wrong direction. It was late in the evening before they were reinstalled in their paddock and the fence securely mended. Toni and I did the last-minute packing. Everything was ready and the lorry due in the morning. I prayed that our troubles were at an end.

At 8 a.m. the next morning everyone came to say goodbye. The lorry arrived on time, the photographers were there, but Toni and I were gone. We were out hunting for the zebroid which had vanished again during the night. Zen was still in the paddock, the fence was intact, but no zebroid. To our complete astonishment we learnt that he had been removed by Amber, his previous owner. While Toni went to placate the transport company and arrange for the lorry again on the following day, I went to town in search of Amber. I found her in her solicitor's office. The minor disagreement at our previous meeting left me totally unprepared for the vehemence of her attack. She clawed, she scratched, she screamed obscenities. Her solicitor had to intervene to rescue me. Dishevelled and shaken, I listened in disbelief – the zebroid was not for sale, it never had been, and she refused to give me my money back.

25
Following the Rift Valley

The lorry was late. I thought it wasn't coming, but it eventually arrived and everything went as planned. We disembarked at Eldoret. I couldn't believe that our safari had actually begun; I doubted I would ever believe it, not during and not afterwards. I wondered what would happen to us. I wasn't happy about the way things had been going. An undismissible feeling of foreboding lurked constantly at the back of my mind. Instead of a wonderful sense of freedom, I felt as though we were heading for a terrible disaster.

In Eldoret we replaced the zebroid with a pack pony. She looked rather like a hippo, having been deformed due to tick-bite fever in her youth. She had a bad temper and tried to bite anyone within reach.

When we set out both Toni and I were on foot leading our three horses, but after two miles we decided that we ought to try riding them. If we didn't make the attempt now, we would keep putting it off, and we might as well find out how the horses were going to react. The gentlest of the three was the big dun, Toroka, which was supposed to be unrideable because he reared. As Toni had only had time for one riding lesson before we left Nairobi, I had made Toroka a bridle with a snaffle bit and we had bought a second-hand saddle with stirrups. I held Toroka's head while Toni struggled to climb on his back – the saddlebags made it difficult for her to mount. Toroka sidestepped. I wedged myself against his right shoulder making it impossible for him to step forwards or to the right, so he stepped to the left, landing his full weight on Toni's foot. In the end she got aboard, however, and all was well.

That left me with my bucking bronco and the pack pony. Both wore bitless rope halters, and Zen had an old carpet-type saddle with stirrups. He had never been mounted without either blinkers or someone holding his head to block his view of the aspiring rider. I was very apprehensive. I led him alongside a sloping bank, pretended to adjust his saddlebags, and swung quickly on to his back. He stood stock still, stunned. I sat equally still and stunned, then commanded, 'Walk on,' and tugged at the pack pony's rope. 'Walk-on,' I insisted firmly, and together they walked forwards along the road. They behaved perfectly all day. In the evening when we camped we hobbled the horses which didn't seem to worry them either.

As we sat drinking our coffee by the dying fire we watched the new moon rising into the velvet black sky. The night was cold. I slung my hammock over the ashes of the fire, a galeforce wind blew up, the hammock rocked merrily, and the fire's embers rekindled, keeping me very warm.

By mid-December we were 10 000 feet high in the Cherangani hills. The hills were a vast moorland plateau which formed one side of the Rift Valley. To the east was the sharp escarpment falling into the desert and to the west was Mount Elgon and Uganda. Our route was a grassy track which led along the top of the highest ridges. The views were glorious, except when the clouds came down from the sky and engulfed us wetly, but generally the days were sunny, windy and cold. It was wild and remote, and we caused great excitement when we rode through villages because no one of this region had ever seen a horse before. The children were so fascinated that they ran behind us for miles. When we asked a tribesman if vehicles ever came this way he replied, 'Yes certainly, we saw a car here, it was fifteen years ago.'

The local tribe were Kalenjen. They were friendly people, and their faces reflected the open honest sweetness of their natures. Despite the simplicity of their lives they were not backward. Many of them spoke Swahili, and the influence of missionaries was apparent in the way that they said grace before drinking each cup of spiced tea. The staple food was potatoes, and as we sat in the smoky huts, firelight illuminating smooth dark skin, knees drawn up to their chests, sitting quietly peeling potatoes, it reminded me of Van Gogh's early paintings in Holland of scenes like 'The Potato-eaters'. Cowbells tinkled outside as the cows waited to be milked and woolly merino sheep bleated impatiently waiting to be allowed into the back section of the hut where they spent the nights. Sometimes a sheep was slaughtered for us – skinning, jointing and hanging all took place in the living-room, and then we would sit in a circle round the carcass, chopping bits off to roast in the fire. Much of the talk was about the Ngorko bandits and cattle thieves who had attacked these people the previous week. We had to hope they didn't attack while we stayed because they would undoubtedly have stolen our ponies.

Our safari seemed to be going well. The ponies had become such firm friends that we didn't have to hobble them, and although Zen was still very wild he never strayed away from the others. They had all behaved perfectly, Toroka hadn't reared, Zen hadn't bucked, and the pack-pony hadn't tried to bite us. Despite Toroka's high spirits Toni was beginning to learn to control him and she hadn't once fallen off. I enjoyed riding Zen and didn't mind always having to lead the pack-pony. It was a new experience for me and I was surprised at how easy it was. The two went so well together that it was possible to trot and canter, though unless the packs were properly balanced they slipped and jolted about. The provisions inside the packs suffered from hard wear and tear. Just imagine putting your hand into a pocket and finding a warm gungy mess of tomato ketchup mixed with mealie meal and toothpaste.

Then a catastrophe – the pack pony went lame. We wrapped

her lame foot in sacking, put the luggage onto Zen, and I led both ponies at a dismally slow walk. It became obvious that she would not recover without several days of complete rest, so we rested, but each day she was no better and finally we were forced to leave her behind. We also had to leave the bulk of our provisions. We loaded as much as possible into the saddlebags of the two horses and left everything else in the care of the local chief. We hoped that after another week of rest the pony would be fit again. I volunteered to return on foot to collect her, and provided she was sound by then it wouldn't take me long to catch up with the others. If she was still not sound I would have to find her a good home.

Toni and I concentrated on being optimistic. It was lovely not to be kept to a plodding walk by a limping horse. We sang carols as we cantered gaily across sunny windswept moorland among giant heather trees, and along grassy paths studded with yellow daisies. Zen gave a couple of leaping cat-bucks, but they were only intended as muscle-stretching exercises and they didn't unseat me. It was easy to feel on top of the world. Our path led over the summit of Kelelaigelat, the highest peak of the Cheranganis, and then ran for many miles at 11 000 feet along the crest of a thin ridgeway above the surrounding hills.

As we crossed an invisible boundary from Kalenjen into Pokot territory, our exuberance was replaced by wariness. It was well known that the Pokot tribes were unfriendly to strangers. The ones with whom we stayed were no exception. They were very primitive people. They wore hides and skins, blankets, kilos of beads round their necks, and up to twelve heavy loop earrings in each ear. Their heads were half-shaven, leaving a band of hair from forehead to neck which was greased into scores of short braids and threaded with beads, buttons and cowrie shells. None of them spoke Swahili. They had closed faces and they looked at us with eyes narrowed in distrust. However, they agreed to let us stay and said the horses would be safe overnight in the central cattlefold.

We let the horses loose there and I blocked up the entrance quite sturdily with branches. When the cattle came home they walked straight through my barricade as if it was made of matchsticks. The cattle took one look at the horses, stampeded in all directions breaking down the cattlefold and vanished into the twilight. Total chaos exploded. Everyone was shouting and waving sticks. This terrified the horses, they bolted out through a gap, and set off in a panic-stricken gallop over the hills. We all gave chase. I could run fast and outstripped the others. I ran up and down five hills and through two bogs before I even paused for breath. From the top of the sixth hill I saw the horses, two hills ahead of me still galloping. I really ran. It grew dark, but the full moon had risen, and eventually I cornered and caught the horses on a cliff-sided hill. On the way back I met Toni and the Pokots, who helped us find a secure place for the horses to stay. Then they sat with us all evening until we fell asleep.

Despite their hostile attitudes, all the Pokot people we met were good to us, and when we chanced upon some Christmas season celebrations they were quite happy for us to stop and join in. The celebrations were a noisy colourful event – dancing black bodies tattooed in dot-patterned tribal scarrings, the women wearing small goatskin aprons and big beaded belts, wide bead chokers from chin to shoulder, and heavy brass earrings which jiggled so madly as they danced that they had to tie them up with string. They taught us their dance which was a series of jumps in half-beats in time to handclapping rhythm and chanting.

On Christmas Eve we came down from the mountains. We had been dreading it because we'd been told that the only route down was that of the cattle rustlers and it was so rough that cattle often died on the way. However, it was a fabulous day. We set off early morning in icy, wet, dense fog. We slid headlong down muddy banks, fell into streams, got lost in bamboo forests, crossed ravines which Toni said were impossible. Somehow or other we found a way round every obstacle. We wanted to reach somewhere special for Christmas Day, so we aimed for the Catholic mission at Ortum. Day faded into night, we picked a star and followed it, riding by the light of the full moon. At 9 p.m. we stumbled wearily into the mission just in time for the nativity play and church service. The nuns asked us in for tea. They were polite, but it was clear that we were not welcome. As a favour they allowed us to sleep in an empty school dormitory.

Christmas Day dawned. There was nowhere we could brew coffee, let alone cook any food, not that we had much because the majority had been left behind with the pack pony. The day was a non-event, and rather sad.

The problem of the pack pony and provisions had now to be tackled. I returned into the hills to try and collect them. When I finally reached the place where we had left them I saw that the huts were deserted – no people, no pony, no cattle or sheep, not a sign of life. I was baffled. Before long I heard running feet. Several warriors rushed past clutching bows and arrows. I followed them, and they led me to a mob of men sitting in a grove of heather trees. They were busily re-feathering their arrows, sharpening their six-foot spears, and preparing to fight the Ngorko cattle rustlers, who were attacking a nearby village. I didn't stay to watch the fight. I went off with two young warriors to search for the pack pony which had been hidden with the women, children and animals somewhere in the forest. Also hidden in the forest were the hideouts of the Nderoboes, the wild men, but my Swahili was too limited to understand what my guides were trying to tell me. When we found a circumcision ceremony in process, they wouldn't let me stay to watch. The pony was still lame, so I went back to see how the fighting was progressing. It was already over.

The chief drew me aside and asked what I intended to do with the pony. I sighed. I knew that her previous owners didn't want her sent back to them, she was such an ugly old hippo, but I didn't want to leave her with an African who would work her to death. No problem said the chief, he would take her himself. He wanted the prestige of owning the only horse in the region. He thought she was the finest animal he had ever seen. Everyone had admired her. No one noticed her crumpled ears and strange-shaped body; they thought that was normal. For the rest of her life she would be considered beautiful.

Taking the remainder of the luggage I rejoined Toni and the horses.

From the freezing cold heights of the Cherangani hills we descended sharply down into the blazing hot desert, where daily temperatures reached 40°C (120°F) in the shade, and the water in our canteens was nearly boiling. With canteens and jerrycans we had the capacity to carry seven gallons of water, but we couldn't use full capacity because of the weight. It was important that the total luggage was light enough for the horses to canter without strain as we had to hurry before the desert dried out and all trace of grass and water was gone. For the first lap we rode north along the base of a mountain range where we found occasional small streams. There was a time of paradise when after a long hard day in the stony thorny dry bush, we stopped beside a stream. It widened into sparkling clear rockpools with sandy shores and clumps of feather-headed reeds, grassy banks, piles of firewood which had been brought by the floods. It was a perfect place. Scarlet dragonflies hovered above the stream, at night the fireflies glittered in the grass and their reflections in the water competed with the starry night, bullfrogs sang, and there were no mosquitoes.

The Turkwell River flowed out of a magnificent gorge in the mountains. It was the largest river in north-western Kenya and it ran a winding two-hundred mile course to Lake Turkana. We planned to follow the river to the lake, and we were pleased to find that it was still flowing with plenty of water. There were crocodiles and herds of buffalo and elephant. There were also tsetse flies but this time they didn't present a problem because in Nairobi I had managed to obtain some serum to protect the horses against sleeping sickness.

Preparing to follow the Turkwell and actually following it were two different things. It was impossible to go along the banks. The river was hidden in a belt of dense palm and thorn forest several miles wide, beyond which the trees thinned out into thorny scrub bushland. When we left the gorge in the morning we didn't bother to fill the jerrycans, we felt sure we'd find a way to the river later in the day. We struck out north-east across the bush on what should have been a short cut. The bush was so thick that we kept having to detour further north, but no matter how far we went the bush didn't become any clearer. Every plant had thorns, some were poisoned, all were needle sharp. As we rode thorny branches hooked into our clothes and skin, tearing us to shreds; walking on foot was just as bad because our legs got lacerated and our clothes glued together with burrs. At midday we tried to go east to the river, but the thorn bushes became so thick that there was no possible way through, so we continued in any direction that we could, stopping often while one of us went off searching for a route. Sometimes we found game trails, but without exception they went in circles coming to dead ends in impenetrable walls of prickles. All the tributary streams were dry, and though we made it to some green trees we found only another dried-up mud pan. The horses sniffed and pawed at the dry mud. Toni and I were also thirsty. We had not yet trained ourselves to resist the urge to drink and all morning we had drunk freely from our canteens. Now they were nearly empty. We rationed ourselves to one sip every two hours. It was agony. Our fear of not finding water made us even thirstier. I would have sold my soul for a tub of cold water, I couldn't stop thinking about it.

It got later and hotter, and we got more and more lost. Our legs, arms, and faces were streaked and clotted with blood, but we had ceased caring. The only important thing was water, and for that we were desperate. There was no sign of the Turkwell which should have been right there in front of us, and we kept on forwards desperately hoping to find it. The heat built up like a furnace. There was no breeze. The land became more open, though so flat that we could get no view.

When twilight came we were going north-east; twilight faded into night, and we kept going. Stones underfoot. Stars overhead. One sip every two hours. Finally we were too exhausted to go on. We unloaded the horses and lay on the ground to wait until dawn. Oh, what terrible thirst. Neither of us could sleep. After about an hour I sat up, I thought I'd heard something like a motor. Toni suggested it might be a heavy vehicle on the road to Sudan, audible only because noise carried so clearly at night. The sound grew louder, and louder. We jumped to our feet and saw a pair of headlights coming slowly towards us. We stood poised to dash to whichever side it was going to pass. It came close, we were almost directly in its route and it was easy to flag it down. The occupants were amazed to see us, and we were amazed at the coincidence of chance that had brought them past this precise spot where we had given up. The driver told us that it was once in a blue moon he came this way. He had been out looking for Ngorko bandits, Toni and I had been very fortunate not to be attacked. Also we were within a few miles of a Catholic mission. It was scarcely credible, but it was true.

At the mission, we all drank bucketfuls of water, then the horses were put in a lush green irrigated area beside the river, while Toni and I slept in blissfully comfortable beds. The mission was empty. Apparently the sisters had left after the last bad raid. There had been a lot of tribal fighting in the district and the previous week thirty people had been killed. It seemed we were lucky to have come through West Pokot unscathed.

We had now crossed into Turkana territory. The Turkana people were much friendlier than the Pokot, but they were equally primitive. Many of the men went naked, others wore short blankets over one shoulder, they had round bone lip-plugs inserted mid-chin, and their hair was caked in mud and decorated with coloured stones and a feather or two. The women looked little different from the Pokot; their bodies were tattooed with dotted tribal markings, they wore beaded goatskin half-aprons, and enormous quantities of beads around their necks.

In the desert the nomadic Turkana built dome-shaped *manyattas* of thorn branches, an ideal hut since any breeze could blow freely through and keep them cool. Inside the *manyattas* were the nomad's possessions – just a couple of old tins, some decorated gourd pots, wooden bowls, and extra bracelets for special occasions. They lived on camel meat and camel milk. Their herds of camels browsed on the thorn trees which grew along dry river beds, and when they needed water the Turkana dug holes in the river beds. In some places water was near the surface, but other holes went over ten feet deep. Chains of women and children linked down into the holes and passed the water out by the cupful. It was the end of the rains; I looked at the deepest holes and wondered how much deeper would they have to dig in the dry season. Sometimes it took us hours to refill the jerrycans.

Our horses managed remarkably well in the desert. We had no bucket for them, but they had learnt to drink from a plastic bag. The land became rapidly more arid, and varieties of cactus flourished, while the remnants of grass were just dry white wisps. We weren't worried about the horses because we knew a sack of cubes was awaiting them in Lodwar, and meantime they scavenged enough to survive. Actually they both looked in peak condition. Their coats shone, their flanks were muscled, their stomachs were nicely rounded, and their unshod feet had grown hard as iron.

We had been travelling for about five weeks. Zen was a great deal less wild than formerly. He still stamped and snorted till his nostrils rattled, but it was only an act. He wanted us to know that he was independent. He proved it often – it was Zen that we left loose to graze, while Toroka was restless and had to be hobbled.

291

Toroka was a beautiful animal, he seemed to delight in being alive. His ears were always pricked forwards and his expressions flickered between curiosity, astonishment, and incredulity at what he saw. He was gentle, affectionate, and spirited. He moved with long strides, eager to gallop; he loved to go fast.

We were camping only about thirty miles from Lodwar. It was in the middle of the night. A terrible noise woke us up, the sound of a horse screaming, then stampeding hooves. Our camp was being attacked. I grabbed the long knife and charged towards the centre of commotion, howling my battle cry in full throat and in varying tones to sound like a mob of people. The attackers ran away. Toni, Zen, and I searched in the dark for many hours before we found Toroka. He was still alive, but his bones were showing whitely through the blood and skin where he had been slashed open, and his front legs had been severed almost in half.

Toroka — we would have done anything to save him, but his legs could never have been mended. We had to kill him. Neither Toni nor I cried, we were too sad for tears. Zen stood beside Toroka all night.

The next day we all felt shocked and miserable; we didn't see why it had happened, there was no sense in it, no reason, unless they did it for his meat. We camped that evening in a dry river-bed only fifteen miles from Lodwar, and again some 'friendly' Turkana attacked. When you're hot, tired, and want to relax, brew food, drink some precious water, the last thing you need is two savage, half-naked Turkana men threatening you, demanding goods, and jabbing sharpened sticks at you. We ignored it — they were young men, perhaps it was just a display of high spirits. They danced round and round us, stamping, yelping, laughing, and bounding in leaps, plunging their sticks into the ground within an inch of us. That made us angry. They retreated a bit, but danced more wildly, and threw volleys of stones at us. Then they closed in again, tried to grab us, got beaten off, so grabbed some of our belongings instead. Their dance went on for another hour, but the more they tried to make us frightened, the more we got angry. Finally they went away. It was too late to start cooking, it was unwise to start relaxing, so we made do with just some sips of water. Then we brought Zen into our camp and I slept beside him with my knife in my hand.

26
Camel Trouble

Lodwar was not the fertile green oasis I had imagined. It was a dry dusty little town made up of Arab-Moorish style buildings, façades of white-painted archways, verandahs, pillars, and flat-roofed houses with stonework balustrades. Most people had built palm leaf huts on their roofs since the nights were too hot for sleeping indoors. The heat was overpowering and the dreams we'd had of lying in cold baths could not be fulfilled because even the water from cold taps was scalding hot. Also the town's water pump had broken, so water was rationed. We stayed with Fred Seren, the livestock officer. Lodwar was the administrative headquarters for a vast tract of desert. One or two men from each government department were stationed there and, apart from a few missionaries, some Turkana and lots of camels, the town's inhabitants were all government staff. Zen was in prison, because it was the only fenced enclosure. He was well cared for – the official noticeboard of prisoners' duties listed: chopping fire-wood, fetching water, tending horse.

Toni and I spent most of our time looking for a camel and growing more depressed with every fruitless search. Nobody wanted to sell a camel. To the Turkana, camels were the symbol of wealth; they had no use for money, so therefore it was point-less to sell a camel. Medical attention and schooling in Lodwar were both free, the Turkanas' food was camel meat and milk, money was valueless. Even if we managed to buy one we would be faced with the problem that Turkana camels were not working beasts, they were untrained, very wild, and apparently could kick and bite viciously. So we abandoned the idea of a camel, and tried to buy two donkeys, but with equal lack of success. We found a man who said he could train a camel if we could buy one. He had trained the government camels, and they were excellent camels, any one of them would have suited us, but they weren't for sale either.

It was a period of desperate frustration. Every day brought fresh hopes which were quickly disappointed. We fell into bleak despair. All the government departments tried to cheer us up. The district vet invited us for lunch (of camel meat), the Inspector of Mechanics and the Ministry of Works came for tea, the Department of Water Development gave us dinner, and when I asked where I could take my torch to be repaired they said I must go to the Ministry of Lighting. Yes, of course, how obvious.

Everyone in town tried to help us find a camel. We were offering to pay more than the normal price, which was between 300 and 600 shillings (about £20), but the only camel we were shown was a scrawny baby one for 1500 shillings. Finally there was nowhere further we could search. We had explored every possibility, tried so hard, but failed. Not even one donkey was forthcoming. It seemed our safari was doomed. Then, when all hope was gone, we were offered a camel. A large, strong, healthy, male camel which had been trained to carry firewood. We had asked about him before and the owner had refused to sell, but now he had taken pity on us. The price was 500 shillings.

It took us one day to learn to control the camel. He only understood Turkana which is a strange language made up of staccato guttural noises and assorted grunts. The command for the camel to lie down is 'Tu tu tu' accompanied by violent hissing, to stand up is 'Ha', and to go forwards is 'Ha ha' or 'Brrr' like an alarm clock. He had never been ridden, but both Toni and I instantly went for rides on him. He was as good as gold, though not very comfortable to ride. He didn't move like a ship of the desert, unless you imagined sitting in the crow's nest during a storm. The saddle was some sacks stuffed with grass, held in place by two sets of crossed poles and ten yards of rope, all tied up in a terribly complicated way. He didn't wear a bridle, he had a neckrope with a secondary rope which looped through his mouth. It was quite alarming putting this bit between his teeth. He opened his mouth and gargled jets of foul-smelling water in his throat, but the trainer said that was normal.

Zen had never seen a camel at close range before, so I took him to meet his new travelling companion. At a hundred yards apart they saw each other. Zen stopped. His eyes went wide with horror, he stared, stamped, snorted, turned tail and fled. And the camel made off at a gallop in the opposite direction. Toni and I decided that for the first few days we would travel half a mile apart, gradually coming closer until they got used to each other. The idea was to go due east for forty miles to Lake Turkana, then north up its shoreline for about 150 miles to the Ethiopian border, and continue north across Ethiopia.

It was 1 February 1978, my birthday. It was about 2 p.m. I was sitting in the scanty shade of a thorn tree in a vast desert, wondering what to do. It had been three hours since the camel ran away and Toni ran after it. I had watched them both growing smaller in the distance, then vanishing over the sandy horizon. Now there was just emptiness.

We had stopped at a dry river bed for the long midday break, and as soon as the camel was unloaded he had broken free and raced away. I hoped that Toni would be able to find this place again. We had been using compass bearings all morning and I had the compass in my pocket. All I could do was wait. The jerrycans had enough water to last Zen and me for one more day, then we would have to set off in search of water. I took another sip from my canteen and re-angled it carefully in the sand to catch the breeze.

It's impossible to explain the heat and thirst of a desert, it would be meaningless unless you had suffered it. You intend to take only one sip of water, but you can't stop, will power and common sense are overruled while the water pours into you, hot and unrefreshing. You've got to stop, but you can't. Your hands will not obey the order to put down the canteen. When you finally succeed in stopping, then you feel guilty because you know that four sips are a luxury, a gulp is just wasteful, and besides, nothing can satisfy your thirst. The more you drink, the more you thirst. We had now taught ourselves not to drink any water before noon, but when noon came, it was difficult to curb ourselves. Toni was afraid of running out of water and dying of thirst. Fear is contagious. I had caught it from her and somehow that fear accentuated thirst and turned it into an obsession. The Turkana nomads could exist happily without water. They greased their bodies with animal fat to retain the sweat.

Still no sign of Toni. I made some alterations and repairs to the saddlebags, then went to check if Zen had finished his meal of cubes. He whinnied when he saw me coming. He felt lost without Toroka. He had regressed back to nervous wildness, and in Lodwar he had successfully escaped from the prison several times by jumping clear over the prison fence. However, he had been very easy to find because the Turkana had never seen a horse before, so when I asked if anyone had seen a strange creature like a giant donkey, they all helped me to trace him.

A dust devil whirled across the empty sands, the air shimmered with heat-haze. No Toni. The camel must have run a long way. He was obviously as alarmed at the sight of Zen as Zen was by him. We had been walking far apart, except when we needed to confer about our route, which we did by cupping our hands and hollering our conversation at the tops of our voices. The camel was so big and strong that without the mouthbit he would have been very hard to control. During the rest hours he had to be secured by tying one front leg close bent at the knee, so that he could hop around slowly to browse palm leaves and thorn branches.

There was a speck moving on the horizon. My eyes narrowed against the glare of the sun. A person, but no camel. It was Toni. I ran to meet her with some water. Her lips were white, dry and frothy, and she had to peel the skin off to open them. She drank quickly.

'I found the camel, but he ignored my commands, so I tied his feet together. I hope it'll hold him. He's about three miles away, we'll have to hurry back with more ropes.'

I saddled Zen and hoisted poor, exhausted Toni onto his back. He began trying to buck, but I held his halter and put my shoulder under his neck so he couldn't get his head down, and together the three of us sort of kangaroo-hopped forwards across the sand.

When we saw the camel we backtracked and hobbled Zen out of sight. We wanted to sneak up to the camel without alarming him. It was difficult to sneak up to a camel in open desert. From his superior height he spotted us immediately. So we played Grandmother's Footsteps, with Toni and me on different sides. When he looked at Toni I ran forwards, then froze as his gaze turned towards me, and then Toni would dash closer. It worked. We caught him and attached a new neckrope, but he wouldn't lie down to let us put the rope loop in his mouth, and we couldn't reach his head because he was about nine feet tall. We tu-tu-tued and hissed ourselves silly, but he disdainfully ignored us. So Toni climbed up on my shoulders, grasped his lower lip, and threaded the rope through his teeth while he gargled, burped, and spat revolting smells at us.

We returned to our camp, the camel lay down, and we tied up both his front legs so he couldn't stand up again. He was beside a tasty thorn bush, and after his day's excitement he should have been tired. Toni and I were too tired to eat, let alone cook supper. We just lay down and fell asleep. In the night the camel started crawling around on his elbows, snapped one leg rope, and ran away on three legs. We chased him by moonlight, but gave up when he vanished. What a way to spend a birthday.

We slept again until dawn, then resumed our search. The camel had run off to the east, but it was likely that he had circled and gone west towards Lodwar. I went back past the camp, hobbled Zen and left him to scavenge for grass, and set off to search the way we had come. The trainer had said that it was impossible for a camel to run on three legs. I reckoned that hobbles were safer – no animal could gallop in hobbles. I glanced back. There was Zen, leaping along in huge galloping bounds, heading north at top speed.

Over the next few days we went backwards as often as we went forwards. The scenery was lunar and colourless. There were strangely shaped depressions, ancient raised beaches, sweeps of gravel, and camel-thorn underfoot. We spent many hours extracting the prickles which broke off in our toes. Dust storms and howling hot winds interrupted the monotony of endless, grilling sunshine.

When water was again necessary we detoured south to the Turkwell River. It was still hidden in a dense palm forest, but there were paths and we hurried along them, spurred on by the thought of all that water. We had spent days dreaming about swimming and bathing in it. However, on arrival we found that the river had dried up.

'Never mind,' we both sighed. 'Let's start digging.'

The water was two feet below the sand. It was pure and cool and we drank it as fast as it welled into the hole. It took a long time for the camel to drink his fill. He needed water every four days, though he could be trained to last for weeks or months. Zen, being a desert pony, also didn't drink often. Once we were beside the lake, water would be less of a problem. The lake was alkaline and we had been told that if we drank it our throats would burn and we'd be ill, but apparently it wouldn't harm the animals.

The lake – Lake Turkana, Rudolph, the Jade Sea – rhapsodised and romanticised by those who had seen it. I wondered what it held in store for us and my heart felt heavy with an ominous foreboding.

The lake was so beautiful that no matter what might happen, it was worthwhile. Flat empty desert rolled right down into the water. Sometimes there were sand dunes beside the shore, and groves of palm trees – dom palms, with dark green, fan-shaped leaves and clusters of reddish, shiny nuts. Flocks of pelicans, pink flamingoes, saddlebilled storks, and sacred ibis waded in calm shallow lagoons, while tumbling white waves surged and receded along the shoreline. The colour of the lake changed according to the wind and sky, though the jade greenness was supposed to be due to algae. I saw no algae. The water was sparklingly clear and where the waves churned it glittered with gold specks of mica. Far out across the lake we could see purple volcanic islands, and dimly beyond those was the mountainous outline of the eastern shore. The sun shone from a cloudless blue sky. We walked along at the water's edge, frequently stopping to tear off our clothes and dive in for a swim. Sometimes we would just lie down in it fully dressed or merely fill our sunhats with water and tip them over our heads. The wet clothes and wet hats in the gentle breeze kept us deliciously cool. The breeze ruffled the lake and turned it a deep azure blue.

Zen seemed quite content to drink the lake water, though he snorted every time a wave splashed up his nostrils. He and the camel had come to terms with each other, though it was at first a tenuous friendship. While I was holding their ropes I watched Zen step forwards and raise his nose towards the camel's head. The camel lowered his head, their noses met, and they softly nuzzled each other. The camel taught Zen to browse on palm leaves and dom nuts. The camel's favourite food was thorn trees which he ate by wrapping his thick lips round tasty branches, and with a sweeping sideways gesture, he ran his mouth along each branch, pulling off the leaves. As for Toni and me, we lived on feasts of spaghetti bolognaise, jam pancakes, porridge, and fish from the lake which we bought from the occasional Turkana. Nile perch of 250 lb had been caught, though an average fish usually weighed about 150 lb.

After exactly one week beside the lake we came to some fresh-water springs. Luxuriant green vegetation sprouted between the dunes and the air was full of bird song. In the evenings the lake was calm as molten lead, the central island glowed with the reflection of sunset, and the sky turned pink with hundreds of flamingoes winging south. I slept on the crest of a high sand dune, spread-eagled across the surface of the world, and I gazed at other worlds thousands of light years away. Some stars fell in blazing trails of fire, the palm leaves rustled, and the waves lapped rippling up the beach.

To start each day watching the dawn and the sunrise over a silver lake, what more could one desire? It was a shame that whenever we thought life was perfect, it would be spoilt by irritating things. Irritations like the flies which besieged us crossing Ferguson's Gulf, the camel walking desperately slowly because his load was unbalanced, Zen playing up because he was bored with the camel's tedious pace, or finding the coffee spilt in the saddlebags because the food compartment hadn't been properly packed.

I lay beneath the night sky and watched the new moon rising above a horizon which flashed sporadically with far distant lightning. Today had been incredibly hot, the wind like the blast of heat when you opened an oven door. Even the lake was warm and unrefreshing. It was mid-February, the weather should not have been changing, but each day was markedly hotter than the last, oppressively hot for a desert. I could feel the stickiness in the air.

I stretched and yawned. It had been a long day. The camel had started oh-so-slowly, the load was straight but the frame poles had slid backwards, and we'd had to sit the camel down, unpack and re-pack him. It wasn't until we had finished that we realised we hadn't included the new sack of horse cubes which we'd been very lucky to find awaiting us in Ferguson's Gulf. We hoisted the sack onto Zen's back, but it slipped when he shied at some Egyptian geese, and that goaded him into a tremendous bucking fit. I held onto his rope as he bucked in circles round me. First the sack came off, then the saddlebags split down the seams. Things flew everywhere. Zen bucked more furiously and didn't stop until he had burst the girth and strewn everything across the sand. There was no shade, so we did emergency repairs in the sun. We re-saddled Zen and put the heavy sack on top of the camel. That made his load top heavy. It rocked perilously, one of the ropes broke, and we had to stop and re-pack him yet again. It took us over an hour.

Then came the midday halt, a snack and some lemon-flavoured water, and pour my grievances into my diary. Toni and I were not working well as a team. The petty difficulties we encountered every day put each of us under a strain. We interpreted each other's remarks as criticism, we never laughed, nothing was fun, nothing ever went right. We seemed caught in an ever-deepening vortex of disasters – a depressing downwards spiral of cause and effect. It was with horror that I frequently caught myself acting against the good of our safari. Maybe it was the contrast in our characters that was responsible for our ill-fated journey. In the same way as we each brought out the worst in each other, somehow the discord was influencing the turn of events. Sometimes I wished that our trip was over. I don't mean that I wanted to call a halt to it, but I wished that I was looking back on it from a point in the future, so that I could forget the bad and remember the good.

I yawned again, more sleepily. We'd had a lovely afternoon. Zen had been docile and as affectionate as a large dog and the camel had swung along speedily in time to the camel song. It wasn't actually a song, but when Toni and I were both calling, 'Hai, ha ha. Hei. Brrr, ha ha,' in varying tones and rhythms, it all blended into a chanting harmony. But then we'd detoured inland to look for fresh water under one of the dry river beds and we'd met a Turkana who told us there was a Catholic mission only five miles away. We'd arrived there hot and tired at about 6 p.m., but when we asked for a drink of water the Irish Catholic father said that we must walk another mile to the tap in the Turkana village. He had a water tank, he had taps for water in his house, he had cold bottles of water in his fridge, but he wouldn't offer any to us. We didn't argue, we went on to the village tap.

That night the lightning seemed nearer. The air was close. At dawn the sky was blanketed in cloud. The wind was dropping – it was ominously hot. How strange to be in a sunless desert. As we continued north the land was also changing. A range of stark, bare, purple mountains began to rise up in the west, and along the lakeside there were no more palm trees. It was barren and desolate.

Our disaster for that day was in the evening when I took Zen down to drink in the lake. He swallowed a wave, jumped, tangled in his rope and bolted inland. I watched him for a couple of miles, and when he was no longer visible I could see his dust trail catching the evening sunlight. It would soon be dark. There was no point in chasing him now, so I went back to Toni. We wondered if we would ever see him again. If he wanted to go off and be a free wild horse, it was his decision. But this was desert country. He wouldn't survive, I had to find him. Later, when we reached fertile green land, then he could go free. My search took me right over to the mountains. I tracked him for five hours and found him resting in the shade of some rocks. I called him, and he came to me.

27
To Ethiopia

North Island came into sight. The lake was aquamarine, the waves were rough, the sandy beach was volcanic black. Yellow spear grass covered the dusty dunes, some thorn trees marked the line of a dry river bed, a fish eagle perched on a dead tree stump, the empty vastness of open space stretched in a circular horizon. Hot day, hot wind – it blew from any direction, at any time, at any strength, with no regular habits or patterns. The clouds built up into a massive cumulus over the lake, lightning began, and it grew dark in the north. We weren't worried because the wind was blowing from the south. Suddenly and without warning the wind changed, the clouds swept round, and we were hit by a sandstorm. A sandstorm which flashed with lightning, it was an awesome combination. We cowered with our animals beside some spindly trees, the roaring wind bent the trees flat to the ground and the storm raged for hours into the night.

I awoke to find myself almost buried in sand. It was a sunny morning.

The following evening the sky again looked angry, and since we were close to another Catholic mission we decided to hurry there, to see if we might shelter, and also to ask for more water. Again we were refused water and sent some distance to a tap.

The Christianity of the Catholics extended only as far as the natives. I'd met people in Nairobi who warned me that these

Catholics were unfriendly, that they hated outsiders and tourists. One of the priests even said to me, 'We are not here to help people like you.'

In the evening as I walked from the campfire to fetch a cooking pot, I felt a sharp stab of pain in my foot. So sharp that it made me scream.

'What is it?' Toni called anxiously.

'I don't know,' I gasped, 'Probably a snake or scorpion.'

I hopped to get the torch and looked at my foot. There was a thin trickle of blood from a mark which hurt like fire. We flashed the torch where I'd been walking. A very large scorpion scuttled away from the light.

'Kill it,' I begged Toni, and I ran as fast as I could towards the mission centre. I had to get there before the poison overtook me. I knew that the Catholic fathers wouldn't come out to help me, but if I could reach the nurse's bungalow they couldn't turn me away.

The nurse laid me on a bed and sent for some antihistamine. The poison moved slowly up my leg and when it reached the glands at the top I nearly broke apart with agony. The nurse had gone back to her supper. I tried so hard to keep quiet. I clenched my teeth on the corner of a cushion and tried to think calm thoughts, even to hum snatches of tunes, but every effort ended with my body writhing in distress and my voice singing the song of pain. Slowly as the poison progressed I grew numb, paralysed. At last an injection arrived. The nurse gave it to me, then sent me away. I couldn't walk. Someone carried me to an open-sided workshop near our camp and he left me on the concrete floor between some puddles of water. Toni was there. I wanted to speak to her, but my mouth and vocal chords couldn't produce proper words. The paralysis was creeping all over me.

Within a couple of hours I was completely paralysed. My chest felt like a small, tightly clenched fist and my heart was thumping faster than if I'd run up a mountain. My saliva glands had gone mad but I couldn't swallow, my throat had closed up; I

was gasping for breath and choking on my saliva. I thought I
was going to die. My clothes were drenched in sweat, I was freezing cold, it felt like the cold of death. Paralysed, but still screaming, trying to speak, only able to grunt, I made Toni realise the
cold and the sweat. I don't know how she managed to haul my
soaked clothes off me. I was limp like a stuffed dummy but I
screamed with pain at the lightest touch of her hand. Then she
covered me with dry things and slept close up beside me to give
me warmth. It was without doubt the longest and most terrible
night of my life. Mosquitoes swarmed around my face, but I
couldn't feel my hands to brush them away. No amount of coverings made me warm, the freezing sweat poured off me. I lay
shuddering and groaning, concentrating on not choking to
death. I didn't think I would last the night through.

As the first rays of dawn paled the eastern sky I could take no
more. I screamed and screamed and screamed my lament. Toni
ran to beg the nurses for help and with great reluctance they said
I could have a bed in the infirmary. They collected me in a Landrover. They told me I was making a fuss about nothing, and
since I couldn't walk to the Landrover they took my arms and
dragged me across the stones.

For two days I lay in the infirmary unable to move. My body
was numb, but I could feel the poison coursing up and down my
limbs. Occasionally my muscles jerked because of their total
inactivity, and that always made me cry out with pain. The
nurses were using the room as a teaching room, and they told me
to shut up. I formed the words to beg for pain killers, but they
said I didn't need them, that I was just pretending to be paralysed, that if it had been a scorpion sting I should be up and
about by now. They never had a kind word or a smile, they gave
me no treatment, and had they thought about my condition they
would have realised that it was something a great deal more
serious than a scorpion sting. But they weren't interested, they
didn't care. I couldn't move, I couldn't drink or eat, my throat
was tightly closed, and in two days all I had was one cup of water.

It was Toni who held the water to my lips, who attended to my needs and looked after me in my helplessness. She was angelic. The infirmary did not cater for the sick, there was no food, no washing facilities, and not even sheets or a pillow for my bed. Toni constructed a pillow for me out of an old briefcase wrapped up in a straw mat.

The numbness passed and was replaced by the permanent jangling of pins and needles. My skin felt as though it was being rubbed with sandpaper, and my fingertips leapt with pain at whatever they touched. Touch was excruciating, and every time I winced my heart would contract and I'd feel the poison shooting up and down again. However, I was at last on the mend. I could swallow thin porridge, I could almost ignore my pains. I spent every moment trying to flex my fingers and wriggle my toes, and by the fourth day with the support of a chair I managed to stand on my feet. They felt like raw stumps of flesh on a carpet of nails, and my legs collapsed when I tried to walk. The nurses watched me fall, didn't come to help me back to bed, and later that day they discharged me from the infirmary saying that I ought to have got better by now. I was happy to leave. I was stunned by their coldness and brutality, and disgusted by the behaviour of the whole mission.

It was good to be back with Toni and the animals. She'd had her hands full looking after them. If the mission had allowed Zen to graze in the fenced playing field her task would have been halved, but Zen had had to be tethered. He had escaped a couple of times, and had grown very wild again. I began practising using crutches. It was only my injured foot which was still useless, though when I thought about it my whole body was ringing with pain. We spent the evening packing up all our gear and preparing to leave the next day, and since I could be little help to her, Toni found a young Turkana boy who agreed to come with us. It rained torrentially all night, and although it stopped by morning it meant that the rivers would be in flood, the camel refused to cross them, so we couldn't travel north along the lakeshore.

However, that didn't stop us going west, inland towards the mountains.

We loaded the animals. Zen was especially difficult because he was afraid of any type of stick and my wooden crutches terrified him. He snorted, rattling his nostrils, and wouldn't let me go near him. Before trying to get on his back I made him watch how. I limped around in distress, and when I accidentally fell over (which I did frequently), he came up and sniffed my hand. From then on he behaved beautifully. He stood firm while I struggled to climb into the saddle, he was more docile and gentle than he had ever been previously.

The Turkana boy came with us only as far as Lokitaung, a small outpost in the mountains, and we left him there because he was so frightened of sleeping out at night. We'd promised to protect him from leopards, bandits, and even kangaroos.

'But there are no kangaroos in Africa, and anyway they aren't dangerous,' we'd said.

'Yes, *ndio*, kangaroos,' he insisted, shaking with fear. He spoke good Swahili and a smattering of English, we couldn't mistake what he said. We were at a loss to know what he could be talking about. He described these kangaroos as fierce killer animals – they were the size of donkeys, black, and they hopped on three legs.

I also was afraid of an unknown creature, whatever had bitten my foot. The boy agreed that had it been a scorpion sting I would have recovered in a day – but had it been the bite of a hunting spider, that would have been many many times worse. I would have been paralysed for several days, with freezing sweat and choking saliva, I would have lain and listened to the poison coursing through my body, exactly as I had done. He described the hunting spider as having a big, hairy body and hairy legs a couple of inches long, and it struck with the speed of lightning. It sounded like the African equivalent to the tarantula.

Ten days after the bite I could walk without crutches and without pain. All that was left was the scar, and the desire not to see any Europeans for a very long time.

In Lokitaung we had a stroke of luck. We found our third sack of horse cubes. I saw it being unloaded from a lorry. If it hadn't been for those three sacks of horsefood, Zen would never have been able to make the journey across the NFD, for though he knew how to eat camel-thorn and to dig for roots, he couldn't have survived on them alone. Another piece of good fortune in Lokitaung, apart from the kindness and helpfulness of the Africans there, was that we received a message from Lodwar confirming that we would be allowed to cross the border into Ethiopia. We had done everything possible to ensure that there wouldn't be any problems. We had an official letter from the Ethiopian embassy stating that we were tourists (not spies), and asking all Ethiopians to help us pass safely through their country. Of course, we also had visas, but the embassy had made a mistake on the month of issue, so they had already expired. Still, that was easily fixed with a pen of matching coloured ink, and we reckoned the alterations were undetectable unless scrutinised.

To reach the Ethiopian border we had to go over the mountains. They were craggy, burnt, red rock, stark and old, born at the creation of the Rift Valley. It wasn't a difficult climb up – gorges with white-trunked trees growing Japanese-style from cracks in tall cliffs, valleys of a million stones led us into a world of rocks. They told stories of blazing volcanic heat, monstrous eruptions, upheavals from the earth's core, the cooling process still being visible in the rocks around us. We slowed down to a snail's pace, stopping every few yards to examine the rocks. Many of them were hollow and when we cracked them open we found they were lined with tiny crystals of quartz or amethyst and rose. The rocks themselves ranged from conglomerates embedded in each other to brittle lightweight lava, sandstone, black basalt. Almost every river bed was filled with translucent red, orange and yellow quartz pebbles. Toni didn't quite share my enthusiasm, but I noticed her collection of stones wasn't much smaller than mine. We called to each other to see and show what we'd found. We both laughed and smiled the whole time with happiness. Nothing could go wrong now.

The mountains should have been waterless, but the freak weather had given life to the springs. Cold water trickled down beautiful terraces of smoothly worn rockpools, then disappeared back underground. Occasionally we met nomadic Turkana herding their goats. We swopped tobacco for pots of fresh goat milk. The men were naked but they stored the tobacco we gave them in their lip-plugs, or in their earrings which were jars of cow-horn. When they took their earrings off, their earlobes hung down to their collarbones. As I stared in fascination they became embarrassed and looped the lobes up over the top of their ears.

The Turkana were amazed at Zen. Several times men had stopped and, standing in front of him, had sung high-pitched songs to him. It was an expression of their reverence for animals.

Our animals were certainly worthy of the highest praise. The camel had become an alpine camel and had already crossed places in the mountains which the Turkana said it was impossible for a camel to pass. The trouble was that we never knew it was impossible until too late. We found ourselves completely jammed in gulleys where the camel could go neither forwards nor backwards, or halfway up mountains that were too rugged for him to climb or descend.

'*Twende*, go on, *twende*,' we yelled. 'Ai-yah, ha ha. Giddey-up,' as he slid inexorably backwards towards seemingly certain death. In situations like that there was no choice but to make him go forwards over whatever obstacle it was that camels couldn't cross. He was good natured and always willing to try. Often Zen showed him the way. Zen was surefooted and brave – there was nothing he wouldn't face.

In the middle of the mountains we came to an area where the land to every jagged horizon was purple – red-purple cliffs, mauve-pink pebbles, violet-coloured sand, and hills with purple lava in solidified flowing tongues. It was stunning: solitary puce anthills ten feet tall and thin, like chimneys; vibrantly green vegetation glowing in the purple valleys, yellow flowers and tender young shoots of grass sprouting in response to the recent rain. Herds of hartebeest, Grant's gazelle, and steinbuck scattered at our approach, and a kalokol wildcat streaked across our path. We journeyed very few miles in a day. We didn't want the mountains to end.

'What's the hurry?' asked Toni, seeing I had started packing up our gear.

'No hurry,' I replied, and handed her the Christmas box that kind-hearted Mrs Jones in Eldoret had given us to keep for Christmas day. It was now early March. The inhospitable mission in Ortum had been too sad for a celebration so we had kept the box and waited for the right time to enjoy Christmas. We ripped open the seal and found the box was tightly packed with mince pies, a tube of cream, packets of dates, nuts and raisins.

After our feast we sat resting, snoozing, and thinking. Zen rolled vigorously in a patch of purple sand. The camel followed his example – he made a ridiculous sight. I heard an almost inaudible rumble of thunder and began putting things away in the packs.

'You *are* packing,' said Toni.

'Just sort of,' I answered, very slowly collecting the ropes. With each faint rumble my pace quickened. Toni joined me, leisurely, then faster, and suddenly it was a mad scramble. We dashed around, frantically stowing everything away, fetching the animals, saddling, loading, roping in place. Within fifteen minutes we were set to go.

We must have looked rather silly. The sun was shining, the storm was nowhere near us. It had circled round and was pouring its wrath on some mountains far behind us.

Only a short time after we'd left, the dry river bed where we had been sitting became a torrent of water, a flash flood, rolling downhill in a solid sheet. One minute you hear a roaring noise, the next you're swept away.

We waited at the Kenyan border while two soldiers went to the Ethiopian border-post to buy some chickens and to tell the guards we would be there by evening. They returned with the message that the Ethiopians didn't want to see us. They wouldn't let us cross the border, they would be watching us through binoculars, with their machine guns trained on us. Not encouraging news, but we went there anyway.

It was several miles to the actual border line, which was marked by stone cairns spaced half a mile apart. We intended to follow exactly along the line on the Kenya side, but there was a swamp in the way, so we had to go across into Ethiopia and then we got a bit lost. Luckily after a while we found another stone cairn, and finally arrived at the cairn which marked the meeting point of Kenya, Ethiopia, and Sudan. We stood on the tip of Kenya and waved white handkerchiefs at the Ethiopian police post on the hill. A soldier came down. We showed him our official letter from their embassy, and he invited us to the police post. There were a dozen soldiers there. They were all friendly and many of them spoke English. They seemed impressed with our letter. So far, so good. Passport formalities came next. The officer stared at the visas with a very puzzled expression.

'There appears to be something wrong with the dates on your visas,' he said.

My heart plummeted. Our attempt at forgery must have been discovered. We were sent outside and there was a long delay. Then one of the soldiers came out and explained the nature of the problem. The Ethiopian calendar is not the same as ours. Each month has thirty days, with a five-day space at the end of the year. Their new year begins on 12 September and their calendar is seven years behind ours. It was now only 1971. The officer's confusion was in understanding the date; our alterations had not been noticed.

After thoroughly searching our luggage they allowed us to proceed up the Omo River, accompanied by three armed soldiers. It took us two days to reach Kaalam because the Omo delta was so swampy and the camel wouldn't walk through the swamps. Mirages rippled in every direction and we kept detouring to avoid swamps that were not there.

We moved slowly across the vast flat plain. Carpets of yellow daisies covered the ground and faint blue mountains loomed on the horizon. The region was inhabited by a tribe who inserted plates into their lips, and by the Rendille, whose menfolk wore mud-castes on their heads, decorated with a long twangy stick which danced around with a pompom of feathers on the end. It was a headscratcher. When a man had an itch, he just bent the stick down and scratched with it. Troupes of young men were returning from circumcision. They carried six-foot spears and marched in formation, chanting strange aspirant, hissing songs, thrusting their chins backwards and forwards with each stamping footstep. We met some nomads moving house, their curved hut poles loaded on donkeys. They had very few possessions. They weren't poor, they simply had no use for 'things'. One of the nomads was reputed to own 20 000 cattle, 1000 camels, and umpteen goats. He was a splendid old man. He had a huge lip-plug which was full of water to drink on the journey.

I don't think we went to Kaalam. We went along the bank of the Omo River and ended up at an army headquarters where we were put under arrest. This border area had been closed for some time and no one was allowed through – a fact which the embassy hadn't known when they gave us permission to go there. It wasn't at all bad being under arrest. We weren't locked up. We camped in some trees by the river and so long as we didn't run away, we could go where we liked. The worst thing was the mosquitoes which were as bad as in the Congo. We were also warned about crocodiles which are reputed to be the longest in the world, but I only saw one. The soldiers and their wives often invited us to their huts for meals of *wat* and *njera*. *Njera* is a millet pancake two feet in diameter and *wat* is a spicy meat sauce. The dish was put in the centre of the floor, and we tore off pieces of the pancake and used them to pick up the meat. Everyone dug in until the food was finished. It is by far the most delicious staple diet in Africa and the traditional drink of *tej* (honey wine) is one of the nicest things I've tasted. Toni and I settled in very happily.

The local tribe here were Galeb people. They didn't know what to make of us. They knew we weren't Kenyan or Ethiopian, so they greeted us with '*Salaam aleikoum*,' and whispered to each other that we were Somali women. It was fortunate they didn't realise that Ethiopia was at war with Somalia.

The lieutenant of the army camp didn't believe we were tourists, he thought we were imperialist spies. Ethiopia was also in the throes of a civil war between the revolutionaries and the imperialists, though most of the imperialists had now been wiped out. Zen didn't help matters by standing on and breaking their water pipeline from the river. That was clearly sabotage.

On our arrival the lieutenant had telegraphed the revolutionary authorities in Addis Ababa to find out what to do with us, and finally, after only five days, the answer was received: 'Send them back into Kenya. They may re-enter Ethiopia at Moyale.' All our permissions, confirmations, and official letters were worthless. We couldn't go to Moyale with Zen and the camel – it was in the very middle of the war zone. We had no idea where to go. Sudan was the obvious answer, but it would mean months of travelling in perhaps waterless desert, then swamps, and more desert. We could have done it, but we didn't want to. In any case, Zen's horse cubes were finished. He couldn't go through the Sudanese desert and he couldn't go back across the NFD.

We had reached the parting of our ways. Ethiopia was a good country for a horse. The grass was green and Zen was well able to survive. His previous owners had told me that when I left him I must kill him because he would never adjust to a new master. No, he couldn't have accepted a new master, but he could be his own master from now on. I patted him for the last time, and inside myself I cried because I would have loved to stay with him in Ethiopia.

For Toni, the camel and me the safari was not quite over. We travelled back into Kenya, back into the purple mountains, and back into the desert. Between the mountains and the desert we declared the safari officially ended. I felt as though we were part of a film which had been played and was now being wound backwards. Ever since Lodwar, when people asked us where we were going and where we had come from, we had replied, 'To Ethiopia, from Lodwar.' Now when they asked we replied, 'To Lodwar, from Ethiopia.'

Our onward travelling was in search of a good home for the camel, but no one wanted to buy him. The only offer we received was in Lokitaung from the local butcher. But our camel was an exceptional camel. He deserved better than to end up as stew. Finally, in desperation, we sold him for a few shillings to a Turkana who promised him a peaceful retirement.

As for Toni and me, chance was still not on our side. We tried to hitch-hike north into Sudan, but bad luck dogged our every move. Unable to continue north, we went south, to Nairobi, and on our first night there the house where we were staying was burgled. I stood among the scattered remains of my belongings. It seemed that I was now back at the beginning, in the car park at Kano with Lesley, surrounded by our fast-diminishing pile of possessions. The film had re-wound.

Toni and I went north-west and travelled for two weeks on the Somali and Ethiopian borders. We had set our hearts on returning to Ethiopia, but the country was now closed to all foreigners. We eventually managed to obtain permission and re-entered, however, although I couldn't stay long because my brother's wedding was drawing close. Ethiopia, with horsemen in flowing robes, volcanic crater lakes in magnificently wild mountains, ancient churches hewn in sheer rock faces – it is the country to which, above all others, I long to return.

On 27 April 1978, over three years after I had left home, I flew back to England. I fell asleep on the plane and dreamt that I was in a market place, bargaining over the price of an elephant. Finally I agreed to a price of five coins, and with the elephant I set out to cross the Milky Way.

OUR CURRENT LIST OF TITLES

Abernathy, Miles, *Ride the Wind* – the amazing true story of the little Abernathy Boys, who made a series of astonishing journeys in the United States, starting in 1909 when they were aged five and nine!

Beard, John, *Saddles East* – John Beard determined as a child that he wanted to see the Wild West from the back of a horse after a visit to Cody's legendary Wild West show. Yet it was only in 1948 – more than sixty years after seeing the flamboyant American showman – that Beard and his wife Lulu finally set off to follow their dreams.

Beker, Ana, *The Courage to Ride* – Determined to out-do Tschiffely, Beker made a 17,000 mile mounted odyssey across the Americas in the late 1940s that would fix her place in the annals of equestrian travel history.

Bird, Isabella, *Among the Tibetans* – A rousing 1889 adventure, an enchanting travelogue, a forgotten peek at a mountain kingdom swept away by the waves of time.

Bird, Isabella, *On Horseback* in *Hawaii* – The Victorian explorer's first horseback journey, in which she learns to ride astride, in early 1873.

Bird, Isabella, *Journeys in Persia and Kurdistan, Volumes 1 and 2* – The intrepid Englishwoman undertakes another gruelling journey in 1890.

Bird, Isabella, *A Lady's Life in the Rocky Mountains* – The story of Isabella Bird's adventures during the winter of 1873 when she explored the magnificent unspoiled wilderness of Colorado. Truly a classic.

Bird, Isabella, *Unbeaten Tracks in Japan, Volumes One and Two* – A 600-mile solo ride through Japan undertaken by the intrepid British traveller in 1878.

Boniface, Lieutenant Jonathan, *The Cavalry Horse and his Pack* – Quite simply the most important book ever written in the English language by a military man on the subject of equestrian travel.

Bosanquet, Mary, *Saddlebags for Suitcases* – In 1939 Bosanquet set out to ride from Vancouver, Canada, to New York. Along the way she was wooed by love-struck cowboys, chased by a grizzly bear and even suspected of being a Nazi spy, scouting out Canada in preparation for a German invasion. A truly delightful book.

de Bourboulon, Catherine, *Shanghai à Moscou (French)* – the story of how a young Scottish woman and her aristocratic French husband travelled overland from Shanghai to Moscow in the late 19th Century.

Brown, Donald; *Journey from the Arctic* – A truly remarkable account of how Brown, his Danish companion and their two trusty horses attempt the impossible, to cross the silent Arctic plateaus, thread their way through the giant Swedish forests, and finally discover a passage around the treacherous Norwegian marshes.

Bruce, Clarence Dalrymple, *In the Hoofprints of Marco Polo* – The author made a dangerous journey from Srinagar to Peking in 1905, mounted on a trusty 13-hand Kashmiri pony, then wrote this wonderful book.

Burnaby, Frederick; *A Ride to Khiva* – Burnaby fills every page with a memorable cast of characters, including hard-riding Cossacks, nomadic Tartars, vodka-guzzling sleigh-drivers and a legion of peasant ruffians.

Burnaby, Frederick, *On Horseback through Asia Minor* – Armed with a rifle, a small stock of medicines, and a single faithful servant, the equestrian traveler rode through a hotbed of intrigue and high adventure in wild inhospitable country, encountering Kurds, Circassians, Armenians, and Persian pashas.

Carter, General William, *Horses, Saddles and Bridles* – This book covers a wide range of topics including basic training of the horse and care of its equipment. It also provides a fascinating look back into equestrian travel history.

Cayley, George, *Bridle Roads of Spain* – Truly one of the greatest equestrian travel accounts of the 19th Century.

Chase, J. Smeaton, *California Coast Trails* – This classic book describes the author's journey from Mexico to Oregon along the coast of California in the 1890s.

Chase, J. Smeaton, *California Desert Trails* – Famous British naturalist J. Smeaton Chase mounted up and rode into the Mojave Desert to undertake the longest equestrian study of its kind in modern history.

Clark, Leonard, *Marching Wind, The* - The panoramic story of a mounted exploration in the remote and savage heart of Asia, a place where adventure, danger, and intrigue were the daily backdrop to wild tribesman and equestrian exploits.

Cobbett, William, *Rural Rides, Volumes 1 and 2* – In the early 1820s Cobbett set out on horseback to make a series of personal tours through the English countryside. These books contain what many believe to be the best accounts of rural England ever written, and remain enduring classics.

Codman, John, *Winter Sketches from the Saddle* – This classic book was first published in 1888. It recommends riding for your health and describes the septuagenarian author's many equestrian journeys through New England during the winter of 1887 on his faithful mare, Fanny.

Cunninghame Graham, Jean, *Gaucho Laird* – A superbly readable biography of the author's famous great-uncle, Robert "Don Roberto" Cunninghame Graham.

Cunninghame Graham, Robert, *Horses of the Conquest* –The author uncovered manuscripts which had lain forgotten for centuries, and wrote this book, as he said, out of gratitude to the horses of Columbus and the Conquistadors who shaped history.

Cunninghame Graham, Robert, *Magreb-el-Acksa* – The thrilling tale of how "Don Roberto" was kidnapped in Morocco!

Cunninghame Graham, Robert, *Rodeo* – An omnibus of the finest work of the man they called "the uncrowned King of Scotland," edited by his friend Aimé Tschiffely.

Cunninghame Graham, Robert, *Tales of Horsemen* – Ten of the most beautifully-written equestrian stories ever set to paper.

Cunninghame Graham, Robert, *Vanished Arcadia* – This haunting story about the Jesuit missions in South America from 1550 to 1767 was the inspiration behind the best-selling film *The Mission*.

Daly, H.W., *Manual of Pack Transportation* – This book is the author's masterpiece. It contains a wealth of information on various pack saddles, ropes and equipment, how to secure every type of load imaginable and instructions on how to organize a pack train.

Dixie, Lady Florence, *Riding Across Patagonia* – When asked in 1879 why she wanted to travel to such an outlandish place as Patagonia, the author replied without hesitation that she was taking to the saddle in order to flee from the strict confines of polite Victorian society. This is the story of how the aristocrat successfully traded the perils of a London parlor for the wind-borne freedom of a wild Patagonian bronco.

Dodwell, Christina, *Travels with Fortune* – the truly amazing account of the courageous author's first journey – a three-year odyssey around Africa by Landrover, bus, lorry, horse, camel, and dugout canoe!

Dodwell, Christina, *A Traveller on Horseback* – Christina Dodwell rides through Eastern Turkey and Iran in the late 1980s. The Sunday

Telegraph wrote of the author's "courage and insatiable wanderlust," and in this book she demonstrates her gift for communicating her zest for adventure.

Dodwell, Christina, *Travels in Papua New Guinea* – Christina Dodwell spends two years exploring an island little known to the outside world. She travelled by foot, horse and dugout canoe among the Stone-Age tribes.

Ehlers, Otto, *Im Sattel durch die Fürstenhöfe Indiens* – In June 1890 the young German adventurer, Ehlers, lay very ill. His doctor gave him a choice: either go home to Germany or travel to Kashmir. So of course the Long Rider chose the latter. This is a thrilling yet humorous book about the author's adventures.

Farson, Negley, *Caucasian Journey* – A thrilling account of a dangerous equestrian journey made in 1929, this is an amply illustrated adventure classic.

Fox, Ernest, *Travels in Afghanistan* – The thrilling tale of a 1937 journey through the mountains, valleys, and deserts of this forbidden realm, including visits to such fabled places as the medieval city of Heart, the towering Hindu Kush mountains, and the legendary Khyber Pass.

Galton, Francis, *The Art of Travel* – Originally published in 1855, this book became an instant classic and was used by a host of now-famous explorers, including Sir Richard Francis Burton of Mecca fame. Readers can learn how to ride horses, handle elephants, avoid cobras, pull teeth, find water in a desert, and construct a sleeping bag out of fur.

Glazier, Willard, *Ocean to Ocean on Horseback* – This book about the author's journey from New York to the Pacific in 1875 contains every kind of mounted adventure imaginable. Amply illustrated with pen and ink drawings of the time, the book remains a timeless equestrian adventure classic.

Goodwin, Joseph, *Through Mexico on Horseback* – The author and his companion, Robert Horiguichi, the sophisticated, multi-lingual son of an imperial Japanese diplomat, set out in 1931 to cross Mexico. They were totally unprepared for the deserts, quicksand and brigands they were to encounter during their adventure.

Hanbury-Tenison, Marika, *For Better, For Worse* – The author, an excellent story-teller, writes about her adventures visiting and living among the Indians of Central Brazil.

Hanbury-Tenison, Marika, *A Slice of Spice* – The fresh and vivid account of the author's hazardous journey to the Indonesian Islands with her husband, Robin.

Hanbury-Tenison, Robin, *Chinese Adventure* – The story of a unique journey in which the explorer Robin Hanbury-Tenison and his wife Louella rode on horseback alongside the Great Wall of China in 1986.

Hanbury-Tenison, Robin, *Fragile Eden* – The wonderful story of Robin and Louella Hanbury-Tenison's exploration of New Zealand on horseback in 1988. They rode alone together through what they describe as 'some of the most dramatic and exciting country we have ever seen.'

Hanbury-Tenison, Robin, *Mulu: The Rainforest* – This was the first popular book to bring to the world's attention the significance of the rain forests to our fragile ecosystem. It is a timely reminder of our need to preserve them for the future.

Hanbury-Tenison, Robin, *A Pattern of Peoples* – The author and his wife, Marika, spent three months travelling through Indonesia's outer islands and writes with his usual flair and sensitivity about the tribes he found there.

Hanbury-Tenison, Robin, *A Question of Survival* – This superb book played a hugely significant role in bringing the plight of Brazil's Indians to the world's attention.

Hanbury-Tenison, Robin, *The Rough and the Smooth* – The incredible story of two journeys in South America. Neither had been attempted before, and both were considered impossible!

Hanbury-Tenison, Robin, *Spanish Pilgrimage* – Robin and Louella Hanbury-Tenison went to Santiago de Compostela in a traditional way – riding on white horses over long-forgotten tracks. In the process they discovered more about the people and the country than any conventional traveller would learn. Their adventures are vividly and entertainingly recounted in this delightful and highly readable book.

Hanbury-Tenison, Robin, *White Horses over France* – This enchanting book tells the story of a magical journey and how, in fulfilment of a personal dream, the first Camargue horses set foot on British soil in the late summer of 1984.

Hanbury-Tenison, Robin, *Worlds Apart – an Explorer's Life* – The author's battle to preserve the quality of life under threat from developers and machines infuses this autobiography with a passion and conviction which makes it impossible to put down.

Hanbury-Tenison, Robin, *Worlds Within – Reflections in the Sand –* This book is full of the adventure you would expect from a man of action like Robin Hanbury-Tenison. However, it is also filled with the type of rare knowledge that was revealed to other desert travellers like Lawrence, Doughty and Thesiger.

Haslund, Henning, *Mongolian Adventure –* An epic tale inhabited by a cast of characters no longer present in this lackluster world, shamans who set themselves on fire, rebel leaders who sacked towns, and wild horsemen whose ancestors conquered the world.

Heath, Frank, *Forty Million Hoofbeats –* Heath set out in 1925 to follow his dream of riding to all 48 of the Continental United States. The journey lasted more than two years, during which time Heath and his mare, Gypsy Queen, became inseparable companions.

Holt, William, *Ride a White Horse –* After rescuing a cart horse, Trigger, from slaughter and nursing him back to health, the 67-year-old Holt and his horse set out in 1964 on an incredible 9,000 mile, non-stop journey through western Europe.

Hopkins, Frank T., *Hidalgo and Other Stories –* For the first time in history, here are the collected writings of Frank T. Hopkins, the counterfeit cowboy whose endurance racing claims and Old West fantasies have polarized the equestrian world.

James, Jeremy, *Saddletramp –* The classic story of Jeremy James' journey from Turkey to Wales, on an unplanned route with an inaccurate compass, unreadable map and the unfailing aid of villagers who seemed to have as little sense of direction as he had.

James, Jeremy, *Vagabond –* The wonderful tale of the author's journey from Bulgaria to Berlin offers a refreshing, witty and often surprising view of Eastern Europe and the collapse of communism.

Jebb, Louisa, *By Desert Ways to Baghdad and Damascus –* From the pen of a gifted writer and intrepid traveller, this is one of the greatest equestrian travel books of all time.

Kluckhohn, Clyde, *To the Foot of the Rainbow –* This is not just a exciting true tale of equestrian adventure. It is a moving account of a young man's search for physical perfection in a desert world still untouched by the recently-born twentieth century.

Lambie, Thomas, *Boots and Saddles in Africa –* Lambie's story of his equestrian journeys is told with the grit and realism that marks a true classic.

Landor, Henry Savage, *In the Forbidden Land –* Illustrated with hundreds of photographs and drawings, this blood-chilling account of equestrian adventure makes for page-turning excitement.

Langlet, Valdemar, *Till Häst Genom Ryssland (Swedish)* – Denna reseskildring rymmer många ögonblicksbilder av möten med människor, från morgonbad med Lev Tolstoi till samtal med Tartarer och fotografering av fagra skördeflickor. Rikt illustrerad med foto och teckningar.

Leigh, Margaret, *My Kingdom for a Horse* – In the autumn of 1939 the author rode from Cornwall to Scotland, resulting in one of the most delightful equestrian journeys of the early twentieth century. This book is full of keen observations of a rural England that no longer exists.

Lester, Mary, *A Lady's Ride across Spanish Honduras in 1881* – This is a gem of a book, with a very entertaining account of Mary's vivid, day-to-day life in the saddle.

Maillart, Ella, *Turkestan Solo* – A vivid account of a 1930s journey through this wonderful, mysterious and dangerous portion of the world, complete with its Kirghiz eagle hunters, lurking Soviet secret police, and the timeless nomads that still inhabited the desolate steppes of Central Asia.

Marcy, Randolph, *The Prairie Traveler* – There were a lot of things you packed into your saddlebags or the wagon before setting off to cross the North American wilderness in the 1850s. A gun and an axe were obvious necessities. Yet many pioneers were just as adamant about placing a copy of Captain Randolph Marcy's classic book close at hand.

Marsden, Kate, *Riding through Siberia: A Mounted Medical Mission in 1891* - This immensely readable book is a mixture of adventure, extreme hardship and compassion as the author travels the Great Siberian Post Road.

Marsh, Hippisley Cunliffe, *A Ride Through Islam* – A British officer rides through Persia and Afghanistan to India in 1873. Full of adventures, and with observant remarks on the local Turkoman equestrian traditions.

MacCann, William, *Viaje a Caballo* – Spanish-language edition of the British author's equestrian journey around Argentina in 1848.

Meline, James, *Two Thousand Miles on Horseback: Kansas to Santa Fé in 1866* – A beautifully written, eye witness account of a United States that is no more.

Muir Watson, Sharon, *The Colour of Courage* – The remarkable true story of the epic horse trip made by the first people to travel Australia's then-unmarked Bicentennial National Trail. There are enough adventures here to satisfy even the most jaded reader.

Naysmith, Gordon, *The Will to Win* – This book recounts the only equestrian journey of its kind undertaken during the 20th century - a mounted trip stretching across 16 countries. Gordon Naysmith, a Scottish pentathlete and former military man, set out in 1970 to ride from the tip of the African continent to the 1972 Olympic Games in distant Germany.

O'Reilly, Basha, *Count Pompeii – Stallion of the Steppes* – the story of Basha's journey from Russia with her stallion, Count Pompeii, told for children. This is the first book in the *Little Long Rider* series.

O'Reilly, CuChullaine, (Editor) *The Horse Travel Handbook* – this accumulated knowledge of a million miles in the saddle tells you everything you need to know about travelling with your horse!

O'Reilly, CuChullaine, (Editor) *The Horse Travel Journal* – a unique book to take on your ride and record your experiences. Includes the world's first equestrian travel "pictionary" to help you in foreign countries.

O'Reilly, CuChullaine, *Khyber Knights* – Told with grit and realism by one of the world's foremost equestrian explorers, "Khyber Knights" has been penned the way lives are lived, not how books are written.

O'Reilly, CuChullaine, (Editor) *The Long Riders, Volume One* – The first of five unforgettable volumes of exhilarating travel tales.

Östrup, J, *(Swedish), Växlande Horisont* - The thrilling account of the author's journey to Central Asia from 1891 to 1893.

Patterson, George, *Gods and Guerrillas* – The true and gripping story of how the author went secretly into Tibet to film the Chinese invaders of his adopted country. Will make your heart pound with excitement!

Patterson, George, *Journey with Loshay: A Tibetan Odyssey* – This is an amazing book written by a truly remarkable man! Relying both on his companionship with God and on his own strength, he undertook a life few can have known, and a journey of emergency across the wildest parts of Tibet.

Pocock, Roger, *Following the Frontier* – Pocock was one of the nineteenth century's most influential equestrian travelers. Within the covers of this book is the detailed account of Pocock's horse ride along the infamous Outlaw Trail, a 3,000 mile solo journey that took the adventurer from Canada to Mexico City.

Pocock, Roger, *Horses* – Pocock set out to document the wisdom of the late 19th and early 20th Centuries into a book unique for its time. His concerns for attempting to preserve equestrian knowledge were based on cruel reality. More than 300,000 horses had been destroyed during the recent Boer War. Though Pocock enjoyed a reputation for dangerous living, his observations on horses were praised by the leading thinkers of his day.

Post, Charles Johnson, *Horse Packing* – Originally published in 1914, this book was an instant success, incorporating as it did the very essence of the science of packing horses and mules. It makes fascinating reading for students of the horse or history.

Ray, G. W., *Through Five Republics on Horseback* – In 1889 a British explorer - part-time missionary and full-time adventure junky – set out to find a lost tribe of sun-worshipping natives in the unexplored forests of Paraguay. The journey was so brutal that it defies belief.

Rink, Bjarke, *The Centaur Legacy* - This immensely entertaining and historically important book provides the first ever in-depth study into how man's partnership with his equine companion changed the course of history and accelerated human development.

Ross, Julian, *Travels in an Unknown Country* – A delightful book about modern horseback travel in an enchanting country, which once marked the eastern borders of the Roman Empire – Romania.

Ross, Martin and Somerville, E, *Beggars on Horseback* – The hilarious adventures of two aristocratic Irish cousins on an 1894 riding tour of Wales.

Ruxton, George, *Adventures in Mexico* – The story of a young British army officer who rode from Vera Cruz to Santa Fe, Mexico in 1847. At times the author exhibits a fearlessness which borders on insanity. He ignores dire warnings, rides through deadly deserts, and dares murderers to attack him. It is a delightful and invigorating tale of a time and place now long gone.

von Salzman, Erich, *Im Sattel durch Zentralasien* – The astonishing tale of the author's journey through China, Turkistan and back to his home in Germany – 6000 kilometres in 176 days!

Schwarz, Hans *(German)*, *Vier Pferde, Ein Hund und Drei Soldaten* – In the early 1930s the author and his two companions rode through Liechtenstein, Austria, Romania, Albania, Yugoslavia, to Turkey, then rode back again!

Schwarz, Otto *(German)*, *Reisen mit dem Pferd* – the Swiss Long Rider with more miles in the saddle than anyone else tells his wonderful story, and a long appendix tells the reader how to follow in his footsteps.

Scott, Robert, *Scott's Last Expedition* – Many people are unaware that Scott recruited Yakut ponies from Siberia for his doomed expedition to the South Pole in 1909. Here is the remarkable story of men and horses who all paid the ultimate sacrifice.

Skrede, Wilfred, *Across the Roof of the World* – This epic equestrian travel tale of a wartime journey across Russia, China, Turkestan and India is laced with unforgettable excitement.

Steele, Nick, *Take a Horse to the Wilderness* – Part history book, part adventure story, part equestrian travel textbook and all round great read, this is a timeless classic written by the foremost equestrian expert of his time, famed mounted game ranger Nick Steele.

Stevens, Thomas, *Through Russia on a Mustang* – Mounted on his faithful horse, Texas, Stevens crossed the Steppes in search of adventure. Cantering across the pages of this classic tale is a cast of nineteenth century Russian misfits, peasants, aristocrats—and even famed Cossack Long Rider Dmitri Peshkov.

Stevenson, Robert L., *Travels with a Donkey* – In 1878, the author set out to explore the remote Cevennes mountains of France. He travelled alone, unless you count his stubborn and manipulative pack-donkey, Modestine. This book is a true classic.

Strong, Anna Louise, *Road to the Grey Pamir* – With Stalin's encouragement, Strong rode into the seldom-seen Pamir mountains of faraway Tadjikistan. The political renegade turned equestrian explorer soon discovered more adventure than she had anticipated.

Sykes, Ella, *Through Persia on a Sidesaddle* – Ella Sykes rode side-saddle 2,000 miles across Persia, a country few European woman had ever visited. Mind you, she traveled in style, accompanied by her Swiss maid and 50 camels loaded with china, crystal, linens and fine wine.

Trinkler, Emile, *Through the Heart of Afghanistan* – In the early 1920s the author made a legendary trip across a country now recalled only in legends.

Tschiffely, Aimé, *Bohemia Junction* – "Forty years of adventurous living condensed into one book."

Tschiffely, Aimé, *Bridle Paths* – a final poetic look at a now-vanished Britain.

Tschiffely, Aimé, *Mancha y Gato Cuentan sus Aventuras* – The Spanish-language version of *The Tale of Two Horses* – the story of the author's famous journey as told by the horses.

Tschiffely, Aimé, *The Tale of Two Horses* – The story of Tschiffely's famous journey from Buenos Aires to Washington, DC, narrated by his two equine heroes, Mancha and Gato. Their unique point of view is guaranteed to delight children and adults alike.

Tschiffely, Aimé, *This Way Southward* – the most famous equestrian explorer of the twentieth century decides to make a perilous journey across the U-boat infested Atlantic.

Tschiffely, Aimé, *Tschiffely's Ride* – The true story of the most famous equestrian journey of the twentieth century – 10,000 miles with two Criollo geldings from Argentina to Washington, DC. A new edition is coming soon with a Foreword by his literary heir!

Tschiffely, Aimé, *Tschiffely's Ritt* – The German-language translation of *Tschiffely's Ride* – the most famous equestrian journey of its day.

Ure, John, *Cucumber Sandwiches in the Andes* – No-one who wasn't mad as a hatter would try to take a horse across the Andes by one of the highest passes between Chile and the Argentine. That was what John Ure was told on his way to the British Embassy in Santiago-so he set out to find a few certifiable kindred spirits. Fans of equestrian travel and of Latin America will be enchanted by this delightful book.

Warner, Charles Dudley, *On Horseback in Virginia* – A prolific author, and a great friend of Mark Twain, Warner made witty and perceptive contributions to the world of nineteenth century American literature. This book about the author's equestrian adventures is full of fascinating descriptions of nineteenth century America.

Weale, Magdalene, *Through the Highlands of Shropshire* – It was 1933 and Magdalene Weale was faced with a dilemma: how to best explore her beloved English countryside? By horse, of course! This enchanting book invokes a gentle, softer world inhabited by gracious country lairds, wise farmers, and jolly inn keepers.

Weeks, Edwin Lord, *Artist Explorer* – A young American artist and superb writer travels through Persia to India in 1892.

Wentworth Day, J., *Wartime Ride* – In 1939 the author decided the time was right for an extended horseback ride through England! While parts of his country were being ravaged by war, Wentworth Day discovered an inland oasis of mellow harvest fields, moated Tudor farmhouses, peaceful country halls, and fishing villages.

Von Westarp, Eberhard, *Unter Halbmond und Sonne* – (German) – Im Sattel durch die asiatische Türkei und Persien.

Wilkins, Messanie, *Last of the Saddle Tramps* – Told she had little time left to live, the author decided to ride from her native Maine to the Pacific. Accompanied by her faithful horse, Tarzan, Wilkins suffered through any number of obstacles, including blistering deserts and freezing snow storms – and defied the doctors by living for another 20 years!.

Wilson, Andrew, *The Abode of Snow* – One of the best accounts of overland equestrian travel ever written about the wild lands that lie between Tibet and Afghanistan.

de Windt, Harry, *A Ride to India* – Part science, all adventure, this book takes the reader for a thrilling canter across the Persian Empire of the 1890s.

Winthrop, Theodore, *Saddle and Canoe* – This book paints a vibrant picture of 1850s life in the Pacific Northwest and covers the author's travels along the Straits of Juan De Fuca, on Vancouver Island, across the Naches Pass, and on to The Dalles, in Oregon Territory. This is truly an historic travel account.

Younghusband, George, *Eighteen Hundred Miles on a Burmese Pony* – One of the funniest and most enchanting books about equestrian travel of the nineteenth century, featuring "Joe" the naughty Burmese pony!

We are constantly adding new titles to our collections, so please check our websites: **www.horsetravelbooks.com** and **www.classictravelbooks.com**

CPSIA information can be obtained at www.ICGtesting.com
Printed in the USA
LVOW042239200612

286980LV00001B/105/A